Access, Participation and Higher Education

THE FUTURE OF EDUCATION FROM 14+

Access, Participation and Higher Education

Policy and Practice

Edited by
Annette Hayton and Anna Paczuska

**KOGAN
PAGE**

First published in 2002

Kogan Page Limited
120 Pentonville Road
London N1 9JN
UK

Stylus Publishing Inc.
22883 Quicksilver Drive
Sterling, VA 20166–2012
USA

British Library Cataloguing in Publication Data

A CIP record for this book is available from the British Library.

ISBN 0 7494 3836 3

Typeset by Saxon Graphics Ltd, Derby
Printed and bound in Great Britain by Biddles Ltd, Guildford and King's Lynn
www.biddles.co.uk

Contents

List of Contributors   *vii*
Series Editors' Foreword   *ix*
Acknowledgements   *xi*

Introduction: Education in Demand?   **1**
Annette Hayton and Anna Paczuska

Part 1 The Changing Context for Higher Education   **21**

1. **Getting In and Getting On: Choosing the Best**   **23**
   Sheila Macrae and Meg Maguire

2. **Challenging Inequality, Choosing Inclusion: Higher Education
   in Changing Social Landscapes**   **40**
   Karen Evans

3. **Increasing Demand for Higher Education in the Longer Term:
   The Role of 14+ Qualifications and Curriculum Reform**   **55**
   Ann Hodgson and Ken Spours

4. **Fair Funding for Higher Education: The Way Forward**   **69**
   Claire Callender

5. **Redefining Higher Education: A Case Study in
   Widening Participation**   **89**
   Patrick Ainley, Jill Jameson, Peter Jones, Dai Hall and Marc Farr

6. **Higher Education: A Risky Business**   **106**
   Louise Archer, Carole Leathwood and Merryn Hutchings

7. **Widening Participation: The Place of Mature Students**   **122**
   Alison Fuller

8. **The Applications Process: Developing an Admissions
   Curriculum**   **137**
   Anna Paczuska

9. **Higher Education Provision and the Change to a Mass System**   **150**
   Ruth Farwell

Contents

Part 2 Developing Strategies for Widening Participation   **163**

10. **A Framework for Institutional Change**   **165**
    Margo Blythman and Susan Orr

11. **Reflections on Widening Access to Medical Schools:
    The Case of Southampton**   **178**
    Angela Fenwick

12. **Mentoring: A Black Community Response**   **189**
    Howard Jeffrey

13. **Making Links with Schools and Colleges**   **201**
    Harinder Lawley, with Ian Stirling and Jan Oztun Ali

14. **Guidance and Choice in a Changing Context**   **212**
    John Beckett

15. **Access: The Widening Participation Success Story**   **225**
    Norman Carey

16. ***Student Voice*: Working to Ensure Successful Transition to
    Higher Education**   **235**
    Julia Dinsdale

17. **The Sussex Coastal Highway**   **245**
    Jacky Harding

    Conclusion: Is Higher Education Gladdening our Existence?   **255**
    Annette Hayton and Anna Paczuska

    Index   *271*

List of Contributors

Patrick Ainley is a Reader in Learning Policy at the University of Greenwich.

Louise Archer is a Researcher at the Institute for Policy Studies in Education, University of North London.

John Beckett is a Higher Education Advisor at the Sixth Form Centre, City and Islington College.

Margo Blythman is Teaching and Learning Coordinator at the London College of Printing, The London Institute.

Claire Callender is Professor in Social Policy at South Bank University, London.

Norman Carey is Head of Division, Vocational Studies at Westminster Kingsway College.

Julia Dinsdale is Widening Participation Officer at University College, Worcester.

Karen Evans is Professor of Lifelong Learning and Head of the School of Lifelong Education and International Development at the Institute of Education, University of London.

Marc Farr is an education consultant with Experian.

Ruth Farwell is Dean of Academic Affairs at South Bank University, London.

Angela Fenwick is a Lecturer in Medical Education at the School of Medicine, Southampton University.

Alison Fuller is a Senior Research Fellow at the University of Leicester.

Dai Hall is Head of Recruitment and Marketing at the University of Greenwich.

Jacky Harding is Project Officer for the Sussex Coastal Highway scheme at the University of Brighton.

Annette Hayton is School Manager at the Institute of Education, University of London.

Ann Hodgson is a Senior Lecturer at the Institute of Education, University of London.

Merryn Hutchings is a Researcher at the Institute for Policy Studies in Education, University of North London.

Jill Jameson is Director of Lifelong Learning at the University of Greenwich.

Howard Jeffrey is Manager of Mentor and Student Initiatives at City and Islington College.

Peter Jones is a Principal Lecturer at the University of Greenwich.

Harinder Lawley is Head of Access Development at the University of North London.

Carole Leathwood is a Researcher at the Institute for Policy Studies in Education, University of North London.

Sheila Macrae is a Research Fellow at King's College, University of London.

Meg Maguire is a Senior Lecturer at King's College, University of London.

Susan Orr is Teaching and Learning Coordinator at the London College of Fashion, The London Institute.

Anna Paczuska is Director of Access and Widening Participation at South Bank University, London.

Ken Spours is a Senior Lecturer at the Institute of Education, University of London.

Series Editors' Foreword

The English post-16 education and training system is at a watershed after several years of growth in the late 1980s and early 1990s. This period saw a steady rise in participation and achievement in all areas of post-compulsory education. New Labour, in its second Parliament, has firmly backed further expansion of the system. The issue is what to expand and how to attract and support those learners who were left behind in the Conservative Government era and who have not traditionally participated in post-compulsory education. While English higher education has been described as a 'mass' system, it still only attracts a minority of young people and, in particular, fails to sufficiently involve those from lower socio-economic groups.

To its credit, this book does not simply take as its focus the current Government 50 per cent participation target, but seeks to take a broader historical and system analysis to discuss what the necessary conditions might be for a further expansion of the size and role of higher education. In doing so, it also highlights a range of practical strategies designed to increase access to this sector.

The central problem the book sets out to debate is the continued imbalance in the social composition of higher education participants. What its historical analysis shows is that while higher education has expanded, it has not fundamentally changed because many of the new participants have simply been absorbed into traditional higher education provision. This 'absorption approach' has meant that in recent years some groups who were traditionally excluded are now relatively well-represented, in particular women and some ethnic minority groups. But this progress lays bare the most glaring limitations of this type of expansion: the lack of participation of young people from working class backgrounds, which the editors attribute to a marketized and class-based approach to higher education during the 1990s.

The editors quite rightly point to a number of factors that together conspire to maintain this position: selectivity, competition and elitism, qualifications and standards, funding mechanisms and student finance. This multi-faceted problem points to the need for a fundamental system-based solution rather than a set of unconnected initiatives aimed at widening participation.

In furthering this analysis, the editors bring together a number of key writers in the field to explore both the underlying problem of the imbalance in the social composition of higher education and policies for widening participation at both the national and local level. While some of the chapters in the book suggest immediate measures for a more inclusive approach to higher education, the main conclusion of the book is that higher education itself has to change radically if it is to attract and serve the needs of a wider range of learners.

In the final chapter, the editors pose some searching questions. In particular, they ask why some groups still continue to reject higher education despite the strenuous efforts to attract them. The editors recognize the influence of the changing nature of labour markets, lifestyles and identities in the way that young people see higher education. This leads them to propose that teaching, learning and curricula in higher education have to change if universities are to play a more central role in what has become a more diverse and complex society.

Arguably, this final chapter lays the basis for another book. The discussion of a new type of higher education goes beyond the parameters of this volume. Moreover, this is contentious territory because it means, among other things, confronting the economic function of higher education and the role of employers and their support for a more diverse concept of higher-level study. It also raises the question of what further social, educational and economic measures might be needed to sustain wider participation. It is difficult to see further higher education expansion being based simply on individual demand for learning.

The editors are right to suggest that a more fundamental review of the role and approach of higher education is required. We would suggest that if higher education is to attract more learners, it also has to provide a whole range of more visible rewards related to economic benefits, social cohesion, cultural identity and awareness, and personal development. This requires the involvement of a whole range of players within and beyond the education system in the project of higher education expansion. This book marks an important step in opening the debate on this issue.

Ann Hodgson and Ken Spours
Institute of Education
University of London

Acknowledgements

This book grew out of several years of activity in the London Region Post-16 Network that included a number of rowdy meetings, a seminar series and two conferences. As we worked with colleagues from schools, colleges, LEAs and universities to plan events and share experiences our understanding of the issues around widening participation grew. Many of those colleagues are represented in this volume but all those that participated have contributed in some way to the ideas behind this volume, so our first thanks is to them.

For their careful reading and comments on draft versions we would like to thank Eileen Ball, Margo Blythman, Colin Chambers, Nadia Deason, Angela Fenwick, Heather Graham, Pam Baldwin, Clive Hayton, Ann Hodgson, Carole Leathwood and Therese Lorphevre.

A special mention is due to Ken Spours who, at an early stage in the discussions about the book, asked the question 'why bother with higher education?'. This changed our approach and set the tone for future work.

We would also like to thank our long-suffering colleagues, friends and families for supporting us, in particular Alan Bashall, Irene Kemp, Naomi Hayton, Miles Hayton-Robinson, Ruth Farwell and the staff in the Access and Widening Participation Unit at South Bank University.

Introduction: Education in Demand?

Annette Hayton and Anna Paczuska

Along with the right to vote the right to education is a freedom which populations throughout history and across the world have struggled to achieve. In the UK at the turn of the 19th century a university education was a privilege enjoyed almost exclusively by the sons of the rich. Undergraduates made up less than 1 per cent of the population and included only a handful of women. There were only 10 universities and these were dominated by the traditions and values of Oxbridge.

Now over 30 per cent of young people embark on some kind of higher education and over half of university students are women. Opportunities for adults to return to study have increased and many universities make provision for part-time study and other flexible forms of delivery. However, participation rates of those from working class backgrounds and some ethnic groups remains very low. Currently about 70 per cent of young people from professional families go on to university as compared to 13 per cent from unskilled manual backgrounds (Social Trends, 2000).

The New Labour Government has the explicit aim of increasing participation in higher education to 50 per cent of 18–30-year-olds and also wishes to include a greater proportion of students without a family tradition of higher education. However, despite a continuing focus on access and progression and an increase in resources specifically directed at widening entry, the participation rate has remained static since 1996. Universities are now actively recruiting undergraduates and encouraging more of the population to become students – a marked contrast to the situation a century ago when under-represented groups were struggling for access to higher education.

In this introductory chapter we look at the origins of the modern higher education system and the motives that drive people to aspire to higher education; and we argue that education systems are constructed and change according to the economic, social and political pressures of particular times and places. We then ask why the participation rate has not continued to increase despite the best efforts of universities to recruit more students. We also ask why the inequalities in participation between different social groups persist, despite numerous initiatives to widen access. We go on to explore the relationship between wider economic, social and political contexts and individual choice. We argue that those from backgrounds without a family tradition of higher education encounter a range of risks and barriers not normally faced by their middle class contemporaries.

We then examine the barriers to progression and successful completion that are embedded in our current systems of admissions, guidance, qualifications and financial support. We also outline the particular problems caused at the period of transition to higher education by the differences in culture and practice between the three sectors of education involved in transition: the school system, further education and universities.

We then consider how far education can tackle social disadvantage. We argue that education, as well as reflecting wider changes in society, has a significant part to play in shaping the future. We also argue that education policies and practices are inextricably linked to particular concepts of society. We consider the motives of the early pioneers who fought for access to higher education and identify four particular motivations for struggle: equal opportunities, empowerment, access to professional knowledge and also pleasure in learning. We conclude by asking how much progress has been made during the last century towards these goals and ask how far that will help to prepare us all for the challenges of the 21st century.

Like those early pioneers who struggled for increased access to higher education we believe in the development of education systems that leave aside outdated elitism and help to build a more equitable society that rejects poverty and discrimination. It is for this reason that we welcomed the opportunity to bring together this edited collection on widening participation and add our voices to the debate about future policy and strategy. We are fortunate in having contributions from individuals who not only share a commitment to promoting social justice but also make this central to their work.

The origins of higher education

In his recent Palgrave paper (2001) Mike Finn stated that 'Universities have changed spectacularly over the last 150 years' – but, despite the changes, higher education is still strongly influenced by the values and practices of the past. Finn reminds us of the monastic origins of the university and the ways in which that legacy continues to influence our organizational structures, the curriculum and the 'culture' of higher education. Fortunately, most would agree, the restriction of celibacy on Fellows has been removed – but as Finn points out, even this did not happen until relatively recently in 1882.

The close association with the Christian Church meant that, as Scott said, universities were largely concerned with the training of clergymen and teachers (1995). As Scott also points out, universities had a socializing function for the sons of the ruling classes:

> Although members of elite social groups passed through the universities, they rarely completed their degrees. The subsidiary mission of the pre-industrial universities was to complete the socialisation of future elites, social and political. (Scott, 1995: 12)

During the 19th century there were significant developments in the higher education system as wider economic, social and political changes occurred and the direct influence of the Church declined. Scott (1995) identifies three 'decisive shifts' which changed the nature of higher education: industrialization, the growth of the professions and demands for greater democracy. The expansion of higher education beyond Oxbridge was initially based on voluntarism with universities, such as University College London and Owens College, Manchester, founded with the explicit aim of extending access and providing opportunities for a different kind of curriculum (Lawson and Silver, 1973; Dent, 1970). At the same time the rise of the middle class and the growth of the professions led to increased demand for access to knowledge and skills that could only be acquired through advanced education. Towards the end of the 19th century government interest was aroused. For the first time the potential of higher education to provide a skilled and educated workforce to support the growth and competitiveness of British industry, and to serve the Empire, was realized by the state.

This represents a significant change in the purposes and nature of higher education during the 19th century. The exclusivity and cultural dominance of Oxbridge was challenged as other pressures and priorities emerged in the new social, economic and political context.

The struggle for higher education

The early 19th century was a time of great economic, political and social change. Industrialization and urbanization changed work and social relationships irrevocably and, as we have seen, the way that the education system developed was inextricably linked to these wider changes. However it is often forgotten that, at the same time, demands for greater democracy and equality were increasing in urgency. The ideas of equity and the 'Rights of Man', founded in the radical thinking of the Enlightenment, were the intellectual spur for the revolutions in France and the United

States. Despite the spectre of revolution, which so unsettled the British ruling classes, the democratic alternative – the right to vote – was won only after a long struggle.

Although access to formal education in the early part of the century was restricted to a minority, this did not preclude working class groups and movements from having an understanding of its importance or a vision of its potential. The Chartist William Lovett regarded free access to education up to university level as an essential part of the struggle for self-improvement and democracy. In a speech in 1837 he pronounced:

> Unhappily, although the time has gone by for the selfish and bigoted posses-
> sors of wealth to confine the blessings of knowledge wholly within their own
> narrow circle, and by every despotic artifice to block up each cranny through
> which intellectual light might break out on the multitude, yet still, so much of
> the selfishness of caste is exhibited in their fetters on the Press, in their
> colleges of restriction and privilege and in their dress and badge proclaiming
> charity schools, as to convince us that they still consider education as their
> own prerogative, or a boon to be sparingly conferred upon the multitude
> instead of a universal instrument for advancing the dignity of man and for
> gladdening his existence. (Rose, 2001: 64)

Struggles for the 'Rights of Man' did not automatically include equal rights for women. As well as women being excluded from the franchise, their access to formal education was severely restricted and the fight for a university education was a major part of the struggle for women's equality. Alice Zimmern, an early feminist, asserts that:

> The chief gain this half-century has brought to women's education is their
> admission to the universities. It is the keystone to the arch without which the
> rest of the fabric could have neither stability nor permanence. Thirty years
> ago it had hardly been seriously contemplated; now eight of the ten universi-
> ties of Great Britain teach their students without distinction of sex...
> (Zimmern, 1898)

The passion and commitment of early pioneers who tried to extend access to higher education is evident but what precisely were they fighting for? Four main strands can be identified: equal opportunities, empowerment, access to professional knowledge and pleasure in learning.

Equal opportunities

Equality of opportunity was a central theme in the struggle for access to higher education. The idea that the working classes might go to university was rarely considered, despite individual exceptions. This view was diffi-cult to challenge as, on the whole, the working classes lacked the economic means to support their study and the prominence of the classics in univer-sities meant that very few were able meet the entrance requirements. Hardy's (1898) novel *Jude the Obscure* describes how Jude, a respected stonemason, struggled for admission to university. Given his ultimate failure to gain entry, the novel also highlights the risks – financial, social and emotional – involved in making the attempt.

Women were specifically barred from university study because of their sex. Before women were able to gain full entry the statutes and ordinances of most universities had to be changed. It is worth remembering that the vestiges of the restrictive system remained well into the 20th century with Cambridge not allowing actual graduation for women students until 1947 (Purvis, 1991). The model of the male scholar was the generally accepted norm so women also had to struggle against popular opinion in order to be accepted, as Bell and Tight point out:

> Nationally, for all too many people, the idea of female higher education remained hilarious as the success of Gilbert and Sullivan's *Princess Ida* (first produced in 1884) demonstrated:
> 'A Woman's College! Maddest folly going!
> What can girls learn within its walls worth knowing?' (Bell and Tight, 1993: 73)

Underlying the exclusion of both women and the working classes was the belief that they were intellectually inferior and incapable of study at higher level. In some medical circles it was believed that too much mental labour could cause infertility in women (Purvis, 1991). Similar arguments based on innate biological differences have been used to justify the exclusion of various groups and are often the basis for explanations of differential performance based on 'race', class and gender.

Empowerment

Exclusion from higher education brought into sharp focus the importance of access to information and opportunities to share ideas and develop critical perspectives that are needed to empower groups and individuals both intellectually and as citizens. Throughout the 19th century groups excluded from the mainstream organized their own educational and political activities. These included 'mutual improvement' societies, friendly societies, lending libraries, the Socialist Sunday schools, colleges for girls and the WEA (Workers' Education Association) (Rose, 2001; Dent, 1970). While some activities were concerned solely with mutual improvement, many had a political dimension and the link between resistance and education was often quite explicit (Thompson, 1974).

Professional knowledge and expertise

Professional knowledge and expertise was a clear benefit of higher education denied to excluded groups. Of course this went along with the resulting increase in earning power, status and independence associated with professional employment. For example, women were barred from most professions, including medicine, and had to fight for entry. As Purvis points out, once women experienced higher education and gained access to the professions this had 'profound implications for their subsequent social placement within the economic structure' (Purvis, 1991: 119).

Pleasure in learning

An often overlooked but enduring motive for further study was the love of learning itself and the pleasure it afforded. As William Lovett said, education can 'gladden man's existence'. Rose (2001) found that this was indeed the case and that 19th century workers were reading a range of literature, poetry and drama, including Shakespeare, and setting up reading and discussion groups on a variety of topics.

So, in the 19th century access to education and, in particular, higher education was regarded as a privilege and something to be fought for whereas today many universities are struggling to recruit students. This leads us to ask what has happened to bring about such a radical change in attitudes and aspirations.

The current context for higher education

The context for higher education as we begin the 21st century is very different from that of the 19th century. The population of the UK is ethnically and culturally more diverse and British culture now includes ideas, perspectives and values from many communities. The Church of England has less direct influence on the state and less importance for individuals. Religious faith – where it exists – is no longer synonymous with Christianity. There is less overt restriction on individuals because of their religion, class, 'race' or gender than there was a century ago. Also, rather than legislation to exclude we have legislation that outlaws discrimination.

Industrialization and the national capacity for manufacturing have been replaced by a very different economic imperatives. Manufacturing engages only 17 per cent of the workforce (LMST, 2000). There has been a phenomenal growth in the 'service' sector and, as a result, the structure of the labour market is quite different. It is now considered normal for women to undertake paid employment outside the home and they make up 45 per cent of the workforce (Skills and Enterprise Executive, 2001). The introduction of new technologies into the workplace has changed the way that we work and has also resulted in a range of new jobs that require new sets of skills.

These changes are taking place against the backdrop of globalization – both economic and cultural. As multinational companies move their investments and activities from country to country the power of the state to regulate the economy and labour market has been severely restricted. Technologies such as TV, film, video and the Internet all open up a range of possibilities for communication for the general population. They enable world-wide marketing of various products – giving rise to complaints of cultural globalization of the worst kind. But technologies also offer us unprecedented access to information about different cultures and new perspectives only glimpsed at 100 years ago.

Old structures, definitions and delineations are eroding and, where they remain, often act as barriers to our understanding. They are being replaced by numerous complex interrelations between different groups, which obscure former certainties. As Barnett argues, universities are operating in an age of 'supercomplexity' where previously accepted frameworks of understanding are being challenged and where uncertainty '… is the condition of our age' (Barnett, 2000: 128).

Participation in higher education

In contrast to the situation 100 years ago, over 30 per cent of the population is now engaged in some form of higher education. This is a startling increase, which has gained momentum in the last 30 years. Scott (1995) has described the change as a move from an 'elite' system, designed to cater only for a privileged few, to a 'mass' system.

There is no doubt that even though higher education has clung to many of its traditional values, there has been massive change. The number of participating students is one example. In 1971 there were just 176,000 students in 45 universities. By the turn of the 20th century the number of students in higher education was more than 10 times greater with 1.8 million students in the system (Scott, 2001).

Participation by previously under-represented groups has changed too. Women and ethnic minorities now have high participation levels relative to their representation in the general population. For example, ethnic minorities[1] now represent 15 per cent of the student population but only 6 per cent of the working age population (NAO, 2002). The comparable data for women is 57 per cent and 50 per cent (NAO, 2002). The gender balance has changed so that now more than half the total number of students are women – although a marked imbalance at subject level remains. The number of women entering higher education undergraduate courses under the age of 21 as a percentage of the 18–19-year-olds overtook the percentage of men in 1992/93 (HEFCE, 2001).

The number of mature entrants to higher education (those entering at age 21 or over) has also increased. The most rapid expansion occurred during the period 1983/84–1992/93 when the numbers entering more than doubled. The rate of increase was most apparent in entrants to full-time undergraduate provision, where traditionally mature students had not been well represented before. The number of mature entrants has remained roughly constant since 1998/99 (HEFCE, 2001).

UK higher education appears to be a massive success story in terms of increasing participation and changing the profile of students in higher education. However, these successes mask significant differential participation rates between different social classes. Generally the largest increase that has occurred in higher education is the number of full-time undergraduate students. There was a 67 per cent increase between 1988/89 and 1993/94. The main driver of this was the increase in participation by 18–21-year-olds – but this has been largely from the professional and middle classes (HEFCE, 2001).

Opportunity for all

The low participation of certain groups has been recognized as an issue by various governments concerned with increasing opportunities for individuals and providing a skilled workforce to support the economy. However, cultural, financial and social factors all play a part in preventing access of certain social groups to higher education and promoting progression for others. The way these factors combine is not constant – they come together in different proportions and in different ways and change over time.

When Ralph Glasser left the Gorbals in Glasgow and went up to Oxford in 1938 he faced all three barriers – cultural, financial and social. Ostensibly, the major barrier at this time was the ability to pay (Tapper and Salter, 1992). Glasser overcame the hurdles of selection and finance by winning a scholarship but the social and cultural barriers remained. Once up at Oxford, he found that people did not know how to behave towards such a rarity as a working class student:

> In pre-war days for a Gorbals man to come up to Oxford was as unthinkable as to meet a raw bushman in a St James club – something for which there were no stock responses. In any case for a member of the boss class, someone from the Gorbals was in effect a bushman, the Gorbals itself as distant and unknowable as the Kalahari Desert. (Glasser, 1988: 1)

Education policy post-1944 sought to remove financial barriers to continuing education and develop a system based on merit rather than privilege: 'courses of higher education should be available for all those who are qualified by ability and attainment to pursue them and who wish to do so' (Robbins, 1963).

The meritocratic system of university entry introduced by Robbins in the 1960s brought with it financial grants and assistance to enable even the poorest students to access university if they achieved the necessary academic qualifications to progress. As we have seen, the number of students has increased significantly and progress has been made in broadening access. One important change has been the increased participation of women in higher education. Now, rather than being exceptional, it is as normal for a middle class girl to continue on to university as it is for her brother.

However, significant barriers to participation remain for those without a family background to higher education. Despite post-war policies introduced to promote access, and despite initiatives introduced by the New Labour Government that are specifically designed to widen participation, working class groups are still under-represented. This indicates that the factors influencing an individual's decision whether to go on to higher education are complex and multifaceted.

Making the choice

Firstly, of course, for a large proportion of the population the idea of going on to university is still not seriously considered – let alone consciously chosen or rejected. Nevertheless, there has been a change in attitudes and expectations and higher education is now more likely to be considered as an option than it was even 20 years ago. As Scott (1995: 173) pointed out, the early 1990s saw the development of what he describes as a 'college culture' where it became normal to continue education after 16 rather than exceptional.

Recent research and surveys (MORI Poll, 2000; Connor, 2001; IES, 1999) show that the choices of prospective students are influenced by a number of factors including:

- social pressure from parents, family and peer group – both positive and negative;
- ability to achieve the necessary entrance qualifications;
- lifestyle and status;
- job prospects and earnings – current and future;
- interest in subject and enjoyment of studying;
- personal confidence.

Ball, Maguire and Macrae (2000) found that these factors are very real and immediate for young people making choices about their future work or education. However, although the statistics clearly show that social background is a key factor in determining the likelihood of participation in higher education, young people tend to regard success or failure as a personal issue unrelated to wider social trends.

As we have seen, education policy post-1944 made provision for those previously excluded from secondary and higher education to continue their studies by removing financial barriers and developing a system based on merit. Although they were not the only factor to fuel expansion, these policies gave unprecedented opportunities to the general population for continuing their education. However, policies designed to tackle social disadvantage, and many analyses that set out to explain it, often overlooked the cultural and social barriers faced by those without a family tradition of higher, or even secondary, education. One of the first studies to explore these barriers was Willis's *Learning to Labour*, published in 1977. Willis interviewed a number of working class 'lads' who had won places at grammar school and, far from feeling grateful for the opportunity to attend, they found the culture quite alien. A significant minority rejected the middle class, academic culture that they encountered there.

It became apparent that economic barriers were not the only obstacles to successful participation in education. Some on the left took the approach that education merely served to reproduce the hierarchical relationships of capitalism and, as Weiner (2002) puts it, teachers were 'cast as hapless and helpless dupes in capitalism's project of creating winners and losers'. Bourdieu (1978) offered a more comprehensive explanation of how certain social groups retain power and privilege. He argued that there are different types of 'capital' and that in addition to economic capital, individuals possess social and cultural capital. As schools – and universities – are based on particular cultures and practices associated with the upper and middle classes, those with different backgrounds will not possess the right sort of capital to succeed in education. In making life choices such as whether to go to university, individuals draw on their stores of 'capital', asking questions such as 'Can I afford it?', 'What will my friends think?', 'Who do I know who can help me?', 'What should I say in my application?' The answers are different, of course, depending on individuals' social background.

Ball, Reay and David (2002) use the ideas of different sorts of capital to identify a range of factors that influence choice amongst young people in Britain today. They code these into two types of 'choosers' – 'embedded' and 'contingent'. The 'embedded' are those who are more likely to go on to university than not. The 'contingent' have a range of influences working against them, which, although not insurmountable, act together to make the decision more difficult. This typology is helpful as it goes beyond the rather simplistic descriptors of 'middle class/working class', 'male/female' or 'black/white' that fail to capture the complexity of an individual's situation, without denying the effect of wider social and economic conditions (see Table 0.1).

Ideal types of higher education chooser

Table 0.1   'Contingent' and 'embedded' choosers

'Contingent' Choosers	'Embedded' Choosers
Finance is a key concern and constraint	Finance is not an issue
Choice uses minimal information	Choice is based on extensive diverse sources of information
Choice is distant or 'unreal'	Choice is part of a cultural script, a 'normal biography'
Few variables are called up	A diverse array of variables are deployed
Choice is general/abstract	Choice is specialist/detailed
Minimal support (social capital) is used	Extensive support (social capital) is mobilized
Ethnic mix is an active variable in choosing	Ethnic mix is marginal or irrelevant to choice
Choosing is short term and weakly linked to 'imagined futures' – part of an incomplete or incoherent narrative	Choosing is long term and often relates to vivid and extensive 'imagined futures' – part of a coherent and planned narrative
'First-time' choosers with no family tradition of higher education	'Followers' embedded in a 'deep grammar of aspiration' which makes higher education normal and necessary
Narrowly defined socioscapes and spatial horizons – choices are 'local'/distance is a friction	Broad socioscapes and social horizons – choices are 'national'/distance is not an issue
Parents as 'onlookers' or 'weak framers'/ mothers may give practical support	Parents as 'strong framers' and active participants in choice

Source: Ball, Reay and David (2002)

For many potential students, embarking on a university degree is a risky business, as Archer, Leathwood and Hutchings explore in Chapter 6. Factors such as those identified above form the basis of their individual 'risk analysis' and their final choices. High-achieving, well-motivated sixth form students without responsibilities and with strong family support but few economic resources may decide to 'take the risk' and go on to higher education, judging that they are likely to get a degree, find a job and so repay undergraduate debts. If they doubt their capacity to achieve, or face opposition from their family, the 'risk' of failure increases and with it the possibility that they will start their working lives half qualified and burdened with debt that cannot be repaid. The extent to which such disincentives can be overcome by young people's belief in their ability to change their life chances by going on to higher education is explored by Evans in Chapter 2.

In a society where choices are increasingly complex, how can education play a part in tackling disadvantage and what can education systems and institutions do to remove barriers to participation?

Barriers to progression

Despite the prominence given to 'Education, Education, Education' in New Labour's 1997 election campaign it is clear that education alone cannot deal with all the factors that lead to social exclusion and educational disadvantage. Nevertheless, education policy at national level and institutional policy and practice at local level do have a direct effect on individuals and their life chances. Decisions about financial support, qualifications, guidance, institutional practices, curriculum, teaching and learning approaches all have an impact. However, as we have seen, the development of effective policies and successful strategies to promote progression to higher education and widen participation has proved particularly complex.

Selectivity and admissions

Selectivity is a key feature of the UK system, and one that, as well as being enshrined in the qualifications system, is embedded into the culture and practices of all schools, colleges and universities concerned with entry to higher education. Selectivity means that it is not enough for a prospective student simply to gain the qualifications necessary to achieve entry to university. In order to progress onto an undergraduate course a candidate has to be 'selected' for entry to a particular institution. The 'elite' universities usually have more applicants than places, leading them to reject many suitably qualified prospective students, and are often referred to as 'selectors'. The tradition of selection means that even so-called 'recruiters' – institutions that have difficulty in filling places – join in the annual ritual of 'selecting' students through a central admissions procedure.

The problem is that the present system has been designed mainly for 'oven ready' students who progress direct from 16–19 study onto single subject and largely academic full-time courses. They go through the UCAS system to Oxford or to 'old' or redbrick universities. At one extreme:

> Students arrive at Oxford in the traditional form: aged 18, 3 'good' A levels with entry points at an average of over 29 out of 30 (3 grade As at 10 points each); from resolutely middle-class backgrounds as revealed by home address postcodes; selected at college interviews the previous December largely on academic achievements-to-date and interviewers' attempts to assess 'potential' as the tie-breaker among so many applicants of similar achievements-to-date, family and school background. (Warner and Palfreyman, 2001: 11)

In Chapter 7 Fuller draws our attention to the increase in mature students that has taken place as individuals redefine and renegotiate their place in society. These students are certainly not 'oven ready' and neither are many of the prospective students that schools and colleges are supporting through the process of application to university. In Chapter 8 Paczuska argues that an 'admissions curriculum' has developed in order to support new constituencies of students into higher education. However, rather than being designed specifically to widen participation, it has grown in a piecemeal way, without clear purposes and objectives.

Advice and guidance

At the point of transition into higher education the provision of accessible, informed and responsive advice and guidance is essential in order to widen participation. However, when we look at the three sectors of compulsory schooling, further education and higher education together, we do not see a coherent system of guidance. What emerges is a picture of fragmented provision.

The growth of careers and guidance provision as a distinct element in education provision is a relatively recent phenomenon. Until the late 1980s most school students relied on perhaps a single 'careers interview' and those destined for higher education were identified long before that took place (Watts and Kidd, 2000). The importance of guidance has been recognized and greater emphasis is given to careers education within schools and colleges. The Careers Service played a significant role but its brief was too wide to provide the detailed and intensive guidance required by 'non-traditional' students. Privatization of the Careers Service and competition between institutions has exacerbated the problem.

Connor and Dewson (2001) found that, regardless of social class, more than half the students in their survey were dissatisfied with the quality of advice and information they had received. Of those who had chosen not to progress to university, 68 per cent would have welcomed more information, indicating a need for a more focused service. Individual schools, colleges and universities have developed their own solutions to the increasingly transparent and pressing issue of student guidance. In Chapter 14 Beckett describes one college's approach to the issue, suggesting that a range of strategies is needed to provide students with the support they require. In addition, specially tailored support such as the black mentoring scheme described by Jeffrey in Chapter 12 may be necessary to support certain excluded groups. However, as he points out, mentoring has become accepted as part of mainstream provision that is successful with all students.

Qualifications and standards

The UK qualifications system has always been a central element in promoting selectivity and determining educational opportunity: 'qualification systems are the key instruments of national policy and have traditionally been the major mechanism for selecting school and college students for employment and HE' (Young, 1999: 177).

For successful progression to take place there must be an articulation between the pre-university curriculum and qualifications and the higher education experience. Traditionally, A levels have served this function and have provided a clear progression route for academically able school pupils. The increase in post-war participation in further and higher education and the greater diversity of the student population highlighted the limitations of A level as a preparation for higher education, or indeed employment. As a result, various 'mechanisms' were developed to enable students to overcome traditional barriers to university entry.

Access courses, which were developed in the 1970s and 1980s, were designed specifically for adults without formal qualifications and proved very successful in increasing participation. In Chapter 15 Carey describes how Access courses at his college successfully widened participation and changed the culture of his institution. 'Mechanisms' such as Access developed outside the mainstream system. Changing the national system is altogether more complex but, as Hodgson and Spours argue in Chapter 3, without changes to mainstream qualifications the number of students that are qualified for higher education study cannot increase significantly.

Funding expansion

The drive behind the Conservative Government's support for the expansion of higher education during the 1980s was primarily economic. Higher education was seen as a key player in the government's plan to increase the 'competitiveness' of the UK by providing high-level training and increasing the pool of high-level skills that would make the UK competitive on the world market. Much of the expansion in higher education at this time was achieved through 'efficiency gains' by increasing staff/student ratios right across the university sector. The former polytechnics suffered a drop of about 25 per cent in public funding per student. Changes to funding and unprecedented government interest in the content and outcome of university programmes led to accusations that expansion had been encouraged solely to subordinate scholarship in higher education to the demands of vocational training – though Watson and Bowden (1999) argue that this outcome may have been accidental rather than planned. Apart from the perceived erosion of the traditional academic freedoms and values, the increase in the staff/student ratio has been of serious concern to lecturers. As the retention of students from 'non-traditional' backgrounds has become an issue the concern about expansion has been brought into sharp focus as the solutions indicate the need for more student support and increased contact with staff.

Student financial support

Reform of the student finance system has been on the agenda for some years, beginning with the erosion of the student grant under the Conservative governments. New Labour has tried to pursue its vision of expanding higher education by using the student finance system as a policy mechanism to fund widening participation. In pursuing its policy it rejected the recommendations of the Dearing report (NCEHE, 1997), which proposed charging fees on a flat-rate basis but maintaining support for living expenses for those in most need. The Kennedy committee's report (Kennedy, 1997), which focused on widening participation in further education, was published at the same time as Dearing. The report highlighted how the higher education student maintenance grant benefited middle class undergraduates and argued that, if New Labour was serious about widening participation, support should be given lower down the system to students in further education colleges.

Maintenance grants for higher education in England and Wales were replaced by loans, and tuition fees were also introduced, which shifted the costs of higher education onto individual students. Callender regards this policy as contradictory, pointing out that: 'The most disadvantaged students, and the very focus of widening participation policies, experience the greatest risks, hardship and financial pressures' (Callender, 2000). Callender describes the impact that this decision has had on poorer university students and considers some principles for a more equitable system in Chapter 4.

Transition into higher education

The process of preparation, application and entry to university is a period of transition for prospective students. This transitional phase is not confined to one area but cuts across the sectoral boundaries of compulsory secondary education, further education and higher education. Each sector views progression differently and has its own distinctive set of concerns. Individuals seeking entry to higher education need to learn about and negotiate a series of separate but linked systems in order to progress. There are also major differences in the amount of control that each of the three sectors has over curriculum and qualifications. In higher education, universities have the freedom to control the content of curriculum and confer the qualification. Conversely, schools work within the constraints of a national curriculum and a nationally defined qualifications system. In colleges the curriculum is defined largely by the qualifications system – but their independence from the national curriculum and their tradition of innovation allows the development of notable exceptions such as the development of Access courses.

The sectors themselves are by no means clearly defined and contain organizational tensions within them – most notably the continued distinction between the 'old' universities and the post-1992 institutions in the higher education sector. The emerging Learning and Skills System, which will be responsible for all non-university post-16 provision, could bring some coherence to the process but at present potential students are faced with separate systems and distinct cultures.

Education for wider participation

So to what extent has education made a difference and promoted a more equitable society? If we look at the four areas that motivated early pioneers in their struggle for access to higher education: equal opportunities, empowerment, professional expertise and pleasure, how relevant are these struggles for students in the 21st century?

Equal opportunities

For present-day students the context in which they make the choice to progress on to higher education is not openly constrained by policies, rules or regulations that have been specifically designed to exclude particular groups. The fight for 'equality of opportunity' has moved into other more complex arenas concerned less with overt discrimination and more with values, beliefs and attitudes and the way that these are embedded in policies and practice. In Chapter 1 Macrae and Maguire describe the first-year undergraduate experiences of four young people from very different social backgrounds. For the two students from families without a tradition of higher education, university culture is almost as alienating as it was for Ralph Glasser in 1938. The formal barriers have been removed but the cultural barriers, with all their mysteries and petty humiliations, remain.

Empowerment

Knowledge is no longer exclusively guarded and accessed by a small elite. Books, newspapers, televisions, CDs, computers and so on are freely available and relatively accessible so, in many ways, opportunities for accessing information and sharing knowledge have never been greater. Certainly the university's role as a repository and disseminator of information is less important. However, because of the growth in communication methods and the easy access to information, the capacity to sift, assess, analyse and interpret information from a variety of sources is increasingly important. A higher education system that recognized the growth of new cultural forms and the importance of developing critical awareness in its students could play a significant role here. The university could provide a space within which students and staff could explore ideas and develop new approaches that might help us to understand and deal with the complexities of post-industrial society. In Chapter 16 Dinsdale outlines the importance of ensuring that the 'student voice' is heard, as the very process of sharing, shaping and formulating ideas helps students to make sense of their situation and move forward.

Professional knowledge and expertise

For students today access to professional knowledge is still a key motivator as possession of a university degree acts as an entry qualification to various professions and can increase an individual's earning power and job satisfaction. However, there are indicators that social background has a significant effect on graduate employment prospects with those from socially disadvantaged groups, including women, less likely to achieve the high salaries traditionally associated with graduates. For those concerned with status other markers define the 'exclusive' in our society today and the move from an elite to a mass system has removed the automatic cachet that a university degree provided. In Chapter 11 Fenwick describes the complexities of encouraging 'non-traditional' students to join an elite university medical school and the strategies that have been developed to achieve this without accusations of 'dumbing down'.

Pleasure in learning

Enjoyment of the subject and 'learning for its own sake' are still significant motivators for prospective students. The IES Student Survey (IES, 2000) found that, regardless of social background, the main reason for young people wishing to go to university was 'to study a subject that really interests them'. But pleasure in learning is rarely the prime focus of the university experience today – even when entry qualifications allow students to take the course of their choice. A more highly regulated university system with harsher assessment regimes combined with increased financial and personal responsibilities often restricts the development of intellectual interest and enjoyment. As we can see from Chapter 6, for many students education is certainly not associated with pleasure:

> [Education]'s boring. No one sits here telling us that... it's going to be thrilling, it's going to be a buzz, it's going to be like a drug where you're going to want more and more and more. I don't get that impression at all. (Jodie, 27, white, unemployed)

The significance of the slowdown in student demand for higher education must not be underestimated and leads us to ask three questions:

1. Are government policies responsive enough and do they encourage and support student progression and participation?
2. Are potential students rejecting higher education because they doubt that it will result in the social and economic benefits traditionally associated with a degree?
3. Is the university agenda itself failing to meet the needs of students and society in the 21st century?

If it is true that many young people do not see higher education as important or relevant, should we accept their view? Or is the case for higher education too important to be abandoned either to government policy or to the vagaries of the consumer market?

Notes

1. This figure disguises marked differences between different ethnic groups but shows a positive trend.

References

Ball, S, Maguire, M and Macrae, S (2000) *Choice, Pathways and Transitions Post-16*, Routledge/Falmer, London

Ball, S, Reay, D and David, M (2002) Ethnic choosing: minority ethnic students, social class and higher education choice, in *Race, Ethnicity and Education*, forthcoming

Barnett, R (2000) Reconfiguring the university, in *Higher Education Reformed*, ed P Scott, Falmer, London

Bell, R and Tight, M (1993) *Open Universities: A British tradition?* SRHE/Open University Press, Buckingham

Bourdieu, P (1978) Cultural reproduction and social reproduction, in *Power and Ideology in Education*, eds J Karabel and A Halsey, Open University Press, New York

Callender, C (2000) *Changing Student Finances: Income, expenditure and the take-up of student loans among full and part-time higher education students in 1998/9*, research report RR215, DfEE, London

Connor, H (2001) Deciding for or against participation in higher education: the views of young people from lower social class backgrounds, *Higher Education Quarterly*, **55** (2), April

Connor, H and Dewson, S (2001) *Social Class and Higher Education: Issues affecting decisions on participation by lower social class groups*, DfEE Research Report RR267, DfEE, London

Dent, H C (1970) *1870–1970 Century of Growth in English Education*, Longman, London

Finn, M (2001) Palgrave/THES Humanities and Social Science prize winner, THES, November

Glasser, R (1988) *Gorbals Boy at Oxford*, Pan Books, London

Hardy, T (1896) *Jude the Obscure*, 1974 edition, Macmillan, London

Higher Education Funding Council for England (HEFCE) (2001) *Supply and Demand in Higher Education*, HEFCE, Bristol

IES (2000) *Annual Graduate Review 1998–1999*, Institute for Employment Studies, Brighton

Kennedy, H (1997) *Learning Works: Widening participation in further education*, Further Education Funding Council, Coventry

Lawson, J and Silver, H (1973) *A Social History of Education in England*, Methuen, London

LMST (2000) *Labour Market Skills and Trends*, DfEE, London

MORI (2001) *Student Living Report*, UNITE/MORI, Bristol

National Audit Office (NAO) (2002) *Widening Participation in Higher Education in England*, HMSO, London

National Committee of Enquiry into Higher Education (NCEHE) (1997) *Higher Education in the Learning Society*, HMSO, London

Purvis, J (1991) *A History of Women's Education in England*, Open University Press, Buckingham

Robbins Report (1963) *Committee on Higher Education*, report of the committee appointed by the Prime Minister under the chairmanship of the Lord Robbins, Cmnd 2154

Rose, J (2001) *The Intellectual Life of the British Working Classes*, Yale University Press, Newhaven and London

Scott, P (1995) *The Meanings of Mass Higher Education*, SRHE/Open University Press, Buckingham

Scott, P (2001) Triumph or retreat, in *The State of UK Higher Education*, eds D Warner and D Palfreyman, SRHE/Open University Press, Buckingham

Skills and Enterprise Executive (2001) *Labour Market Trends Issue 3/2001*, Learning and Skills Council

Social Trends (2000) Dataset: *Participation Rates in Higher Education: By social class, 1991/92–1998/99*

Tapper, T and Salter, B (1992) *Oxford, Cambridge and the Changing Idea of University*, SHRE/Open University Press, Buckingham

Thompson, E P (1974) *The Making of the English Working Class*, Penguin, Harmondsworth

Warner, D and Palfreyman, D (eds) (2001) *The State of UK Higher Education: Managing change and diversity*, SRHE/Open University Press, Buckingham

Watson, D and Bowden, R (1999) Why did they do it? Conservatives and mass higher education, *Journal of Education Policy*, **14** (3), pp 243–56

Watts, A and Kidd, J (2000) Guidance in the United Kingdom: past, present and future, *British Journal of Guidance and Counselling*, **28** (4), pp 485–502

Weiner, G (2002) Auditing failure: moral competence and school effectiveness, (forthcoming) *British Education Research Journal*

Willis, P (1977) *Learning to Labour: How working-class kids get working-class jobs*, Saxon House, Aldershot

Young, M (1999) Reconstructing qualifications for FE: towards a system for the twenty-first century, in *FE and Lifelong Learning: Realigning the sector for the twenty-first century*, eds A Green and N Lucas, Bedford Way Papers, Institute of Education, London

Zimmern, A (1898) *The Renaissance of Girls' Education*, A D Innes and Company, London

Part 1

The Changing Context for Higher Education

1

Getting In and Getting On: Choosing the Best

Sheila Macrae and Meg Maguire

Introduction

In this chapter we explore the perceptions and experiences of a small group of young people who have successfully gained admission to an undergraduate course in two pre-1992 universities. In so doing, we intend to open up aspects of 'choice' and 'choice-making' in order to question the ways in which 'choosing' is socially situated and socially constituted. Our point is that selecting a university is as much related to habitus, dispositions to choose, beliefs about value/status (the 'best' university) as anything else (Bourdieu and Passeron, 1990). Any policy attempts to widen the participation rates of non-traditional students need to be sensitive to this reality. Through a brief exploration of some key concerns that relate to the process of transition to higher education, we suggest that widening participation is not the whole story. Institutions need to be aware of the dilemmas that can arise once the student has enrolled; the issue is not just one of widening participation but also of supporting and retaining these students. In what follows we also want to consider the ways in which aspects of elitism continue to exercise influence in relation to choosing and participating in higher education.

Elitism and access to higher education

To be celebrated, to be wealthy, to have power requires access to major institutions, for the institutional positions men occupy determine in large part their chances to have and to hold these valued experiences. (Wright Mills, 1959: 11).

Woodrow *et al* (1998) believe that there are two 'distinctive positions' on broadening access to higher education, which resonate with issues concerning elitism. One view is that any significant increase in access from non-traditional applicants 'raises the spectre of lowering standards' (Woodrow *et al*, 1998: 112). The role of the university in its 'quest for quality' (Goodlad, 1995) may be thrown into jeopardy by increases in access. If more people are admitted to higher education, this may involve a dilution of the curriculum, a change in pace and a general 'dumbing down'. The second view holds that many people have been excluded from participation 'as a result of socio-economic disadvantage, exacerbated by an elitist higher education system' (Woodrow *et al*, 1998: 112) which constitutes a significant waste of talent. What is needed is a systemic shift in higher education, 'not in the sense of lowering standards, but as a process of providing a learning environment which recognizes and respects a diverse student body' (Woodrow *et al*, 1998: 114). In part, this second thrust reflects a human capital perspective but it also incorporates a social justice trajectory where 'elitism' is recognized as a rationalization for exclusion.

Elitism and increased participation

Woodrow *et al* (1998) point to some of the contradictory outcomes that may arise from policies of increased non-traditional access. One outcome could be that non-traditional students might become concentrated in 'access-type' institutions: institutions that may be lower in the 'reputation' league tables (Robertson and Hillman, 1997). If recruitment to higher education rises from 30 to 50 per cent, 'bright students from poorer backgrounds' may be 'creamed off' by the 'old' (pre-1992) universities' (Ball *et al*, 2001). Thus, one outcome of increased participation might be to 'ghettoize' most low-income students in low-status institutions. As participation rates increase, the situation for those who are excluded becomes even harsher; those without higher education credentials become even more at 'risk' of exclusion (Beck, 1992). For those in the low-status institutions, access to high status and elite occupations may be just as far away as ever.

Somewhat ironically, then, greater inclusion and widening participation may merely serve to ratchet up (relative) patterns of exclusion and reinforce the binds of elitism in society, while working to legitimate claims for a meritocratic society. As Young has argued:

> A social revolution has been accomplished by harnessing schools and universities to the task of sieving people according to education's narrow band of values. With an amazing battery of certificates and degrees at its disposal, education has put its seal of approval on a minority, and its seal of disapproval on the majority who fail to shine from the time they are relegated to the bottom streams at the age of seven or before. (Young, 2001)

Paradoxically, New Labour's commitment to increased participation rates in higher education might work to reinforce patterns of elitism or, at the very least, produce a more internally differentiated and reconfigured pattern of elitism in higher education provision in the UK. However, a research concern with the role of higher education in allocating access to high-status occupations and preserving the advantages of the middle classes has a long history (see Halsey *et al*, 1980; Bourdieu and Passeron, 1990; Kerckhoff and Trott, 1993). Much of this work has pointed to the relationship between social class and participation rates. What has some-times been forgotten is the way in which these advantages are socially situated processes which are evoked and reworked in the experience of higher education itself. In this chapter, it is these socially situated processes we want to open up for consideration.

New transitions and reworkings of elitism

As we have said, the question of widening access is not just about recruit-ment, it is also about retention – and some students are better placed to navigate a route through higher education and stay the course than others. Traditional choosers, for whom going to university is part of a normalized process of 'what you do', are in a privileged position. Their social and cultural capital are in good supply, and for them, participation in higher education is part of a broader set of long-term expectations and assumptions about their place in the world. Those who 'choose' or 'select' a traditional high-status university may well buy into discourses of elitism – where only a 'good' university would ever be seen as a viable prospect (Bourdieu and Passeron, 1990). They may have family and schools to enable them success-fully to 'read' the workings of the university and empower them to steer themselves successfully through many of the 'disruptions' or unexpected events that might de-rail those with less social capital at their disposal. Others, who recognize the ways an elite higher education provider can endow them with status and market advantages (perhaps) on graduation, may have less capacity to manoeuvre themselves through a complex and unfamiliar set of predicaments, experiences and different people. Non-tradi-tional choosers, without the appropriate cultural capital or relevant social capital, may potentially find themselves in the 'wrong' place or on the 'wrong' course, with higher risks of dropping off their course.

The research study

The data we draw on in this chapter come from an Economic and Social Research Council (ESRC) funded study. In this three-year longitudinal research project we focus on one cohort of single-honours undergraduate mathematics students from two traditional city-based English universities.

We refer to these higher education institutions as Waverley University and Marmion University. They were chosen because they are highly regarded for teaching and research and attract large numbers of well-qualified applicants. The average A level scores for mathematics students in both universities were 23 (QAA, 1998), which compares with national average scores of 19 points (QAA, 2000). The proportion of female students admitted to mathematics courses in both institutions is approximately one-third, which compares with national average figures of 38 per cent females and 62 per cent males (QAA, 2000). In one institution, the ethnic composition of the cohort is predominantly white (approximately 95 per cent) while the other has around 45 per cent 'Britasians' (Sing-Raud, 1998), 45 per cent white and 10 per cent Chinese. We aim to work with this cohort of 225 students (79 female and 146 male) during the three years of their degree course in order to understand better the reasons why they experience their mathematics programmes in different ways and why some maintain or develop more positive attitudes than others to the subject.

In the rest of this chapter, and using a series of vignettes, we draw on questionnaire, interview and observational data to examine some of the ways in which four students talk about their first-year experiences of the mathematics course and of university life in general. These four students should not be seen as representative of the cohort but they do characterize the transition from school to university and their responses demonstrate the ways in which prior educational, social and 'ethnic' experiences shape and influence their reactions to their mathematics courses and to university life in general.

Vignettes of four students

Tracy

Tracy is a tall, slim, serious-looking white student with long, dark hair. She is an only child who lives at home with her mother. She had attended an 11–18 mixed comprehensive school where she gained the following A levels: mathematics A, Latin A, French C and general studies D. No one in her family had ever gone to university and there was no pressure on Tracy to move into higher education. Neither parent played any significant role in her university choices and she wrote in her pre-course questionnaire that her father's views were 'particularly unhelpful'. Her mother, who has the equivalent of GCSEs, is an office receptionist and her father is a taxi driver, with no academic qualifications.

As with the majority of students in our study, Tracy chose to study mathematics at university because 'I was quite good at it at school and it's my favourite subject as well'. Also in common with a large number of the cohort, Tracy had no career in mind when she began her course but was firmly of the view that a degree was necessary in order to get a 'good' job. A good job in Tracy's opinion paid more money than one without a degree.

From this description, Tracy can be described as a 'pragmatic chooser', according to the typology constructed by Macrae *et al* (1997). The aim of such choosers is to improve their employment prospects. A mathematics degree was seen by many students as having higher status than degrees in the humanities. It showed, Tracy's teachers had told her, that one could 'think in a clear, logical manner'; an attribute she hoped would be viewed favourably by future employers. At the time of interview, she had no idea what she wanted to do: 'I'll definitely get a job but I haven't got a clue what I'd like to do'. She is enrolled on the three-year course because she 'thought the four-year course would be too hard for me'.

Marmion University had been chosen by Tracy largely because it had been recommended by staff at her school for its good reputation in teaching and research. She had visited some other, lower-status city universities but had rejected them on the grounds that, 'Well, I didn't like where they were, really. It was all just horrible buildings and not nice and I didn't really like them.' Furthermore, they were not high on her teachers' recommendation lists. Marmion was preferred, 'mainly because it looks nice outside and it's near the river. That's it really'. It was also her teachers' first choice. At one level, such choice-making may appear arbitrary and trivial but, at another, location, reputation, 'niceness' or 'nastiness' were crucial factors found also by Ball *et al* (2000) in their study of students' selection of post-16 institutions.

On being asked to summarize her first term at Marmion, Tracy immediately referred to the gap between A level and university mathematics.

Tracy: Yeah it was massive. Bigger than from GCSE to A level, I would say. I didn't realize it would be like that.

Interviewer: You didn't? Can you say more?

Tracy: It was, well, it was just so much more because at school the teachers always made sure you understood things before they moved onto something else and it was just slower and you had time to understand each step. But here it's not like that. You just get so much and nobody really bothers to find out if you're keeping up and so it's up to you and that was a surprise that nobody ever said, nobody ever bothers to ask if everything's alright and if people are following what's going on.

Interviewer: You came here, and you found this big gap.

Tracy: Mmm, it was a problem, a big worry really, at first. Yeah, but now I'm getting used to it.

Interviewer: So how did you feel at first?

Tracy: Well, it was a bit daunting. I thought I was going to find it all hard and I'll never get used to it and I was spending all my time going over the work and that and I was really worried that I'd never keep up and I was just working all the time and I was scared to stop in case I fell behind.

Interviewer: And you were scared to stop in case you fell behind.

Tracy: Yeah, because it was all so fast and that and I thought if I don't work I'll fall behind and never catch up.

The fear of falling behind and being unable to catch up is repeated several times throughout Tracy's interview. She no longer has teachers to support and guide her; she has no yardstick by which to measure her progress and, therefore, can never be sure she has done enough. To add to her anxiety, she is both surprised and concerned that 'nobody really bothers to find out if you're keeping up'. Furthermore, the pace of university mathematics is beginning to speed up. At school, the delivery had been 'slower and you had time to understand each step'.

Tracy is a loner; she sits apart from her peers during lectures and wanders around on her own between teaching sessions. She looks unhappy and rarely smiles. When asked if she shared her anxieties with her mother, Tracy said that there was no point because her mother knew nothing about university. Neither does she approach lecturers or tutors with her worries.

Interviewer: Do you use the lecturers? Do you go to them at all for any help?

Tracy: No.

Interviewer: Why don't you go to them if you're worried about how you're doing?

Tracy: Because they're too busy and it's obvious you're supposed to do it on your own. They don't want you bothering them.

Interviewer: Why do you think that?

Tracy: Because it's just what I think. They don't, like, say things that make you think they'd want you coming to them... Like I say, they don't want that, not really. They're not like teachers at school. They really want to help you because they're teachers and that, but here they're not really teachers. Somebody said they really just want to do research and they have to teach but I don't know about that. But I don't think they're really teachers, not like at school anyway.

To add to Tracy's isolation, she did not belong to any university clubs and reported that she had no social life because she had 'no time for one'. Nor does she have time for a part-time job. From her comments, she studies every weekday evening and for approximately six hours on both Saturday and Sunday. In common with most students in the cohort, Tracy does her homework on her own, but unlike her peers, she never seeks help from other students when she gets stuck. She uses the same ways of coping with the course as she did with her A level mathematics; the only difference is that she has no staff to support her. She employs the same study and revision techniques and continues to use her library at home to borrow books; the university library is 'too big' and is used simply as 'somewhere I'll get a bit of peace and quiet'. She complains of feeling tired and 'weighed down' by the responsibility of 'keeping up' and the fear of 'falling behind'. She adds at the end of several responses, in a voice tinged with desperation and determination, 'but I stuck at it'.

It seemed difficult for Tracy to answer several interview questions. For example, in response to what did she like best and least about GCSE and A level mathematics (these appeared as four separate questions on the pre-course questionnaire), she replied that she did not know. Similarly when asked in interview what, in her view, made a good lecture and then a good lecturer, she again said she did not know. Probing seemed to unsettle and discomfit her. Tracy, apparently, does not share her thoughts about mathematics with anyone and perhaps has never considered some of the issues we are interested in exploring. She clearly relied heavily on her school teachers for guidance and support and in their absence is finding it difficult to keep afloat. All her hard work and 'sticking at it', however, paid off and she did relatively well in her end of year examinations, passing seven of the eight modules and gaining an average of 56.9 per cent.

Janusz

Janusz describes himself as half British and half Polish. He is a tall, blonde, gentle young man who shares a flat with his older brother and his brother's friend, who are both medical students. Janusz attended a boys' independent school throughout his secondary education and in his A levels gained mathematics A, physics A, French A and English A. He was one of only a handful of students in our cohort who had had out-of-school tuition during his A levels; the tuition was in French oral, to perfect his accent. He is enrolled on the four-year mathematics course. Both parents have first degrees; his mother is a librarian and his father, a teacher of engineering. Going to university was clearly important to his parents and not just for academic reasons:

> I mean Dad's always saying that university is about making social connections and networks for when you're older. It's not just about learning things. He says no other experience in your life will be like university and you've got to make the most of it, enjoy it, meet people, do things you'll never, maybe never do again and experience all sorts of new experiences. And he always used to reminisce when he was at uni. and the stuff they got up to.

Janusz had studied politics and philosophy for a year at another university (having been persuaded by his parents to do an Arts subject) before deciding that 'I don't think I was suited to it. I can't really read that quickly, and it was mainly a reading course, speed reading'. He then decided to study mathematics because he wanted, 'something completely different' and, like Tracy, had both enjoyed and done well in mathematics at school. He had chosen Marmion for two reasons. His older brother studied medicine there and he had met some politics and philosophy students who seemed happy there and 'so it seemed the natural place to go, really'.

In his interview, Janusz frequently related his experiences on the mathematics course to those on the politics and philosophy course he had left and here he gives his reasons for enjoying and preferring mathematics to politics and philosophy:

> I just like the structure and knowing the limits of what you're trying to do. In politics and philosophy, it felt limitless and so I didn't really know where I stood but in maths, I think I do know where I stand and what's expected of me. It all feels tighter and more secure and if I keep working within the limits of what's expected I should be all right. But in politics and philosophy I didn't know what the limits were, or if there were any. It felt as it didn't have any limits.

Many students spoke in similar terms about the 'security' of mathematics, about knowing the boundaries and what was expected of them. Feeling 'in control' was also important to students as this added to their sense of security:

> I feel more in control of maths in a way. I know what I have to learn. I know when I've got it right and I think I understand the structure of the course and what bits go together. I never felt that with politics and philosophy. It just all felt so immense and it was like I was always doing little bits of things and I never had any idea where it would lead or how big the thing was that it was part of. I just never felt I had any control and I don't know if it was just me or if that is what politics and philosophy is like. I don't know, but maths is different and I'm enjoying it much more. It feels smaller somehow, or perhaps it's just how it is at the moment but I do know that maths as a subject is immense but maybe it's the way it's taught, that makes it seem as if you can manage it, do it and get it right.

Although students spoke about the security of mathematics, a frequent complaint voiced by them was that their courses were more demanding than those in humanities. Students living in university halls, for example, described arts students as being able to lie in bed most mornings and working only in short, sharp bursts before essay deadlines. Attending lectures seemed, for these arts students, to be an optional extra. Students of mathematics, on the other hand, reported that in theory, they regularly had to get up for morning lectures and tutorials and hand in weekly home-work. In practice, of course, many students admitted they did not meet these demands. They did, however, recognize the problems associated with copying other people's notes, sometimes at third or fourth hand until they resembled something like 'Chinese whispers'. Janusz, rather than seeing regular attendance as a drawback, described the benefits of attending lectures, even those with full course notes:

> Sometimes you read it [in course notes] and you think, well I think I under-stand that but then you hear it and it might even be the same words as are in the notes but somehow you hear it differently to what you read. And some-times it just clicks that way. There's something different in hearing it and reading it. I'm not sure what it is but that has happened a few times and that's good. I like when that happens because it usually means that it sticks in my head.

Janusz spoke positively about his experiences on his course and was equally pleased with the teaching staff. Unlike Tracy, he was quite happy to approach lecturers for help:

> I've had most of them for teaching as well as in tutorials so I know they always welcome questions. They've always been really accommodating, and you don't feel intimidated at all by them to be honest, although normally, sometimes it's a bit limited actually to ask questions during the lecture. I wait until it's over and then go outside and wait to ask them outside of the lecture. They all have these hours, some of them actually encourage you to go to their office any time if you've got a problem, so you get on with most of them.

Janusz's parents had been concerned that he was pushing himself too hard on the politics and philosophy course and that he was likely to 'burn himself out' if he continued working at the same rate on the mathematics course. They had advised him to 'ease up', so he decided 'to pace' himself during the first year: 'I'm not looking for top grades this year'. He passed all eight modules and achieved an average of 67.7 per cent in his examinations.

Florence

Florence is a white student of average height and build with many rings and studs in her ears, lip and nose. She is enrolled on a three-year mathematics with philosophy course and lives in university halls. Florence attended an 11–16 mixed comprehensive school followed by a sixth form college where she gained A levels in mathematics A; further mathematics B (AS); physics B and English language C. She has one older sister who has a sociology degree; both parents have degrees and were teachers. Her mother is now an advisory teacher and her father has re-trained as an educational psychologist.

One of the reasons given by a large number of students in our cohort for choosing Waverley or Marmion was that they did not want to be 'stuck out' on a campus with all the imagined boredom that would entail. Being part of city life was important to many of our students, including Florence, who had attended school in a small, rural area. Many parents who had been to university were able to offer useful advice but Florence wanted to make her own choices. She forbade her parents from accompanying her to the different institutions she visited but they did have some influence over her choice:

> Yeah, well they [her parents] kind of know about these things and they said, well so many people have degrees these days and that, that it's better if you can say, well I've got a degree from some older, more established place that people have heard of like [Marmion], rather than from, say, an old redbrick poly or something. I wasn't actually that bothered but that's what they said, so.

31

While she claimed not to have been 'bothered' about whether she went to a new or more traditional university, the choice of where to study was important to Florence, who visited only elite institutions. Being able to imagine herself there and feeling she would fit in were specific criteria she applied as she did the rounds. Despite large sums of money spent on promotion of courses and marketing of institutions, the decisions to choose or reject places to study are frequently based on the flimsiest of evidence:

> I dunno, it was the kind of student union facilities, they were really poor. It [another university] just seemed to be a place where they did lots of work and that was it. And that was a bit overwhelming. I didn't really want to go there and there was just an atmosphere there – it was very, kind of, there were people in the canteen talking about the work and I just thought, gosh everybody here takes it really seriously and I just didn't like it. It was a big, pale grey block. It wasn't very friendly at all. The place was dull looking, not nice and I just thought, no, I don't want to be here. I dunno, it was just the feeling I got when I went there. I didn't think I'd fit in if people were just talking about work all the time like the people I listened to in the canteen.

Conversations overheard, the colours of walls in rooms, the height of ceilings, the walk from the car park to the entrance, all contributed to students' decision-making. Several reported turning down university offers because of traumas experienced at interview. For others, rejection came as relief. These students usually described the interview process as being over-rigorous and frightening. Maguire *et al* (1999) describe the ways in which interviews are used by prestigious institutions as a tactic for selection. Below, Florence talks about her particular interview experience at another institution:

> They asked me really, really hard stuff which I didn't really mind but I did quite well in it and they gave me a low offer because of that. But it scared me. It was just unnecessary really, because they asked me about stuff that I'd only kind of touched on and they asked me to take it all a lot deeper and I just felt really under pressure. And I thought, well if it's like this at the interview before I've even come here, what will it be like if I come. It just seemed like high pressure and work and asking searching questions and that scared me, to be honest. Yes, they gave me an offer but it wasn't friendly and I thought it might be like that all the time and that just put me off.

Before starting her course, Florence had enjoyed a gap year which she described as 'a kind of recovery period for me, because my A levels stressed me out a lot'. During this time she had worked as an accounts manager for a hardware company where she had been 'indispensable' and had managed to save enough money, she estimated, to meet her costs for the next three years. Mathematics was a natural choice to study at university because, not only was she good at it, but also:

> It seemed like a really important subject that everyone should know. I couldn't understand how people couldn't see how everyone should know maths, because it applies to everything. I used to think I was so lucky because I could see how important it was to everything we do.

Now, however, just over a term into her course, Florence is beginning to question this assumption:

> It's just got so obscure now that it doesn't seem to relate to reality in any way at all. But I mean I still enjoy doing it. I just think while I do it, I'm actually thinking, oh dear, this is not going to be much use. I can't see how, what we do, can matter really, can be useful in everyday life because it's getting more and more obscure.

Florence had found her first term extremely hard, partly because, like Tracy, she did not know what standards were expected of her and had spent most of her time studying and partly because she went to Sussex every weekend to see her boyfriend. She had no social life during the week and found living in university halls very difficult:

> My halls were a bit of nightmare, they still are a bit of a nightmare. They're very noisy and it's hard to sleep and stuff, so I was generally feeling really run down and more and more tired last term and it just got worse and worse as time went on... there's always people running round the corridors and stuff, and there's construction going on outside as well which is annoying and there's one kitchen between 17, so... you have to like wait for the kitchen for about three hours in the evening so you can never eat when you're hungry, you have to starve yourself and then eat later. So that's terrible, that was really annoying me last term because I wasn't eating properly and I wasn't sleeping properly or anything.

We were unprepared for the strong feelings expressed by students living in university halls. Some transcripts run to several pages on this topic as they vent their spleen on the inconsiderate habits of their fellow students. For example, the horrors of unhygienic shared kitchens, dirty dishes, stolen food and the expense of living on takeaway food were described in graphic detail. Almost all students living in halls reported a series of minor health problems which they related to poor eating habits, lack of sleep and living in close proximity to other students.

However, despite these drawbacks, Florence's natural ability and hard work paid off. Her average mark at the end of first year was 88.4 per cent. She had passed all eight modules, came third in her year and won third prize in a competition open to all mathematics students at Marmion University.

Raj

Raj, an only child, spent the first nine years of his life in the Punjab and is one of only a handful of minority ethnic students studying mathematics at Waverley University; a fact that both surprised and unsettled him during his first term:

> You come here and it's like, basically, you know you're different, and plus, because there was no people, like, come from my background [working class]. There was no Asians either, kind of thing, so the whole culture thing was different, you know, and I didn't know, I just couldn't handle it because I'd never been here before and I was like, 'why aren't there any Asians?'... There's only about two or something, two or three of us, I think. Whole mass of teachers Asians, doctors Asians, lawyers Asians, chemists Asians, dentists Asians, so I thought, maths Asians, but no, there weren't.

He had attended a mixed, 11–18 comprehensive school in a deprived inner-city area. 'My school which is, like, really quite bad in all categories. I think there's sixteen schools in our borough and it's the fifteenth in the table, chairs flying out of windows all the time, common practice'. There he gained A grades in the following A levels: mathematics, physics, biology and Punjabi. Such success had not been seen at his school before, where staying on beyond the statutory leaving age was unusual and doing A levels even more unusual.

Raj's parents are both factory workers: his mother, a seamstress and his father, a sheet metal worker. Neither parent speaks much English and Raj has acted as interpreter, dealing with workmen, solicitors and government officials since he was in primary school. While neither parent has academic qualifications, they are both highly ambitious for their only child. Several studies (for example, Bird, 1996; Modood and Shiner 1994; Modood and Acland, 1998) have found that, despite minority ethnic students' less advantaged parental occupational profile, 'most minority groups are producing greater proportions of applications and admissions to higher education than the rest of the population' (Modood and Acland, 1998: 37). Mirza (1998), however, provides evidence of the troubling racial divide between the intakes of the new and old sectors of higher education, where, for example, Asians are over-represented by 162 per cent in new universities, along with students from working class backgrounds (Cohen, 2000).

Raj telephones his mother every day and wants to do well, not only for himself, but also for his mother who has to 'keep face with the Asian ladies she works with'. These 'Asian ladies' are frequently mentioned in his interviews.

> Living in that Asian community, kind of thing, it's very close knit. What other people's sons and daughters are doing, you know, they all want to know. Especially my Mum working in a factory, kind of thing, with all the Asian

ladies, they all talk, 'oh, your son's at university now', you know. It was quite funny last year getting my four As in my A levels. Basically, coming from the school I come from, it's never happened before, so I became a bit of a superstar kind of thing with the Asian ladies, you know. And everyone's like, 'OK, you done that', and now they expect great things of me now, kind of thing, and they ask my mum, 'oh what's your son doing at university? Oh maths, very good', and all that, you know. You just find ladies ask all this stuff and so I've got my mum to think about as well.

As no one in his family had been to university and his school friends were not planning on going, Raj had to turn to his teachers for guidance. 'I wasn't too sure, like wasn't clued up about the whole university thing, where they are and everything. And I wasn't very clever about the whole thing, to be honest, I just went along with what my teachers, my teacher, like helped me and that'. He chose to study mathematics largely on their advice but the choice of Waverley had been his own. 'I was like looking at the league calibre of universities and stuff like that. Waverley was quite good... and I've always aimed high so I thought, "yeah, go for it"'.

Of all the students interviewed to date, none has expressed such surprise at the reality of university life as Raj. He was living in university halls and described his first term as 'terrible'. He was quite unable to settle to work because of feeling socially and culturally dislocated:

I was like thinking, I don't, like, fit into this whole university thing, to be honest. And are, are they all the same, are they all like this? Why did I ever think I would fit in here? People like me don't fit in to places like this. Why did nobody tell me? I can't believe this. What am I doing here? And I was gobsmacked and, like, in my classes there were three students at my school who was doing A levels. There were three maths students, yeah. One was above me, one year above me kind of thing, resitting A level maths and one was my mate and she was resitting GCSEs kind of thing.

I was a bit like, a bit depressed in all probability being away from home, missing my mum, kind of thing. And because I'm living on my own, I ended up first of all I wasn't mixing with other people because, if you like, I dunno, they're better than me. They know things I've like never even heard of. They've been places I've never been. Their lives are like really different, kind of thing to be honest. I'm not like one of them because of my background and that. But a lot of the maths students either come from really good comprehensive schools or grammar schools even, kind of thing, and there's a whole different culture mind, from what kind of background I come from and what they came from basically kind of thing. And I just like don't feel I belong and that. I just like don't fit in because I found myself hard to relate to them kind of thing, and I think this is not my type of people. I can't mix in with them. I never have, and never will, type of thing, and I find it really hard to like mix in and because there's not one person, not one like the people at my school because I looked around and I thought, no there's not one like anyone who went to my school.

None of this unhappiness was evident to the casual observer. Raj could usually be spotted in lectures, wearing a selection of baseball caps and sitting about two-thirds of the way back. He was always with other students, smiling and chatting to them. On the surface, he appeared a happy, well-adjusted student with lots of friends. However, his disorientation meant that he found it difficult to work and while he attended most lectures he soon stopped going to tutorials as he was not handing in homework and wanted to avoid confrontation.

As his school sixth form was so small, teachers often could not be spared to teach such low numbers. Work was set for these students and Raj resorted to teaching himself A level biology and physics from textbooks but when he tried this technique at university, he encountered some problems:

> At my A levels, I would often get a lot of books and read that and sort of teach myself, and I come to university, there are books that you can't read, you can't get for your modules and the ones I did get are either, they were above my head or they were wrong for the module, weren't the exact books for the module. But if I really needed some books, because that was what I did with my A levels, kind of teach myself from books, but here I am with, like, more books than I seen in my life, never seen so many books and I can't find one that will help me. That's quite funny, I thought, all these books and I can't even find one.

Raj frequently described himself as lazy; his teachers had told him so, his mother continued to tell him so. There appeared to be little in the way of a work ethic in his school. He was accustomed to waiting until he was nagged by teachers before getting down to his studies. 'I liked the school teachers, even if you didn't work, they would often catch up with you and get you to work. Like sit you down and talk to you about being stupid, wasting your life playing stupid cards, helping you make the most of yourself.' At university he was waiting for the same thing to happen but it never did. 'I dunno, no one really bothers about you. If you don't do it, you don't do it. It's up to you kind of thing and once I realized that, I pushed it. I took it to the limit basically. How much do I not need to do?' At school, he had developed the habit of leaving his studies to the last minute and working very hard before examinations. He assumed he could catch up with all his missed university work over the Christmas holiday. This, however, was not to be. He was so relieved to be back home, socializing with family and friends, that all plans to study were forgotten. When he did try to revise, he found he did not have sufficient information and could not find suitable books to help. The result was that he failed several modules in his mid-sessional examinations. Ever pragmatic, Raj summed up his early experiences as follows:

> It was probably the worst start I could have hoped for. But, to be honest, I couldn't realize what it was going to be like because I really hadn't a clue what was involved in going to university. Hadn't a clue when I applied and

then I came here and it was like the biggest eye opener I could imagine, just being here. Nobody told me, nobody knew and I never knew what to ask, kind of thing because I never really thought much about it. And nobody I knew knew much because people at my school don't go to university. My mum and dad's never been so nobody could tell me.

In the second half of the year, Raj joined an Asian students' social club where he was able to mix with others who shared his cultural heritage. This enabled him to settle down a little and slowly he began to feel less like a 'fish out of water', although getting down to serious study is still eluding him. In his end of year examinations he managed to gain an average of 40.4 per cent.

Widening participation – is elitism the issue?

In this chapter we started with a brief discussion of the role of elitism in higher education. Drawing on Woodrow *et al* (1998: 112), we argued that increased participation rates of non-traditional applicants can sometimes be seen as a problem: a problem of 'lowering standards'. However, issues related to elitism are far more complex and far-reaching than this. It is evident from national data sets (HEFCE, 2000) and related research (see Archer *et al* in this collection) that working class participation continues to be low. From the small number of narratives reported here, it is evident that discourses of elitism are interwoven into the beliefs, perceptions and attitudes of these four undergraduates, all of whom have chosen to attend high status universities. These discourses of elitism are grounded in different and sometimes overlapping sets. Tracy, for example, holds a pragmatic view where she recognizes the improved final pay-off gained from attending a 'good' university regardless of the disruptions/dislocations involved. Janusz and Florence share a recognition of the access to elite groups and life-enhancing networks extended at university. All of the four students are influenced to some degree by fears, anxieties and desires for security and advantage in a competitive world.

From what these four first-year undergraduates say, it is evident that their biographies and identities play a powerful role in the ways in which they experience higher education. For those who lack familiarity with university life or whose parents did not participate in higher education, the pathway is frequently disjointed and isolated. There is no obvious back-up; there is no clear person to turn to for advice or support. In their immediate pasts, teachers in schools might have been able to offer suggestions, or, in some cases, these young people were able to develop their own tactics through which to manage their studies. Now they are on their own. For newcomers like Raj, the pressures of coping on their own can sometimes be exacerbated by needing to satisfy a wider community. Perhaps the social and cultural capital newcomers like Tracy and Raj have brought with them have been exhausted. They are at a point where they are gaining a different set of understandings but, as yet, they are teetering on the edge, hanging on, not fully able to manage in this novel setting. They are perhaps in, but not of, the university.

Others do not experience this disruption and dislocation in quite the same way. They have moved seamlessly from home to school to university. They have always been aware of the power of higher education to access networks and enriching experiences. They have also been made aware of the need to attend a 'good' university. For undergraduates like Florence and Janusz, the continuity they experience and the capacity/capitals (Bourdieu, 1984) that they have to draw upon offer a wider set of strategies through which they can bring off additional access to tutors or other support systems. This does not mean that they have no difficulties; the dilemma of poor-quality provision in halls of residence was experienced acutely by many students and while non-traditional students like Tracy were more likely to live at home, those like Florence and Raj, who lived in university accommodation, reported health problems related to their living conditions.

Thus, in terms of any policy attempts to widen participation in higher education for young, non-traditional students like Tracy or Raj, while there is a need to consider access, there is also a need to consider issues related to support and retention. Direct discussion, by tutors, of dilemmas such as anxiety, pacing and keeping up as well as better on-course support systems could make a difference. The problem is not just one of widening participation but ensuring that participation extends to on-course processes. It is worth repeating what Raj said because in his comments lies a clue to widening the participation rates of non-traditional students:

> I really hadn't a clue what was involved in going to university... Nobody told me, nobody knew and I never knew what to ask... and nobody I knew knew much because people at my school don't go to university.

References

Ball, S J, Maguire, M and Macrae, S (2000) *Choice, Pathways and Transitions Post-16: New youth, new economies in the global city*, Routledge Falmer, London

Ball, S J, Reay, D and David, M (2001) Ethnic choosing: minority ethnic students, social class and higher education choice, paper presented at British Educational Research Association Conference, 13–15 September, University of Leeds

Beck, U (1992) *Risk Society: Towards a new modernity*, Sage, Newbury Park, CA

Bird, J (1996) *Black Students and Higher Education: Rhetorics and realities*, Open University Press, Milton Keynes

Bourdieu, P (1984) *Distinction*, Polity Press, Cambridge

Bourdieu, P and Passeron, J-C (1990) *Reproduction in Education, Society and Culture*, Sage, London

Cohen, P (2000) What kind of place is this? Cultures of learning, student identities and the process of disqualification in British higher education, in K M Gokulsing and C DaCosta (eds) *A Compact for Higher Education*, Ashgate Publishing Ltd, Aldershot

Goodlad, S (1995) *The Quest for Quality*, Open University Press, Buckingham

Halsey, H, Heath, A F and Ridge, J M (1980) *Origins and Destinations: Family, class and education in modern Britain*, Clarendon Press, Oxford

HEFCE (2000) *Students' Early Statistics Survey 2000–1*, October 2000 http://www.hefce.ac.uk/pubs/HEFCE/

Kerckhoff, A C and Trott, J M (1993) Educational attainment in a changing educational system: the case of England and Wales, in *Persistent Inequality: Changing educational attainments in 13 countries*, eds Y Shavit and H Blossfeld, Westview Press, Oxford

Macrae, S, Maguire, M and Ball, S J (1997) Whose 'learning society'? A tentative deconstruction, *Journal of Education Policy*, **12** (6), pp 499–509

Maguire, M, Ball, S J and Macrae, S (1999) Promotion, persuasion and class-taste: marketing (in) the UK post-compulsory sector, *British Journal of Sociology of Education*, **20** (3), pp 499–509

Mirza, H S (1998) Black women in education: a collective movement for social change, in *Race and Higher Education*, eds T Modood and T Acland, Policy Studies Institute, London

Modood, T and Shiner, M (1994) *Ethnic Minorities and Higher Education: Why are there differential rates of entry?* Policy Studies Institute, London

Modood, T and Acland, T (1998) Conclusion, in *Race and Higher Education*, eds T Modood and T Acland, Policy Studies Institute, London

Modood, T and Acland, T (eds) (1998) *Race and Higher Education*, Policy Studies Institute, London

Quality Assurance Agency (QAA) (1998) *Subject Review Report: Mathematics, statistics and operational research*, QAA, London

QAA (2000) *Mathematics, Statistics and Operational Research 1998–2000*, Report, Q07/2000, QAA, London

Robertson, D and Hillman, J (1997) *Widening Participation in Higher Education by Students from Lower Socio-economic Groups and Students with Disabilities*, Report 6, Higher Education in the Learning Society, National Committee of Enquiry into Higher Education, London

Sing-Raud, H (1998) *Asian Women Undergraduates: British universities and the dangers of creedism*, paper presented at the European Conference on Educational Research, 17–20 September, University of Ljubljana, Slovenia

Woodrow, M with Foong Lee, M, McGrane, J, Osborne, B, Pudner, H and Trotman, C (1998) *From Elitism to Inclusion: Good practice in widening access to higher education, Main Report*, CVCP, London

Wright Mills, C (1959) *The Power Elite*, Oxford University Press, New York

Young, M (2001) Down with meritocracy, 29 June, www.guardian.co.uk/archive/article

2

Challenging Inequality, Choosing Inclusion: Higher Education in Changing Social Landscapes

Karen Evans

Unravelling factors that account for the apparently intractable problems in widening access to higher education among disadvantaged socio-economic groups in the UK has preoccupied the national educational press in recent times. Many initial commentaries pointed to the deterrent effects of the changes in funding support for students and the introduction of tuition fees, but more considered analyses have identified a host of interacting factors associated with low participation. Many of these have been set out in the National Audit Office (NAO) report (2002). The NAO study showed that higher education institutions themselves have been inclined to blame low entry rates from non-traditional groups on relatively poor examination performance at A level or equivalent among working class pupils, and have pointed to evidence that working class students who do achieve two A levels are as likely to proceed to higher education as their middle class counterparts.

The NAO report (2002) has shown that a significant proportion of universities in England discriminate against students from working class and disadvantaged backgrounds. According to the report, qualified working class applicants were 30 per cent less likely to be offered a place at some universities than their counterparts from higher socio-economic groups. Once in higher education, drop-out was associated with A level scores. At this stage there was very little correlation with social class. Social class differences became apparent again at the end of higher education, in the form of disparities in the earning power of people with equivalent qualifications on entering the labour market. Graduates from social classes IV and V earned on average 7 per cent less than graduates from social class I.

Young people from working class families and disadvantaged backgrounds take a financial risk if they decide to go to university. It has been argued that these groups take more risk and are more debt averse than their middle class counterparts and are less certain of the benefits of higher education. In addition they do not have role models within their families and communities for successful participation in higher educations and careers. This chapter considers these factors in the light of comparative data from England and Germany. The comparisons allow the effects of socio-economic, labour market and cultural contexts to become more visible and help to uncover some assumptions which underpin analysis and argument in the area.

The comparative findings come from the ESRC Youth Citizenship and Social Change Programme research on young people in England and Germany (Evans, 2001). This international research has explored how far young adults aged 18–25 feel in control of their lives in relation to higher education, unemployment and work settings in England and the new Germany. The 900 young adults in the study came from three cities in England, eastern Germany and western Germany, each of which represents a labour market undergoing structural change. In this chapter their experiences are considered in relation to the changing context of higher education in the two countries and to the significance attached to wider participation and social support. The chapter explores features of the student experience in the University of Derby, a 'new' English university, and makes selective comparisons with the experiences of German students attending a local university in the cities of Hanover and Leipzig.

The data allow an exploration of four questions that are central to the widening participation debate in the UK:

- What are the subjective perceptions of 18–25-year-old higher education students in England and Germany about the effects of social characteristics in determining life chances?
- How do part-time work and financial support impact on their lives as learners in higher education?
- How do differences in planning dispositions relate to participation in higher education?
- How do choices, pathways, participation patterns and experiences reflect the wider socio-economic environment, particularly with reference to forms of regulation and the operation of markets?

Features of German higher education

German universities differ from those in the UK in a number of important ways. They tend to be more 'traditional' and conservative than their UK counterparts, and less diverse, although there are newer and older institutions with slightly different missions. On the whole, young Germans attend their local university. Higher education tuition in state universities is free. In universities 46 per cent of the students are female, compared to 34 per cent in *Fachhochschulen,* which are universities of 'applied science' similar in some ways to the former English polytechnics. In universities the primary route into higher education is through the *Gymnasium* (grammar school). In the 'new *Länder*', or eastern Germany, 54 per cent and in the 'old *Länder*', or western Germany, 74 per cent came through this route into university in 1998. In *Fachhochschulen* the share of students with 'non-academic' backgrounds is higher. In 1998, 33 per cent of students in the 'old *Länder*' of western Germany and 62 per cent in eastern Germany came from non-traditional backgrounds. Social background plays an important role in the orientation of young people when they first enrol in higher education, both in determining whether they can take a 'semester abroad' and in the financing of their studies and participating in additional part-time work.

Germany has a clear 'academic/vocational' divide, but the right of young people to attend their local university means that the system is non-selective once the threshold of the basic university entrance qualification has been gained. In 2002, the head of the Centre for Higher Education Studies (Frankfurt) blamed the 'outdated' allocation of study places by the Central Office for Allocating Admissions (ZVS) for the lack of student mobility. Only 18 per cent of places are allocated according to the grade of the *Abitur,* the academic school leaving certificate and university entrance qualification. Critics say that this system 'compounds the mediocrity built into the German education system, and [it] reinforces the dropout rate of 33 per cent' (THES, 2002). Some want to abolish the central admissions system and allow selection, pointing to the competitive nature of the growing number of private universities.

These systemic features are reflected in the populations of 18–25-year-olds in the Anglo-German research. In Germany most of the respondents had enrolled in higher education immediately after passing the *Abitur* examination. Only 15 per cent had previously begun any vocational training. Many English students move straight from A levels into higher education. However, about 50 per cent of the Derby sample reported having left full-time education at a younger age (16 per cent at age 16 and 39 per cent at up to age 18). This indicates that many probably had some experience of work or unemployment. For German students, studies may last for seven or eight years, although according to the national survey (Bargel *et al*, 1999) more students than previously are claiming that they are hoping to finish their studies as soon as possible, anticipating the beneficial effects of their move into the labour market. Students in their first semester in all subjects expect to stay about five years at university or four years at *Fachhochschule*.

Although students aspire to reduce their time at university, most of them stay longer than the period within which the course should have been completed both in the old and the new *Länder*. In 1999, in the old *Länder*, the average age of a university student was 24.9 years and 26.3 years for students at *Fachhochschule*. A tenth of students were older than 30 years and 'still doing their first degree'. These are not 'mature students' as we would understand them in the UK. They have registered as conventional students but have then extended their studies over a long period, often undertaking part-time work in parallel with their studies. According to these students there are two factors that slow down their progress through their studies: first, course regulations and second, part-time work.

Non-traditional students in English higher education

One of the most striking findings has been the almost universal recognition by young people in all of the groups studied of the importance of qualifications in influencing life chances, employment and higher education. The means for achieving their goals have diversified in both countries, but more in England than in Germany. Respondents in the two German cities were more aware of the effects of the ascribed characteristics of gender, ethnicity and social class than their counterparts in the English city. More respondents in Derby considered that qualifications override other social characteristics in shaping life chances. The pattern of response in the higher education group is given in Table 2.1.

Table 2.1 Opinions on the importance of social characteristics in affecting life opportunities (numbers and percentages)

	Sex/ Gender	Race	Social Class	Family Background	Education Qualification
Derby					
Higher Education	20	24	32	28	87
Employed	13	13	21	22	80
Unemployed	26	29	32	21	77
Total	59	66	85	71	244
%	19.7	22.0	28.3	23.7	81.3
Hanover					
Higher Education	26	45	46	31	97
Employed	39	58	42	36	94
Unemployed	29	52	46	25	90
Total	94	155	134	92	281
%	31.3	51.7	44.7	30.7	93.7
Leipzig					
Higher Education	46	80	58	37	96
Employed	37	71	53	25	95
Unemployed	35	67	57	28	81
Total	118	218	168	90	272
%	39.3	72.7	56.0	30.0	90.7

Numbers rating social characteristics as 'of considerable importance' in affecting life opportunities (n=300 in each city)

Group interviews with higher education participants in the three cities explored the importance of social characteristics for life chances, as perceived by the successful entrants to the university system. In Derby, the group discussions contained many participants from non-traditional backgrounds, reflecting the policy of the University of Derby in relation to widening participation. For the most part the significance of social class was discussed in relation to university life. One group focused on 'how you were seen by others' and a second group focused on access to and financing of higher education courses. There was some tension between the views of participants in both groups. For some students the 'area you come from' was important in shaping experiences in higher education. One research participant, for example, felt that no matter how well she did, people of a 'higher' social class would not look beyond the fact that she came from one of the poorer council estates in the area and was a single mother. Another young woman in the group expressed the view that social class was not important within the university:

> Daphne: I've never really experienced any divisions in social class really. Not like, especially not university, you don't really care. Nobody really cares how much your parents earn, whether they're employed or not. You know, it's you they're interested in, not your background.

> Dawn: Depends what area you come from though. Geographic. Say if you were on a border of like a posh area and you know like a council estate or something, if you went and had friends in the posher area they might sort of look down at you rather than look at you as someone else.

> Denise: It doesn't matter what you try to do here, they just won't let you cross that barrier. It's fair enough I might be doing a degree and I might be doing better than someone who lives in a really nice area but they never let me past the fact that I'm a single parent from a council estate. They just won't let me do it.

On the issue of the effects of policies on tuition fees, there were perceptions of 'unfairness' from several points of view. Some articulated the view that it is unfair that some must 'scrape' by on what they receive from the state whilst others 'blow their parents' money', others observed that the recent move away from government grants towards loans was excluding the poorest from higher education, and that it is those in the middle whose parents earn slightly more than the cut-off figure for entitlement to a grant who suffer the most. There was also a degree of confusion about what the entitlements actually were:

> Dionne: So, I do think in a way the [influences of] class come in there, because if you're middle class then you tend to suffer, you know middle, middle class, you tend to suffer more than if you're top end of the scale or bottom end of the scale. I think that is a big effect money-wise... I do think

that the classes still are affected, especially when it comes to coming to university because although people tend not to be 'oh you're middle class, you're high upper class, you're lower class', there always seems to be a band that, I mean if you've got no money at all you get a full grant, you get a full loan...

Darren: I think, I think you're missing sort of, I feel the main point here is that, is that with the government stopping the grants it prevents the sort of lower classes of people going to university, so that you get those people who can go to university are going to be the people who can afford to pay the fees so you're going to eradicate the sort of people who couldn't normally afford to go. So I think that's, that's...

Davina: Going back to the pre-historical the rich get educated and the poor...

Darren: Yeah, yeah I mean I thought that had been abolished sort of ages ago, but now it's sort of re-occurring.

Dionne: But if you think about it, the, the poorer, as they say, those with less money are getting the full, are getting an extra loan on top of er...

Davina: But they don't.

Dionne: That's what I got.

Darren: If, if, if it's a loan then you've got to pay it back.

Dionne: Oh yeah you've still got to pay it back.

Many students are employed part-time in casual jobs, often in addition to receiving parental support. This applied to 68 per cent of respondents in Derby, 74 per cent in Hanover and 75 per cent in Leipzig. A survey of students in Germany (Bargel *et al*, 1999) revealed an extensive change over the last 15 years in relation to the employment behaviour of German students while still in higher education. In particular, paid employment during the semester has increased dramatically, alongside the interest free loan and grant system. Today, about two-thirds of all students nationally work during term-time. The survey found that 50 per cent of those who worked did so in order to finance their studies. Others worked to earn additional money. Gaining practical experience and bettering post-graduation chances on the labour market were reasons for working given by one-third of students. This is paralleled by increases in part-time working among students in England. Tensions surrounding financial structures were most marked in the English sample studied.

One of the most prominent themes to emerge from the interviews with students in Derby was difficulty in making choices between earning money, borrowing money from the state, accepting parental support and time spent studying. These decisions and their outcomes were a considerable source of stress for many students:

Dionne: But in the back of your mind you're always thinking you know when I come out I'm going to have to pay off like £10,000 worth of debt and it's just a nightmare to think about it like that. But still.

Dorothy: And I mean my parents would contribute but I don't want to ask them to, you know what I mean, I'd rather pay my own way, because I'm independent even though I still live at home really. So I mean I do struggle with money a lot.

Darren: Through term, I only work week-end at the moment, I used to, used to work, in the second year I used to work like three or four days a week or five days a week. I found that, looking back I found that that was too much and now I only work sort of Saturday and Sunday and I find that a lot better, because I've sort of made it so that I get paid the same amount of money on the week-end and I can still have time to do my work as well Monday to Friday.

Interviewer: And that makes a better balance between your study time and your work?

Darren: Yeah, 'cause I feel that because I only get the grant and a student loan it doesn't sort of cover my expenses, so I feel that I have to work to support, because if I didn't work I would be in that much more debt so, so rather than get in that much more debt I'd rather work as well as study.

Davina: I, myself, have only got the money that I have here. I have no other savings or anything. I saved all my money up and had jobs while I was at college and at school and saved all my money up and basically spent it getting stuff to get me here. Because my parents recently got divorced and so we didn't have anything to send me here with, so I had to buy all my pots and pans and bedding and everything which is unbelievably a large amount of stuff. So I have no money, so presently I have minus four hundred and some-thing pounds. So next to nothing.

Interviewer: So money is a bit of a struggle?

Davina: A little bit. But I don't think I'd have time for a job really.

Dionne: I mean I don't have a problem, I am a very strict budgeter, I have to be, because of what I'm living on, I'm basically feeding myself on a thousand pounds a year, I get no help from my mum or my father and I just live on my loan and what I earned so. But I know it is a big problem for some of the other people that are in my house, they don't budget. And therefore, they end up with no money at the end, spent it all at the beginning and that is stress-ful, but in a way that's mismanagement as well, so I mean I don't think there is anybody there to teach you either.

Plans for the future

Most of the English students in the sample stated that both of their parents had encouraged them to stay in education when they reached the end of compulsory schooling. The German students were more likely to report that their parents had left the decision up to them.

In all three towns a large proportion of students are partly dependent on their parents (61 per cent in Derby, 55 per cent in Hanover, 51 per cent in Leipzig). In Derby, 24 students were financially independent of their parents, a striking comparison with Hanover and Leipzig where only 16 and 8 persons respectively feel independent.

One of the few attitudinal and dispositional variables significantly associated with social class (defined on the basis of the English Registrar-General's scale) was a disposition towards long-term planning. While life chances may have become more strongly influenced by abilities to be proactive and to plan for the future, the findings confirm that dispositions towards planning found in our respondents have structural foundations in social class. When planning dispositions were examined in relation to social class, in the total sample of 900 young people, long-term planning dispositions and the alignment of decisions and choices with long-term goals was found to be strongly associated with the social class of the respondents (see Figure 2.1). This presentation, however, masks differences between the three groups in the sample.

When analysed separately, the findings for the higher education group show that the higher education group with the strongest long-term planning disposition was from the 'skilled non-manual' class (3A). While the numbers were insufficiently large for strong conclusions to be drawn, the results intuitively make sense. For those from managerial and professional

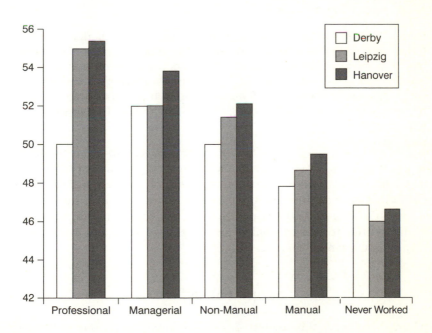

Figure 2.1 Planning dispositions by social class (control 5) (n = 900)

families the process of going to higher education is often one of simply staying on the escalator (getting off it would require the planning). Those non-traditional applicants who actually enter higher education appear to have done so via a process of planning that is untypical for the broader population of young people from working class backgrounds. This again adds to the evidence that there are features of both middle class and working class experiences that keep young people in the socially reproductive 'line of least resistance'.

The majority of students assert in questionnaire responses that 'their own plans' led to their present professional situation. These were 67 per cent in Derby, in Hanover 75 per cent and in Leipzig 80 per cent. An examination of the interviews for the assessment of this question puts the high figures into context. Students talk of the way that their parents played a considerable role in their development: they have been socialized in such a way that alternatives were not seriously considered. Their life and professional 'planning' followed the line of the parents, with no conscious awareness that this was the case. Possibly for some students the naturalness of the 'taken way', the easiness of the decision, the lack of weighing up of possibilities and a lack of assessment of the alternatives led – retrospectively – to the opinion that their 'own plans' were more decisive for their current situation than was actually the case.

In Derby a significant number of the sample were the first from their families to go to university and in Darren's case this made him feel that his situation was solely down to him:

> Darren: Because I'm going in a completely different path to both my parents, I'm sort of forging new links so to speak. I'm the first person out of the family that'll get a degree. So their advice is sort, is not really sort of valid. And they can only sort of say 'this is what I feel', 'cause they haven't had the experience of going to university and doing a degree, their sort of advice isn't really relevant to me. I feel that I'm going through life in what I think more than what my parents think.

This case underlines another factor hypothesized as important in impeding take-up of places. Role models, tacit knowledge and experience in a person's immediate networks are often taken for granted and their power underestimated in supporting or impeding transitions into higher education. But as Heinz (1999) has pointed out, networks provide very significant differential resources, which people engage with and translate into outcomes in the labour market.

Scope for action

In German society, the regulated socio-economic environment requires young people to clear more hurdles than their UK counterparts in entering the labour market. Once in jobs they have more stability than in the UK. English young people use more 'trial and error' approaches. Young Germans experience more 'hurdle jumping' and have to respond to more highly structured external demands to make their way. Standardized careers and more clearly defined options provide clearer maps. The higher education respondents in all three cities reported positive life experiences, including feeling a sense of achievement and high levels of personal responsibility. We asked how far 18–25-year-olds are active agents in their lives outside work and training, and how this compared with their 'institutionalized' lives and work values.

Respondents in the two German cities reported more fulfilling experiences in their personal lives, revealing a cultural norm and an expectation that one ought to make constructive use of personal time and that not to do so is wasteful. Our findings have shown that individualized market-oriented behaviours are shown most strongly in the setting in which markets have been deregulated and individualized behaviours have been most strongly encouraged or enforced, that of the English labour market. While the German groups from both Hanover and Leipzig were less proactive in relation to the labour market, they showed higher levels of politically active group behaviours involving activities such as participation in political events and engagement in political discussions.

In their views of the future all higher education respondents were optimistic. Among the Derby students there was a sense that they had to remain optimistic if they were to succeed in achieving their goals.

> Dominic: I'm hopeful. I'm quite confident.

> Danny: You've got to be fairly optimistic really else you'll never achieve anything.

> Daphne: If you thought at the end of it you weren't going to get a job then you'd just think well what's the point in studying for a degree. You know you've got to think at the end of it there's really going to be something that's made it all worthwhile. And you've got to think optimistically or you'd never do all this work and everything, I think you'd probably get a job now.

> Dionne: I don't know! I don't know at all. Erm, I guess I was at first, I mean I had a big setback this summer when everything was rosy and now it's gone, so I mean I had a big setback, but in certain ways yes, I'm optimistic that I'm going somewhere. But I'm not sure where.

> Danny: I just think that if you've got a positive attitude then you can do almost anything really. I mean if you can sort of get yourself to think yeah I can do that no problem, then you have that confidence and that confidence shows.

German higher education students also showed optimism, with a sense of demands, risks and limits:

A: I see a lot of possibilities to do anything in my future instead of recoiling from the risks, or, I mean, there is no other way of handling it, is there? If you do not do it, you will come a cropper. It would be really terrible. As I see it, there is not a better and enjoyable time as the time the future will bring and I am looking forward to it already.

L: The question was how I see my future prospects, right? It is not only my future. I regard it as a general problem. There is every indication that it will be a positive future, I think.

E: Well, I would describe the future with one singe word: demanding. I do have the feeling that there is something demanding and straining; this responsibility of the organization of your life that now lies in your own hands; and also all the temptations and possibilities that are also part of that. So active but nonetheless very, very exciting and thrilling. It is like 'conquering' something I suppose.

N: That is right. Conquering something – I like the idea very much. In fact, I share your opinion. I think that the future will be positive for us, that is, not only for myself but for everybody else too. So, I do not limit it to myself. It is absolutely breathtaking what we can do, what possibilities there are, what we can learn. That is simply terrific! I think it is good.

Evidence from the wider study (Evans, 2001) has shown that 'agency', as represented by young adults' beliefs in their ability to change their life chances by their own efforts, operates in differentiated and complex ways in relation to the individual's subjectively perceived frames for action and decision. Thus a person's frame has boundaries and limits that can change over time, but which have structural foundations in ascribed characteristics such as gender and social/educational inheritance, in acquired characteristics of education and qualification and in the segments of the labour market into which these lead. In this and other respects, the hypothesis that a 'structured individualization' process is apparent in the experience, values and behaviour of young people is supported.

While structured individualization accounts for the variety of experiences in all social groups as well as for the class-based and gender-based linkages in planning dispositions and horizons, it shifts the attention back onto the operation of structures rather than understanding agency and the agency–structure interfusion. Goldthorpe's answer to the agency problem (1998) is that a calculation of costs and benefit is involved, while accepting that rationality operates within individuals' horizons and social norms and calling for more cross-cultural studies to illuminate this. Our cross-cultural researches did not set out to study the rationality, objective or subjective of our respondents' decision-making, but they revealed the apparent rationality of our respondents' perceptions and actions in relation to the features of the three labour markets involved and their positions in the 'social landscape'. However, these are as well explained by the individually perceived need to maximize their options and minimize social risk as they are by any calculation of 'cost and benefit'.

Furthermore, our findings support the arguments that social divisions are becoming obscured by a universalized belief in competence. This was most advanced in the market-oriented environments of the English labour market of Derby. Our group interview transcripts demonstrated how social differences are perceived and collectively experienced but how, in discussion, questions of 'competence, will and moral resolve' permeated and often dominated the discourse. This was particularly marked in extended discussions of gender differences.

Our further analysis is considering ways in which our English participants in higher education were converting social and cultural inheritance into action in new but socially differentiated and bounded ways. The apparent differences in orientations to 'life project planning' may be explained in part by interactions between the generations, and the extent to which parents are able to secure the prospect of 'better lives and opportunities' for their children. The changing but bounded aspirations and expressions of agency may also be explained by socio-cultural influences experienced in their peer groups and institutional settings, as well as by the contingencies inherent in life transitions. There are some important indicators of 'collectivities' in perceptions of the social landscape and common experiences that are well articulated (and may therefore be surmised to be well internalized). Socially bounded agency means that roles and social relations may be redefined as part of the strategy to 'take control of their lives', and these redefinitions may have collective and cultural features that extend beyond the scope of the present research.

Policy implications

The evidence supports the view that the most insecure and flexible system (represented by the English labour market of Derby) necessitates greater pro-activity and the maintenance of a positive approach to 'opportunities'. This arises out of individual attributions of success and failure, which are themselves linked with beliefs that 'opportunities are open to all'. For young adults in eastern Germany, our previous findings showed that market signals were picked up quickly and, in our 1996–98 case studies, behaviours in the eastern city were aligning with those of our English counterparts as unregulated ways into the labour market opened up. The subsequent reassertion of the dual system and the introduction of programmes to stabilize and regulate 'broken' transitions into the labour market for 18–25-year-olds is similarly reflected in their orientations and expectations five years on. For young adults in the case studies carried out in 1996–98, agency and active behaviours created chances for some of those in the most precarious situations to gain newly appearing footholds in the labour market. Our current respondents show, by comparison, less short-term pro-activity and renewed hopes of ways back to standardized careers through a government created labour market. This is associated with a longer-term planning orientation, a different kind of pro-activity.

But as actors move in these social landscapes, spaces for action open up which are not wholly reducible to the effects of social reproduction or underlying structural features. The concept of 'bounded agency' provides a focus for further consideration of policy issues. Young adults do manifest agentic beliefs in relation to education, work and their social environment, but encounter frustrations in expressing or acting upon them. There are obviously some constraints in the 'social landscape' that will be very difficult to move or remove, but others might be reduced through new policy initiatives or foci. This point is relevant to a range of services including, for example, teachers, university staff, careers advisers, mentors, employers, health workers and social workers and the research has attracted interest from all of these groups.

Over the last decade the German post-school education and training has come under considerable pressure, particularly the highly regulated and institutionalized dual system. The data concerning future prospects showed that the research participants were quite aware of the limited vocational mobility a vocational training in the dual system offers. In Germany, it would be an advance for the structure of employment and vocational training to be regarded as a system consisting of basic vocational training, higher education and continuing education. The historically separated sectors of the education and training system need systematic links in order to remove 'cul-de-sacs' and barriers. In the more fluid and changing higher education environment in England, our findings highlighted a belief in meritocracy and the existence of opportunities for all. But young people entering 'mass' higher education are certainly not blind to class-based inequalities and discriminatory behaviour. Policy needs to address more directly the muddle and disincentives in the financing of higher education studies, and the stress of juggling competing demands in the short duration UK full-time degree. It also needs to recognize more generously that it takes considerable self-belief and courage for people from disadvantaged social backgrounds to make their way even in the most open of UK higher education institutions under present labour market and policy conditions.

Acknowledgement

Grateful acknowledgement is made to the Economic and Social Research Council (ESRC) for its funding of the Major Award Number L 134 251 011, Youth Citizenship and Social Change Programme. The full end of award report is available through REGARD, the ESRC database.

My thanks also go to John Dobby, Senior Statistician, National Foundation for Educational Research and Louise Dartnell of University of Surrey, for their invaluable help in data preparation and analysis.

References

Bargel, T, Ramm, M and Multrus, F (1999) *Studiensituation und studentische Orientierungen*, No 7, Studierendensurvey an Universitäten und Fachhochschulen, Kurzfassung, BMFP, Bundesministerium für Bildung und Forschung, Bonn, pp 30ff.

Evans, K (2001) *End of Award Report to the Economic and Social Research Council, Youth Citizenship and Social Change Programme*, Economic and Social Research Council, Swindon

Goldthorpe, J H (1998) Rational action theory for sociology, *British Journal of Sociology*, **49** (2), pp 167–92

Heinz, W R (1999) *From Education to Work*, Cambridge University Press, Cambridge.

National Audit Office (NAO) (2002) *Improving Student Achievement in Higher Education*, NAO, London

THES (2002) *Times Higher Education Supplement*, 18 January 2002, p 11

Further reading

Ball, S, Macrae, S and Maguire, M (2000) *Young Lives at Risk in the Futures Market*, Policy Press, Bristol

Beck, U (1992) *Risk Society: Towards a new modernity*, Sage, London

Beck, U (1998) *Democracy without Enemies,* Sage, London

Behrens, M and Evans, K (2000) Taking control of their lives? Paper presented at the British Educational Research Association Conference 2000, Cardiff (to be published in *Comparative Education Journal*)

Bloomer, M (1999) Learning careers: exposing the complexities of learning, young lives and transformations, *British Educational Research Association Annual Conference, September 1999*, University of Sussex, Brighton

Bloomer, M and Hodkinson, P (2000) Learning careers: continuity and change in young people's dispositions to learning, *British Educational Research Journal,* 26 (5), pp 583–98

Bourdieu, P (1993) *Sociology in Question*, Sage, London

Bynner, J and Roberts, K (eds) (1991) *Youth and Work: Transitions to employment in England and Germany*, Anglo-German Foundation, London

Christie, H and Munro, M (2000) *Working all the time?* Youth Research 2000 Conference, Keele

Emirbayer, M and Mische, M (1998) What is agency? *American Journal of the Sociology of Education*, **103** (4), pp 964–1022

Engel, U and Strasser, H (1998) Global risks and social inequality: critical remarks on the risk society hypothesis, *Canadian Journal of Sociology*, **23** (1), pp 91–103

Evans, K (2001) Relationships between work and life, in *Citizens: Towards a citizenship culture*, ed B Crick, Blackwell, Oxford

Evans, K and Heinz, W (1993) Studying forms of transition: methodological innovation in a cross-national study of youth transition and labour market entry in
England and Germany, *Comparative Education*, **29** (2), pp 145–58

Evans, K, Behrens, M and Kaluza, J (2000) *Learning and Work in the Risk Society*,
Macmillan, London

Furlong, A and Cartmel, F (1997) *Young People and Social Change?
Individualisation and risk in late modernity*, Open University Press, Buckingham

Gille, M and Kruger, W (2000) Unzufriedene Demokraten. Politische
Orientierungen der 16-bis 29-jahrigen im vereinigten Deutschland, DJI
Jugendsurvey 2, Leske und Budrich, Opladen

Hodkinson, P and Sparkes, A (1997) Careerships: a sociological theory of career
decision-making, *British Journal of Sociology of Education*, **18** (1), pp 29–44

Ragin, C C (1991) The problem of balancing cases with variables in comparative
social science, *International Journal of Comparative Sociology*, **XXXII** (1–2),
pp 1–8

Roberts, K (1995) *Youth and Employment in Modern Britain*, Oxford University
Press, Oxford

Rudd, P and Evans, K (1998) Structure and agency in youth transitions: student
experiences of vocational further education, *Journal of Youth Studies*, **1** (1), pp
39–62

Rudd, P W (1999) From socialisation to post-modernity: a review of theoretical
perspectives on the school-to-work transition, *Journal of Education and Work*, **10**
(3), pp 257–79

Sennett, R (1998) *The Corrosion of Character: The personal consequences of work in
the New Capitalism*, W W Norton, New York and London

3

Increasing Demand for Higher Education in the Longer Term: The Role of 14+ Qualifications and Curriculum Reform

Ann Hodgson and Ken Spours

Supply mechanisms alone cannot affect the two major factors that currently limit the expansion of HE: an inadequate supply of younger applicants qualified to Level 3, and unclear signals from employers about demand for graduates with qualifications other than first degrees. (HEFCE, 2001: 32)

Section 1: Expanding higher education – is the 50 per cent target realizable?

The Government has a target of 50 per cent of young people participating in higher education before the age of 30 by the end of the decade. Its policy in this area has primarily focused on four strands: increasing the overall supply of higher education places; providing financial incentives for higher education institutions to widen participation to non-traditional learners; introducing a diverse range of initiatives to encourage non-traditional learners to apply for higher education and to support them through their courses; and bringing in a new two-year foundation degree. At first glance, this appears to be a rational policy approach rooted in a sense of social and educational justice.

As in other areas of post-compulsory education, however, the Government is committing itself primarily to a 'supply-side' strategy – focusing broadly on the supply of provision to stimulate learner demand. We would contend that historical analysis of participation trends in higher education suggests that sustainable expansion takes place when effective demand for learning has been generated (Hodgson and Spours, 2000). The largest rise in higher educational participation, which took place in the late

1980s and early 1990s, was underpinned by equally large rises in post-16 participation and achievement and by changes in occupational structure leading to increased demand for undergraduate degrees (HEFCE, 2001).

In the recent period, however, many universities, particularly the post-1992 institutions, have experienced a shortfall of demand for places, which suggests that the prospects of success for supply-side approaches alone should be questioned. Moreover, many of the new universities experience high 'drop-out' rates, largely due to the fact that they tend to recruit students with relatively low previous levels of attainment and from more diverse social groups. In addition, these students are often living at home, may be more involved in the local labour market and face a range of external pressures but without clear signals from employers that they value higher education qualifications (HEFCE, 2001).

As we have suggested in earlier work (Hodgson and Spours, 2000), there has been a slowing down in the rate of participation in higher education since the mid-1990s that makes the level of expansion the Government is aiming for less secure than it might wish. Our contention is that current Government policies to widen and increase participation in higher education rely too heavily on the idea that there is a latent unmet demand for higher education. The underlying assumptions behind all of these policies are that there is a pool of sufficiently qualified under-30s who can be encouraged to see higher education as a relevant and attractive option and that education policies on their own can bring about changes in the behaviour of young people.

In this chapter, we suggest that both these assumptions are questionable and that more radical long-term policies involving both the education system and the labour market may be necessary if the Government is to create sustainable demand for higher education by both students and employers. To this end, we pose a number of key questions:

- Where are the students going to come from if the 50 per cent target is to be met?
- Should the expansion of higher education participation be based on increased demand for learning of the younger age group (eg 14–19-year-olds) or can increased demand for learning be largely confined to 20–30-year-olds?
- In either or both cases, what reforms are required to the education and training system to ensure effective demand for learning and, therefore, a strong supply of students capable of sustained participation in higher education?
- Finally, what changes are required in the labour market and higher education itself if the 50 per cent target is to be realized?

We begin to address these questions by examining briefly recent trends in post-16 participation; how learners currently progress through earlier stages of the education and training system and what appear to be the drivers and inhibitors to participation in higher education. We confine our discussion to the under-30s partly because of the focus of the current Government target in this area and partly because other chapters in this volume examine trends for more mature learners. In this section of the chapter, we also look at the important effects of labour market trends and the role of employers in higher education participation. In the second part of the chapter we focus on the recent reform of advanced level qualifications for 16–19-year-olds, known as Curriculum 2000, and speculate on the effects that these changes to the previous stage of education might have on higher education participation. We conclude by suggesting that, while current Government initiatives to widen participation in higher education are valuable, longer-term more radical reform of the education and training system from 14+, including more active involvement by employers, will be needed if we are to encourage more young people to enter and to succeed in higher education over the next few years. Finally, we suggest that the nature of higher education itself will need to change if it is to prove attractive to and worthwhile for the new cohort of students that the 50 per cent target envisages.

Section 2: Trends in participation and achievement 14–19

'System slowdown'

While it is difficult to get to the bottom of where the target for participation in higher education originated and what rationale lay behind the figure of 50 per cent, there are nevertheless strong arguments for wanting the majority of under-30s involved in some form of higher education. Research suggests that significant economic and wider social benefits are derived from this activity (Bynner and Egerton, 1999; Brennan *et al*, 2000).

In the late 1980s and early 1990s, expansion of higher education took place without explicit targets but as a result of rapid rises in both full-time participation and examination attainment of 16–19-year-olds. Similarly, as participation and achievement rates for 16–19-year-olds began to level out in the mid-1990s, so too did the expansion of participation in higher education for this age group. It is clear, therefore, that reaching the Government's target for higher education expansion will rely both on stimulating participation and achievement in the previous phase of education (ie amongst 14–19-year-olds) and on increasing demand among those in their early-20s in the workplace to undertake a form of part-time higher education.

By considering both of these approaches, it is more likely that not only will we reach the Government's target, but that participation in higher education will be more appropriate and there will be some change in the social composition of participants. Moreover, by considering the role of both 14–19 and 20–30-year-olds, the higher education target can be based on considerations of what should be achieved at level 3 (the area where the UK is recognized to be most deficient when compared internationally), rather than being seen as somewhat disconnected from wider education and training policies and debates.

Taking what we will term a 'system-based' long-term approach rather than an 'initiatives-based' short-term approach to higher education expansion among the under-30s (which is the main Government approach in this area currently), requires a historical analysis of participation and achievement trends among 14–19-year-olds and their influence on the expansion of higher education. In our view, the outcome of such an analysis suggests that we are currently trapped in what we call 'system slowdown' and that only through tackling some of the significant barriers to participation and achievement for 14–19-year-olds and ensuring continued employer demand for graduates will we be able to bring about the necessary 'system acceleration' that the higher education target demands.

Trends in participation and achievement

Participation trends in full-time education and the work-based route for 16–19-year-olds

Statistics on participation and attainment amongst 16–19-year-olds suggest that the post-compulsory education and training system in the UK has, for approaching a decade, been moving into a distinctive new phase that we term 'system slowdown'. This describes a situation in that there is little or no growth in many of the major participation and attainment indicators for 14–19-year-olds.

This period of system slowdown started in 1994 with the peaking of participation rates in full-time education at 16, following several years of strong growth (Hodgson and Spours, 2000). Currently, 71 per cent of young people stay on at school or college after 16 and 58 per cent at 17 (DfES, 2001a). These full-time participation levels have remained static during the last five years. Furthermore, the same flattening trend has spread to the work-based route. Between 1997 and 2000, participation in Advanced Modern Apprenticeship (AMAs) plateaued, following rapid growth in the early and mid 1990s, and overall participation in other types of work-based training has actually declined (DfES, 2001b).

Attainment trends in general education 14–19

Attainment trends in GCSEs and A levels have broadly followed the same pattern – rapid rises in the late 1980s and early 1990s and then a slowing trend over the last five years or so. Currently, 50 per cent of 16-year-olds achieve five or more A*–C grades at GCSE and improvement in attainment at this level has been increasing by only one percentage point per year in the late 1990s, about half the rate of growth a decade ago. Attainment rates in A levels and Advanced GNVQs have grown at an even slower rate and by 2000 were virtually static with just under 35 per cent of 17-year-olds gaining two or more A levels or equivalent (DfES, 2001c). Moreover, qualifications outcomes from all types of training, including AMAs, have also plateaued over the last three years (DfES, 2001b).

These trends will inhibit higher education expansion since statistical evidence suggests that attainment at A level is vital for increasing the demand for higher education places among young people in all social groups. As stated in a recent IPPR report: 'once a working student has defied the odds and obtained two A Levels, [he or] she is highly likely to take up a university place' (Piatt and Robinson, 2001: 12).

The factors affecting these trends are, arguably, structural. They are related to barriers in the qualifications system which deter many young people from studying and achieving beyond 16. In particular, there are issues related to the achievement of five A*–C grades at GCSE (the threshold for entry to advanced level study) and poor progression rates between post-16 level 2 and level 3 courses. In addition, the gap between GCSE and A level has been difficult to bridge for many learners.

The problems of attainment in the work-based route are somewhat different. These relate mainly to the lack of incentives for young people to achieve qualifications in apprenticeships which will have to be addressed in further reform of the Modern Apprenticeship System (Keep, 2002). In cases of both full-time education and the work-based route, there is a need, therefore, for further reform of the 14+ qualifications system and of labour markets if demand for higher education is to be stimulated.

Patterns of higher education participation – the historical influence of system factors

The major expansion of undergraduate higher education from the late-1980s to the mid-1990s was based largely on the full-time participation of 18–21-year-olds (HEFCE, 2001), although the numbers of mature students also increased during this period. This trend brought about some changes in the composition of higher education students. There was a dramatic increase in the number of females involved in higher education – by 1996 they constituted 51 per cent of participants compared to 26 per cent in 1962. Moreover, many ethnic minority groups became more than proportionately represented in higher education, although the majority of these students are concentrated in the post-1992 universities (NCIHE, 1997). However, there has been a much slower change in the social composition of higher education. Despite the doubling of the proportion of entrants from semi-skilled and unskilled socio-economic groups, the general social composition of undergraduate higher education remains largely unchanged (NCIHE, 1997; NAO, 2002). This may be related to the fact that there has been much less change in the balance between full-time and part-time students during the expansion period (HESA, 2000) and because there is a strong correlation between social class and educational attainment among younger learners (HEFCE, 2001).

At the same time, according to demographic trends produced for the Government Actuary, while there will be a steady increase in the number of 18–21-year-olds over the next 10 years, the social composition of this group is likely to change in favour of those who have traditionally partici-pated least in higher education (HEFCE, 2001).

The HEFCE report recognizes this problem: 'the largest potential for growth comes from young people from poor backgrounds. If their school staying-on rates and examination achievements at Level 3 increase to the national average, this alone will require 100,000 further places in HE' (HEFCE, 2001: 22).

Both these arguments about the social composition of higher education and the potential for change are related to the need for two deep structural reforms. First, it is necessary to increase significantly the attainment of these social groups in the compulsory and post-compulsory education system (ie among 14–19-year-olds); second, there is a need for changes in the mode of higher education participation with a greater emphasis on part-time study. Again, this takes us back to our arguments about the need for reform of the qualifications system from 14+ and changes in the labour market and its relationship to higher education.

Section 3: Reforming the 14+ qualifications and curriculum system and changes to the labour market

Since its election in 1997, the Labour Government has attempted to reform qualifications in some areas. What we will demonstrate below is that this has been a piecemeal approach that has not sufficiently addressed the underlying education and training system issues discussed above. Similarly, it has attempted to reform Modern Apprenticeships and to encourage employers to become more involved with the education and training system (eg new Sector Skills Councils, the National Skills Taskforce and the Learning and Skills Council system). However, none of these initiatives as yet constitutes the basis for the kind of labour market reform we see as essential to support the higher education participation target. We examine both of these issues below.

Reforming advanced level qualifications – Curriculum 2000 as an island of reform

In September 2000, students on advanced level programmes began to take up the new qualifications resulting from the *Qualifying for Success* (DfEE,1997) reform process. Responding to long-standing pressures for changes to what were regarded as narrow, wasteful and divisive advanced level qualifications, the Government introduced AS/A2 levels to replace the old A level; Advanced Vocational Certificates of Education (AVCEs) to replace Advanced GNVQs; a new Key Skills Qualification in Communication, Application of Number and IT; and proposals for Advanced Extension Awards with the eventual promise of some form of overarching certificate.

The reforms aimed to broaden advanced level programmes of study; to provide a 'stepping stone' from GCSE to A level; to introduce vocational qualifications which are of the same size as AS/A2s and with external assessment to encourage external recognition and parity of esteem for academic and vocational qualifications. The Key Skill Qualification was meant to provide a more applied and employment-related focus for all 16–19-year-olds. A further key aim was to support greater participation, attainment and progression in advanced level study. Curriculum 2000 was therefore, by definition, seen as a way of stimulating greater demand for higher education.

While demands for a baccalaureate-style award were at this point rejected, there was a Government expectation that year 12 students should take up to five subjects in the first year of study; that there should be more mixing of academic and vocational qualifications and that all students should be engaged with key skills.

However, while all advanced level students (bar a few in more traditional vocational programmes) had to take the new qualifications, it was up to schools, colleges and students to decide how many and what combination of subjects they would study. Moreover, it was left to universities to decide what qualifications they would recognize and require. The Curriculum 2000 reform package was, therefore, largely voluntarist and it was left in the main to the market to determine the outcome of the changes.

The first year of Curriculum 2000 ran far from smoothly and led to a review of the reforms by Professor David Hargreaves, Chief Executive at the Qualifications and Curriculum Authority (Hargreaves, 2001a, 2001b). What research on the first year of the reforms indicated is that a slim majority of advanced level students did take four or more subjects; that there was a significant increase in taught hours; that students welcomed the flexibility and choice provided by the new and smaller qualification blocks (Savory *et al*, 2001a; Spours *et al*, 2002). So, on the positive side, advanced level students are more focused, are doing more and are working harder. This may provide benefits for participation in higher education in terms of attitude to study and achievement at level 3. It is also possible that more students may be attracted into advanced level study as a result of the more accessible AS level and good results in the AS in the first round of examinations.

These positive developments, however, have been offset by a number of more negative factors related to Curriculum 2000. The rushed, over-assessed and overloaded nature of the AS qualification has encouraged a didactic approach to teaching and has afforded little time for students to develop the research and study skills required for further and higher learning (Savory *et al*, 2001b, 2002; Spours *et al*, 2002). Moreover, full timetables have given students less time for independent study and for extra-curricular activities, both of which have traditionally been seen as a good preparation for higher education. In addition, recent research suggests that students are continuing and even increasing their engagement with part-time work (Payne, 2001; Fowler *et al*, 2002).

While students on AS programmes have experienced the benefits of the easier climb from intermediate to advanced level study offered by the AS (in most subjects) and have had reasonable examination success at the end of the first year of the reforms, students taking AVCEs have had a rather different and potentially off-putting experience. This is as a result of the requirement for level 3 achievement from the beginning of the course and the consequent low pass rate in these awards. Key skills has proved to be a particularly problematic aspect of the reforms, being both unpopular with students and teachers and largely rejected by higher education providers (Hodgson *et al*, 2001).

Early evidence about the performance of Curriculum 2000 in stimulating demand for higher education is, therefore, very mixed. On the one hand, there will be a rise in the number of students achieving the equivalent of three A levels as a result of increases in the size of programmes of study at advanced level (Spours *et al*, 2002) – a trend also suggested in provisional attainment statistics for 2000/01 (DfES, 2001c). On the other hand, the new programmes of study have been hard work, even laborious, and there is some evidence that this may have deterred some students from considering higher education (Spours *et al*, 2002).

Perhaps most importantly, Curriculum 2000 has been affected by the confused position of end-users, a position not helped by confusions in the reforms themselves. Comprising many different qualifications blocks and initiatives implemented in a rush, Curriculum 2000 suffers from not having a clear identity, unlike either the old A level or baccalaureate awards in other countries. Currently, our local research suggests that employers are unaware of Curriculum 2000 (Fowler *et al*, 2002) and it is unclear what incentive they have to understand it better. Universities too are confused and their unclear and diverse responses to the reforms have not helped schools and colleges to encourage students to significantly broaden their programmes of study or to experiment with new combinations of subjects or key skills (Savory *et al*, 2001b; Spours *et al*, 2002).

We would suggest that the problem related to Curriculum 2000 and end-users has just as much to do with the reforms themselves as with the 'cautious' response of higher education providers. The elective nature of Curriculum 2000 has left universities uncertain about what schools and colleges were going to offer and what students would achieve, and many were anxious not to demand qualifications that might not be taken by their 'traditional market'. In this respect, higher education's position can be seen less as direct opposition to Curriculum 2000 than as a rational response to a voluntarist reform in a market-led system in which universities wished to secure a predictable flow of high-quality applicants.

Taken overall, the emphasis in the reform on breadth and standards rather than on progression, and the fact that Curriculum 2000 emerged as an 'island of reform' unconnected with changes to GCSE or the curriculum in higher education, mean that there is no holistic strategy for progression into higher education for the 14–19 age group. The result is likely to be that Curriculum 2000, in its current form, may well have only a 'neutral' effect on the expansion of higher education.

A new and coherent approach to 14+ education and training

It is clear from the earlier analysis in this chapter that participation rates in higher education rose mainly as a result of increasing participation and attainment amongst 16–19-year-olds. While we have demonstrated that there is currently a broadly plateauing trend in this area, we do not believe that the level of participation in higher education among 18–21-year-olds (currently around a third) has reached saturation point, and the UK still lags behind many other countries in this respect (HEFCE, 2001). But we argue that further increases will only be the result of more deep-seated and connective reform related to the whole 14–19 age group as well as reform to the labour market. This latter point we address at the end of the chapter.

The Government's current focus on 14–19 education and training provides an opportunity to take a more strategic approach to this important education phase and to create long-term effective demand for further learning in the younger age group which goes beyond the current initiative-led approach in this area.

We would suggest that the first issue to tackle will have to be an over-haul of GCSE so that more learners are encouraged to continue to study up to the age of 19, rather than experiencing a sense of failure at 16 and opting out, as is currently the case. As we have seen earlier, only if there is a significant growth in the number of younger students from all social classes succeeding at intermediate and then at advanced level will there be sufficient throughput to increase the numbers eligible for entry to higher education. We envisage this throughput being achieved through the development of a multi-level English baccalaureate system from 14+ which allows learners to progress at different rates at different ages, but with the majority of the cohort achieving a single and recognizable advanced level award at 18 or 19 in both general and vocational education. We see such a system as the only way of increasing level 3 achievement among younger learners while, at the same time, providing them with the skills, knowledge and motivation to succeed in higher education.

An English baccalaureate system from 14+ would also provide the opportunity to raise the profile of vocational education, not by creating yet another separate routeway for certain students (traditionally the lower achievers), but by bringing technical/vocational study into a single mainstream 14+ system. This would require the creation of a high-profile vocational baccalaureate variant which would contain the strong general education component common to all baccalaureates, together with an equally strong and specialized technical/vocational strand recognized by the best employers. This development does not imply full-time education for the whole cohort. A vocational baccalaureate could be designed for the apprenticeship system. Moreover, the linking of the award of apprenticeship to the achievement of such a vocational award could significantly improve qualification rates in the work-based route and allow greater opportunities for progression to part-time higher education.

The development of an English baccalaureate as a recognizable single product achieved by the majority of 18–19 year-olds could provide a transparent and confident signal to both higher education providers and employers of the capabilities and achievements of successful learners. In order to ensure this recognition, however, it is imperative that employers and higher education providers, as well as teachers and policy-makers, are involved in the design of the baccalaureate system so that they not only trust what it produces but can see how they might build upon its outcomes.

The limits of qualifications reform – engaging with the labour market

While we think that a 14+ English baccalaureate system could contribute significantly to creating an increased and sustainable demand for higher education from younger learners, this reform in itself will not address all of the factors that currently suppress demand among this age group. In our earlier analysis, we indicated that changes to the labour market and the demand for qualifications by employers also have a fundamental shaping role in young people's desire to undertake higher education. In this respect, we see the need to consider three major connected developments in relation to the labour market and the role of employers.

First, as we have already argued above, it is important for employers to become more fully involved in the process of qualification at advanced level through the provision of high-quality apprenticeships leading to a vocational baccalaureate, by involvement in the design of such a system and by their willingness to work in partnership with colleges and to demand higher-level qualifications as entry to or promotion within certain types of occupations (that is to say, by adopting a 'licence to practise' approach to training and qualification). A limited number of sectors already operate in this way, but it is important for this development to become more widespread, particularly in growth areas such as the service sector.

Second, there is a need to engage employers around the issue of 'learning and earning' among full-time 16–19-year-olds. Presently, local studies suggest that between 70 and 80 per cent of 17–18-year-olds are involved in part-time work during term-time (Hodgson and Spours, 2001; Fowler *et al*, 2002). Furthermore, a large national study also suggests that those in year 13 working more than 10 hours, or in year 12 working more than 15 hours, are likely to jeopardize their achievement at A level by up to two grades (Payne, 2001).

Our local research on this issue undertaken in South Gloucestershire suggests that part-time work might have a contradictory effect on progression into higher education. On the one hand, it may provide funds for future participation, but it is more likely to diminish students' appetite or capacity to progress to a selective university because of the way part-time employment compromises the aspirations and achievement of some learners. These we refer to as 'risk-takers' (Hodgson and Spours, 2001). What is needed is more active employer understanding of this issue and dialogue with education providers about the demands of advanced level study, so that all full-time students reap the benefits of part-time work without undermining their achievement and aspirations for further progression (Fowler *et al*, 2002). This new research suggests that some kind of compact between students, employers and education providers could create the basis for a more productive relationship between learning and earning.

Third, there is a need to stimulate increased participation in higher education by the 20–30-year-olds who are currently in work. This will require connecting study and achievement at level 4 more closely with promotion, advancement and meeting new and rigorous occupational standards. Currently, participation in HND-style provision is decreasing but it is hoped that the new foundation degrees will reverse this trend (HEFCE, 2001). It is interesting to note that a major area of expansion in part-time undergraduate study has been in the allied medical field (HESA, 2000), where there has been significant change in the occupational structure and levels of responsibility leading to increased demand for higher education courses and qualifications. While this area of engagement is beyond the 14–19 age group that is in focus in this chapter, it underlines the importance of the relationship between changing labour markets demands and higher education participation.

A longer-term strategy

The development of a coherent 14+ English baccalaureate system, allied to labour market changes, is clearly a long-term strategy for increasing the demand for higher education in both general and vocational learning. As Curriculum 2000 has demonstrated, it is vital to take a long-term and carefully managed approach to qualifications reform because of its systemic nature. The kind of reforms we envisage will not necessarily produce the flow of students to meet the Government's higher education target by 2010, though they may do so 5–10 years later.

The current initiatives approach to raising levels of participation in higher education (eg Excellence Challenge, financial support for students, increased information about the costs and benefits of higher education) would have far more chance of success as complementary strategies to the development of an English baccalaureate system from 14+. There are limits to initiative-led reform in this area, because it tries to bring about changed behaviour without addressing the fundamental barriers to educational participation. In our view, while clearly valuable, current initiatives to stimulate higher education expansion are likely to enjoy only limited success.

Finally, qualification and curriculum reforms from 14+ allied to reform of the labour market and the expansion of the higher education system all point to the need for the development of a different type of higher education. Undergraduate education will not in the future be predominantly about single-subject full-time Honours degrees. It is more likely to be part-time, more alternance-based, modular and with more labour-market connection and, as a result, it is likely to involve students from wider social backgrounds because higher education will be more related to working life rather than being a deferral of it.

References

Brennan, J *et al* (2000) Lifelong learning for employment and equity: the role of the part-time degree, *Higher Education Quarterly,* **54** (4), pp 411–19

Bynner, J and Egerton, M (1999) *The Social Benefits of Higher Education: Insights from longitudinal data*, Centre for Longitudinal Studies, University of London Institute of Education, London

Department for Education and Employment (DfEE) (1997) *Qualifying for Success: A consultation paper on the future of post-16 qualifications*, DfEE, London

Department for Education and Skills (DfES) (2001a) *Participation in Education and Training of Young People 16 and 17 in Each Local Area and Region 1995/96 to 1999/2000* National Statistics First Release SFR 14/2001, DfES, London

DfES (2001b) *TEC/LSC Delivered Government Supported Work-Based Learning in England: Volumes and outcomes*, National Statistics First Release SFR 47/2001, DfES, London

DfES (2001c) *GCSE/GNVQ and GCE A/AS/VCE/Advanced GNVQ Results for Young People in England, 2000/01 (Provisional Statistics)*, National Statistics First Release SFR 45/2001, DfES, London

Fowler, Z, Hodgson, A and Spours, K (2002) *Strategies for Balancing Learning and Earning: Student, teacher and employer perspectives in the context of Curriculum 2000*, University of London Institute of Education, London

Hargreaves, D (2001a) *Review of Curriculum 2000 – Report on Phase One*, QCA, London

Hargreaves, D (2001b) *QCA's Review of Curriculum 2000 – Report on Phase Two*, QCA, London

Higher Education Funding Council for England (HEFCE) (2001) *Supply and Demand in Higher Education*, HEFCE, Bristol

Higher Education Statistical Agency (HESA) (2000) *Student Enrolments on Higher Education Courses at Publicly Funded Higher Education Institutions in the UK for the Academic Year 1999/2000*, Statistical First Release SFR 38 HESA, Cheltenham

Hodgson, A and Spours, K (2000) Expanding higher education in the UK: from 'system slowdown' to 'system acceleration', *Higher Education Quarterly*, **54** (4), pp 295–322

Hodgson, A and Spours, K (2001) Part-time work and full-time education in the UK: the emergence of a curriculum and policy issue, *Journal of Education and Work*, **14** (3), pp 373–88

Hodgson, A, Spours, K and Savory, C (2001) *Improving the 'Use' and 'Exchange' Value of Key Skills Broadening the Advanced Level Curriculum,* IOE/Nuffield Series Number 4, University of London, Institute of Education, London

Keep, E (2002) *The Tethered Beetle Takes One More Turn,* Open Lecture Series No 4, School of Lifelong Education and International Development, University of London, Institute of Education

National Audit Office (NAO) (2002) *Widening Participation in Higher Education in England*, The Stationery Office, London

National Committee of Inquiry into Higher Education (NCIHE) (1997) *Higher Education in the Learning Society*, Crown Copyright, London

Payne, J (2001) *Post-16 Students and Part-Time Jobs: Patterns and effects: a report based on the England and Wales youth cohort study,* DfES Research Report 323, DfES, Nottingham

Piatt, W and Robinson, P (2001) *Opportunity for Whom? Options for funding and structure of post-16 education*, IPPR, London

Savory, C, Hodgson, A and Spours, K (2001a*) Planning and Implementing Curriculum 2000: Institutional approaches*, Broadening the Advanced Level Curriculum, IOE/Nuffield Series Number 3, University of London Institute of Education, London

Savory, C, Hodgson, A and Spours, K (2001b) *Teachers' Views on the Changes to A Levels and GNVQs Resulting from Curriculum 2000*, a research report of a survey by the National Union of Teachers in collaboration with the Institute of Education, NUT, London

Savory, C, Hodgson, A and Spours, K (2002) *Excellent in Theory but a Nightmare in Practice – Further education lecturers' views of the first year of Curriculum 2000*, report of a joint IOE/NATFHE survey, NATFHE, London

Spours, K, Savory, C and Hodgson, A (2002) *Curriculum 2000: The significance of the student experience in the reform of advanced level qualifications*, Broadening the Advanced Level Curriculum, IOE/Nuffield Series Number 6, University of London, Institute of Education, London

4

Fair Funding for Higher Education: The Way Forward

Claire Callender

Introduction

On 4 October 2001, Estelle Morris, the Secretary of State for Education and Skills, announced a review of student support arrangements that aims to:

- Simplify the system, especially in the area of hardship support.
- Provide more up-front support for students from less well-off backgrounds.
- Ensure that all students have access to sufficient financial support throughout their years of higher education.
- Tackle the problem of debt and perceptions of debt (DfES, 2001a).

The review is a response to two main issues: first, the problems arising from New Labour's reforms of student aid in their first term of office, including issues voiced on the doorstep during the 2001 election campaign; and second, the Government's concern about its ability to deliver its election manifesto target of increasing participation in higher education to 50 per cent among young people (Labour Party, 2001). At the time of writing, the outcome of the review was unknown.

Increasing and widening participation were positioned at the heart of New Labour's higher education initiatives in its first term of office, and appear central in its second term of office too. On 22 October 2001 Estelle Morris declared:

> Our pledge to increase participation is one of this Government's highest priorities... Universities are not a birthright of the middle classes. None of us can defend the position where five times as many young people from professional backgrounds enter higher education compared with those from unskilled and manual backgrounds – 73–74 per cent compared with 13–14 per cent – and when that gap has not narrowed in recent time. (DfES, 2001b)

In New Labour's first term of office, the main policy mechanisms used for funding this increased and widened participation of full-time students were the 1998 reforms of student funding, namely, the introduction of tuition fees and the complete replacement of student maintenance grants with student loans.[1] However, this chapter will argue that these reforms were inconsistent with New Labour's commitment to widening access and fairness in educational opportunities, and undermined their desire for higher education to contribute to greater social cohesion.

This chapter focuses exclusively on full-time undergraduates in England and its concerns are threefold: first, how the 1998 reforms of student financial support came about; second, the effects of the reforms; and third, what issues should inform any future reforms of the student funding system. The chapter starts by briefly tracing the development of student funding policies under New Labour. Next, it assesses New Labour's policies and policy objectives, drawing upon the findings of a major survey on students' income and expenditure (Callender and Kemp, 2000). So, it explores some of the intended and unintended consequences of the 1998 reforms, especially for poorer students. Finally, it outlines some of the issues that need addressing when considering yet more changes to student funding arrangements, in particular the principles informing future policies.

New Labour's vision of higher education

New Labour's higher education agenda in its first term of office was influenced by the Conservatives' legacy of student loans, first introduced in 1990. Its approach to higher education, therefore, needs to be understood both as a response to policy reforms set in motion by the Conservatives, and as a desire to reshape the sector.

David Blunkett (the then Secretary of State for Education and Employment) saw higher education playing a major role in securing economic competitiveness; meeting the needs of the economy and employers; ensuring a democratic society and an educated citizenry; and securing social cohesion and social justice. He claimed:

> In a knowledge-economy, higher education becomes a potentially powerful instrument of social justice, since it serves not only as a driver of wealth creation, but *as a critical determinant of life chances*. As we expand access, and participation becomes the norm rather than the exception, so the higher education system will increasingly underpin social justice within the community... rather than reinforcing social stratification. (Blunkett, 2000: paragraph 66) (emphasis added)

Here, both economic prosperity and social inclusion were positioned as the key goals of New Labour's higher education policies. They were to be achieved by increasing and widening participation.

New Labour's student financial support policies

New Labour announced its first set of changes to student support arrangements on 23 July 1997, the day the Dearing report was published – thus rejecting the report's suggestions on student funding.[2] The 1998 Teaching and Higher Education Act (Part II) and subsequent regulations enacted most of the reforms.

From 1998/99, new entrants had to contribute towards the costs of their tuition, which were set initially at a maximum of £1,000 and were to be means-tested. Grants were abolished for students entering higher education in 1999/2000, who instead were to receive support for living costs solely through student loans, a quarter of which were income-assessed. The repayments on these loans were linked more directly to graduates' income, but the point at which graduates had to start repaying their loans was lowered to £10,000.

New Labour had accepted the principle that students should contribute to the direct costs of their education, as recommended by the Dearing Committee (DfEE, 1998). Its replacement of grants with loans completed a process begun by the previous Conservative administration. New Labour had unashamedly embraced this part of the Thatcherite legacy, along with arguments about the social and economic returns of higher education.

New Labour's reforms came under attack eventually from a variety of quarters. So, since the 1998 reforms New Labour has had to try to restore the principle of public funding for disadvantaged students through selective assistance (see DfEE, 2000 for details). This has resulted in a complex, confusing and bureaucratic system of support and an array of national and institutional support packages, which in turn has led to further criticisms and demands for reform (NAO, 2002a). Scotland, Wales and Northern Ireland now all have different student funding arrangements from each other and compared with England, which just adds to the confusion and reflects their rejection of Westminster's policies – one of the unanticipated consequences of devolution.

Such criticisms suggest that the 1998 Act is failing to meet its stated objectives. To assess how far it has, we turn to Blunkett's (2000) vision of the role of student financial support. He asked, what were the components of a modern policy for higher education and its contribution to social cohesion and prosperity?

> The first is a system of student support, which both adheres to progressive principles and facilitates access. The system of full public support for tuition fees and maintenance... did not meet these criteria. It failed over the decades fundamentally to transform the socio-economic mix of the student intake, whilst at the same time it redistributed resources from ordinary taxpayers to the better off... it... subsidised those benefiting from higher education at the expense of those denied access. (paragraph 69)

> The new system of student support balances the contributions made by individuals and the community as a whole. It is more progressive than in the past, and it directs resources to those who need them most. Critically, it secures an income stream for higher education of fee contributions and loan repayments, which underpins expansion and the widening of opportunities...
> (paragraph 70)

The new Secretary of State, Morris, has not demurred from these objectives, but has echoed Blunkett's thoughts and said on 22 October 2001:

> Whenever I have conversations about access and about participation, many connect those issues to student finance. We want to think again about any obstacles – real or imagined – that could discourage young people from low-income families from taking up higher education. All of us would like to produce a system of student support which is simpler than the present one... The principles of the reforms that David Blunkett announced in 1997 were absolutely right and we will stick to them. Those who benefit from higher education should contribute to its cost. It would be utterly unfair for graduates... to be completely subsidised through their entire university education by those who do not have their advantages and who can afford it far less easily. (DfES, 2001b)

Morris, like Blunkett, links facilitating access with student funding but recognizes it may act as deterrent. She too implicitly calls upon progressive distributive principles. However, she attempts to shift the debate by downplaying the role of student funding and access.

The effects of changes in student financial support policies

This section seeks to assess whether New Labour's 1998 reforms of student support fulfilled Blunkett's vision of its role, namely, whether it is more progressive and facilitates access. It relies heavily on a survey of student income, expenditure, debt and financial hardship, which was based on a nationally representative sample of over 2,000 full-time home undergraduates studying at 87 higher education institutions in the UK in the 1998/9 academic year (Callender and Kemp, 2000).[3]

Progressiveness

Does the system of student support adhere to progressive principles and is it more progressive than the previous funding system? Student funding in the UK has been heavily criticized for being regressive because it largely benefited the middle classes, the prime consumers of higher education (National Commission on Education, 1993). As Morris recognizes, despite

New Labour's efforts to widen participation, the socio-economic mix of the student intake has remained unchanged. Consequently, the bulk of funding in higher education continues to go to the better off.

The introduction of fees and student loans and the abolition of grants shifted more of the costs of higher education onto individual students, but unequally. Low-income students shouldered a larger share of the financial burden than students from better-off families. Using some simple modelling techniques, we find that between 1989 and 2002, the amount of state subsidy going to a student from a high-income family fell by around 2.5 per cent, but for a student from a low-income family it declined by about 35 per cent. This is because student loans cost the government anything between 30 and 50 per cent of their face value (Barr and Falkingham, 1996). The value of state support wealthy students now receive via student loans wipes out any losses in state support they incurred following the introduction of tuition fees. The greater decline in public subsidy for less well-off students is primarily because student loans attract less subsidy than student maintenance grants. And as a result of these developments, parents have been contributing less towards the costs of their children's higher education, especially those from the highest social classes (Callender and Kempson, 1996; Callender and Kemp, 2000).

There was, therefore, a major structural contradiction in the 1998 reforms. New Labour made the student funding system more 'progressive' by implementing a regressive funding regime. Its policies were regressive because low-income students benefited the least, and had had to pay relatively more towards the costs of their education than higher income students.

Facilitating access

Since New Labour came to power in 1997, it has succeeded in increasing participation and has overseen a small rise in the number of full-time first-degree students entering higher education. This expansion, however, has not led to a widened participation with increases in the proportion of students drawn from under-represented groups (Watson and Bowden, 2001). What impact, if any, did changes in student financial support have on these developments in the UK, or are likely to have on widening participation more generally?

Student loans

The replacement of grants with student loans and the introduction of tuition fees led to a radical restructuring of students' incomes. Between 1988/89 and 1998/99 students' income from grants and their parents fell while their 'income' from borrowings and savings rose. They borrowed more money to fund their education, and consequently were more in debt.

73

However, poorer students have become particularly reliant on borrowings and earnings from paid employment (Callender and Kemp, 2000).

Most of students' borrowings consist of student loans – so any changes to the loan system affects student debt. With the phasing out of grants, more students are taking out loans and borrowing larger sums of money. For example, loan take-up rose from 28 per cent in 1990/91 to 78 per cent in 2000/01 while the average size of loans increased from £390 in 1990/91 to £2,900 in 2000/01 (DfES, 2001c). With their growing value, student loans also form a larger share of students' total income, especially for students from low-income families. However, not all students are equally reliant on student loans.

Our survey showed that lone parents were the most likely of all students to have taken out a loan – nearly all of them had done so. In addition, the larger a student's maintenance grant, the greater the chances of him or her having taken out a loan. So, students from low-income families were more reliant on student loans than those from better-off families. Those students least likely to take out loans were Asian students – under half had done so, and they borrowed the smallest amounts. Students living at home with their parents were far less likely to have taken out a loan compared to students living independently, as were students attending universities in London. This is because students in London were more likely than students elsewhere to live at home and to come from an ethnic minority (Callender, forthcoming).

Nearly one in three students who had not taken out a loan claimed that they did not need one. However, 56 per cent of students were without one because of their, or their family's, concerns about debt and borrowing. Students from the poorest backgrounds and those most under-represented in the student population were most debt-averse. Their debt-aversion highlights the contradictory nature of the current student funding policies. Ultimately, such groups may be deterred from entry into higher education because of worries about escalating debt, yet they are the very focus of widening participation policies.

Student debt

In 1998/99, nearly nine out of ten students had outstanding debts compared with just over seven out of ten in 1995/96. The move from grants to student loans resulted in a threefold increase in the level of student debt between 1995/96 and 1998/9 (Callender and Kemp, 2000). By May 2001, students had debts averaging £5,961 but anticipated owing up to £12,000 by the end of their studies (Barclays, 2001).

Students who are poor before going to university accumulate the largest debts. In our study, the most financially vulnerable groups were lone parents and students from social classes IV and V. A more recent survey (Unite/MORI, 2002) conducted in 2001, shows the increasing disparity in the levels of debt between students from low- and high-income families.

Between 2000 and 2001, students from poorer families saw their debts rise by 46 per cent – over three times the growth (14 per cent) experienced by students from the highest social classes. Thus debt is increasingly becoming a class issue. Without further changes to student funding arrangements, low-income students' debt is soon likely to equal the average gross annual earnings of full-time manual workers. Will low-income students be able to jump over the psychological barrier of having to borrow more money than their parents may earn in a year?

The consequences of rising student debt

Financial hardship

Being in debt is not the same as living in hardship. However, the financial struggle associated with undergraduate life may act as a deterrent to prospective students, especially when the labour market is tight. Once again, social class appears to be a discriminator in terms of students' financial situation. In 2001, twice as many students from low-income families as those from high-income families found it a constant struggle to keep up with their bills and credit commitments (Unite/MORI, 2002).

In our study, lone parents and students from classes IV and V were the most likely to express financial concerns. They had had to economize the most, and juggle their bills, to make ends meet. As importantly, these students in particular strongly believed that financial hardship affected their academic performance and their progression. For example, 76 per cent of students from social classes IV and V felt that financial difficulties had negatively affected their academic performance, compared with 53 per cent of students from classes I and II.

Paid employment

One way students avoid debt and hardship (or more debt and hardship) is through paid employment. It is well established that since the introduction of student loans, the proportion of students working has grown (Ford *et al*, 1995; Lucas and Ralston, 1997; Smith and Taylor, 1999; Unite/MORI 2002). By 1998/9, more than three in five students worked at some point during the academic year; around half worked during term-time and four out of five took summer vacation jobs (Callender and Kemp, 2000).

The pressures to work do not fall evenly on all students. Working, like debt, is a class issue. Our study, like others (eg Barke *et al*, 2000; Unite/MORI 2002), revealed that students from less well-off backgrounds were more likely to engage in term-time work than those from better-off families, and to work longer hours. Students from the most disadvantaged backgrounds also were working longer hours than they did in 1995/96.

Consequently, their earnings have become a much more important source of income compared to students from high-income families (Callender and Kemp, 2000).

Students are far more likely to report that paid work affects their studies adversely rather than positively. In our study, only one in ten students identified his or her term-time working as having a positive impact, but nearly half believed it harmed their studies. This was because they could not devote enough time to their studies, they got very tired, felt constantly overloaded, or missed lectures. Not surprisingly, the more hours students worked, the more likely they were to think their academic work suffered (Callender, 2001). This is borne out by other research, which has measured the effects of term-time work on students' actual examination results. It confirmed that students working in term-time were more likely than non-working students to get lower grades (Barke *et al*, 2000). Thus students' educational attainment, achievement and progression is being compromised by term-time working (NAO, 2002b), especially for the most disadvantaged students.

The risks of higher education

The accumulating evidence suggests that with rising student debt, entering higher education has become an increasingly risky investment decision, especially for low-income students. Research in the United States (Mortenson, 1990; Mumper and Vander Ark, 1991), and now in the UK, shows that low-income students are less likely to complete their studies, and those who do are less likely to do well in terms of their grades and the jobs they obtain on graduation (Naylor *et al*, 2001). For instance, in the UK students from social classes IV and V earn on average 7 per cent less than graduates from social class I and II (Elias, *et al* 1999). This also means it will take them longer to pay off their debts. The prospect of being saddled with huge debts for years after completing their course is likely to affect some of these students' participation.

Even when students from low-income backgrounds do take this risk, our study clearly shows, they are more likely to experience financial difficulties while studying and to engage in paid work, which in turn is likely to affect their performance and chances of completing their courses successfully. The risk of failure may discourage prospective students from less advantaged backgrounds from borrowing the large sums of money now needed to go to university.

The way forward for further reforms

The 1998 reforms, outlined above, were aimed at funding wider participation in higher education. The money raised through tuition fees and saved through the abolition of grants was designated for this expansion. However, as the analysis shows, these policies have failed to meet their stated objectives. They have neither adhered to progressive principles nor facilitated access. The most obvious solution, therefore, is to change the policy approach and the mechanisms employed for widening participation so they are more effective, and to introduce different policies to ameliorate the harsher effects of the 1998 reforms. This latter approach appears to be the focus of the current student funding review, and is articulated within its aims.

Yet such a strategy begs a series of fundamental policy questions:

- What principles should inform the student funding system?
- What is the aim and purpose of the student funding system, and what are its objectives?
- How should student financial support be delivered, and what should guide methods of delivery?
- What distributive principles should inform the student funding system?
- What should be the outcomes of student funding policies?

This section will attempt to address these questions by drawing on the analyses that have emerged from official inquiries into student funding, namely, the Cubie, Rees and Dearing reports. It will discuss the main policy aims of student funding policies; their objectives (what the policies are trying to do); the approach (the mix of benefits recommended for student) and especially the distributive principles underpinning the approach (who should get funding and who should bear the costs); and the policy outcomes.

What principles should inform the student funding system?

The Cubie report

The Cubie report on student finances in Scotland developed the most coherent and accessible set of four 'guiding principles' to assist the development of ideas and policies for student support in both further and higher education. The first, overriding principle was that 'student support should maximise opportunity for all to be able to access high quality life long learning' (ICISF, 1999: 18). This desire for maximizing opportunity informed what the funding should promote. In other words, this principle encapsulated the overall aim of the student funding system.

The report then went on to articulate what it described as the 'administrative principles' of student funding. These principles focused on the practical side of student funding, at the point of delivery. In addition, they were seen as having a role in endorsing and supporting the government's agenda and goals of higher education. In other words, if the student financial arrangements were simple, easy, and well delivered, they would not act as a potential barrier to participation. Thus the second guiding principle was – student support should promote social inclusion, the knowledge economy and an enhanced civil society by having a system which is:

- clear, simple and easily accessible;
- comprehensive and consistent;
- flexible and responsive;
- based on fairness and equal opportunity;
- easily administered, with learner focus;
- adequately resourced (ICISF, 1999: 19).

The third set of principles focused on the funding framework, which set out to inform who should pay for student support. Whatever the source of funding, it was recommended that students should have an adequate level of funding so their income did not fall below the poverty line. In addition, the level of funding should be sufficient so students' ability to undertake their course was not compromised by, for instance, having to do excessive amounts of paid work, to the detriment of their studies, or from excessive financial stress, which in turn may lead to non-completion. Thus, the report declared that 'support should ensure that students in all modes of study are enabled to access a sufficient package of funding, whether from families, employers, graduates, government or through paid employment, none of which should be to the detriment of their studies' (ICISF, 1999: 20).

The fourth, and final, guiding principle concerned targeting for equity. Unlike the other principles, which were to act as a means of checking the workings of the student funding system, this principle specifically aimed to tackle the problems of social exclusion proactively. In other words, it sought particular policy outcomes and proposed targeting resources to achieve these outcomes.

To achieve this, the government should remove barriers to widening access and participation by:

- targeting resources effectively on sections of society under-represented in both further and higher education programmes;
- providing flexible means of support to accommodate the changing nature of the student population;
- assisting, in particular, those students who may not otherwise obtain sufficient support so that education is available to all those who have the ability to benefit from study (ICISF, 1999: 20).

From the principles set out in the Cubie report, the overall aim and purpose of student funding policies is quite clear – maximizing opportunity. The key objectives of the policies, namely, the promotion of social inclusion and the provision of adequate funding, are embedded in both the administrative principles and the funding framework, while the outcomes of the policies are encapsulated in the fourth principle – targeting equity. The policy approach is the subject of the report's main recommendations, but all four principles were to shape them. What is missing from these principles are any which explicitly focus on distributive strategies to inform any policies adopted, namely, who should get funding and who should bear the costs of student support. However, it could be argued that the prioritization of support is implicit in the targeting of those under-represented in further and higher education.

The Rees report

The guiding principles informing the Rees report (IIGSHFW, 2001) on student hardship and funding in Wales are practically identical to those formulated in the Cubie report but add the need for a system that:

- …is enabling for the learner, regardless of age or chosen mode of study;
- recognizes parity of esteem for different modes of study, and contexts of learning, such as full- and part-time study, distance learning, further and higher education, workplace learning, and other courses for adult learners which may or may not carry credit (IIGSHFW, 2001: 2).

These were included because the remit of the Rees report included both full- and part-time students and those in higher and further education, and the demand for regard to the needs of English and Welsh speaking communities and rural and urban communities.

The Dearing report

The principles informing the discussion of student funding policies in the Dearing report had to cover all the various aspects of higher education and not just student funding, unlike the Cubie report. In addition, Dearing's principles had to be considered within the constraints of the government's spending priorities and affordability, unlike Cubie's.

At the outset of the report, the two principles specifically concerned with student support were that 'arrangements for student support should be fair and transparent' (NCIHE, 1997: 84) and 'the various beneficiaries of higher education should share its costs, and public subsidies should be distributed equitably so that individuals are not denied access to higher education through lack of financial means (NCIHE, 1997: 85).

The Dearing report questioned whether the balance of cost sharing was the right one, and who should pay for higher education. It concluded that greater contributions should come from graduates in work, as they were the chief beneficiaries. However, it also recognized that the benefits of higher education are

> ...unpredictable for the individual and realised over a long period of time. We believe it would be unjust and inefficient if those who did not have immediate access to the necessary finance to participate in their higher education were, for that reason, denied the chance of receiving any of its benefits. (NCIHE, 1997: 86)

These two principles also had to support the other principles informing the Committee's work, particularly the promotion of equity of access among individuals irrespective of their social background. Other relevant principles included the maximum participation in higher education having regard to the needs of individuals, the nation and the future labour market; and students being able to choose between diverse courses, institutions, modes and locations of study (NCIHE, 1997: 81–82).

These principles, according to the Dearing report, are meant to guide the development of higher education policy (NCIHE, 1997: 86). It is difficult to see, however, how the first one alone can be classified as the aim or purpose of the student funding system. It can only be classified as such within the context of the other principles, namely, as a means of facilitating maximum participation and promoting student choice. Nor can the second principle be seen as an aim of student funding; rather it is a distributive principle that can inform the overall policy approach to student support.

The report, when discussing student support and how graduates can contribute more towards the costs of their higher education, also asserts that it is necessary 'for the state to provide equitable financial support for students who want to study in different ways or whose personal circumstances require it' (NCIHE, 1997: 304). It then goes on to identify the following issues.

The country should have a student support system which:

- is equitable and encourages broadly based participation;
- requires those with the means to do so to make a fair contribution to the costs of higher education;
- supports lifelong learning by:
  - making choices between full- and part-time and between continuous and discontinuous study financially neutral;
  - reducing the disparity between support for students at further and higher education levels.
- is easy to understand, administratively efficient and cost-effective (NCIHE, 1997: 304).

These issues are both a mixture of policy aims, objectives, approaches and outcomes, and a mixture of the four principles informing the Cubie report.

The overall aim or purpose of the policy is to encourage participation, a somewhat weaker version of Cubie's call for maximizing participation. The key policy objective is to support lifelong learning. The demand for a system that is easy to understand reflects Cubie's administrative principles, as does the desire for an equitable system, but neither have the focus of Cubie's principles. Finally, the call for a fair contribution is again a distributive principle for informing the policies actually adopted. However, Dearing, unlike Cubie, does not set out specific policy outcomes.

It is clear from the analysis of the policies introduced by New Labour in 1998 that they do not fulfil the principles set out in these three reports. Nor do the terms of reference of the current review of student funding cited at the beginning of this chapter. And to a large extent, the lack of clear principles informing current student funding policies along with the absence of concise policy aims, objectives, approaches (including distributive principles), and articulated policy outcomes underpin the failings of the current policies. The unintended consequences of the policies arise from this lack of clarity, focus and overall policy framework and, in turn, help explain the contradictory nature of New Labour's policies.

A new student funding system and beyond

So what would a new student funding system look like if it were informed by a coherent set of principles? What would we want to see if the overriding aim of the policies was indeed to facilitate access and widen participation, as New Labour espouses? What ideas should inform student funding policies and the system of student support, if the desired outcome is social inclusion and a transformation of the socio-economic mix of the student intake?

Such a system of support would need to go beyond ensuring that the costs of higher education (whatever they are) do not prevent some people from entering higher education or deter them from participating in higher education. It would need to go further than just facilitating equal access and equal educational opportunities, and produce a level playing field between students of different social classes and with different abilities to meet the costs of higher education. As Halsey (1998) has observed, 'class remains the stubborn barrier to distribution by merit'.

In contrast to the current approach, a system of student support aimed at widening participation and changing the mix of the student population would need to consider the outcomes of the policies, just as Cubie did in his fourth guiding principle. Just as importantly, the system would have to be rooted in the student experience, and the reality of the lives of both higher education students drawn from low-income families and those who decide not to enter higher education. Hence, the funding system would need to adopt a stronger notion of equality and move away from the notion of equal opportunities, to encompass the idea of equity. Thus, it would need to operate proactively with the clear aim of facilitating the redistribution of opportunities.

One way the funding system could do that is if it provided a positive incentive to enter higher education, and actively encouraged people who would not otherwise participate in higher education. The funding system, therefore, would need to help compensate for previous inequalities, and the subsequent under-representation of certain groups. Thus, it would facilitate access by focusing on certain groups' participation, namely, those currently under-represented in higher education. Here we move from a model of student funding which acts as a disincentive (or is neutral in effect and is neither a disincentive nor an incentive), to a model which acts as an incentive.

To some this may appear extreme, and smack of social engineering. However, the incentive model of student funding already exists. For instance, the 'Secondary shortage subject scheme' for undergraduates on initial teacher training courses gives means-tested grants of up to £7,500 a year. Students on postgraduate teacher training courses in England do not have to pay tuition fees, and receive non-means-tested training 'salaries' (ie grants) of £6,000. An additional 'golden hello' of £4,000 is available for recent graduates teaching shortage subjects. And as announced in the 2001 White Paper *Schools: Achieving success*, the student loans of newly qualified teachers in shortage subjects will be written-off as from September 2002.

Students studying subjects allied to medicine in England currently receive income-assessed bursaries from the NHS of up to around £5,000 a year. For those training to be nurses or midwives on diploma courses the bursaries are not even means-tested. Undergraduate medical and dental students are eligible for bursaries and help with tuition fees in their fifth year of study and beyond.

All these funding arrangements are far more generous and advantageous than those for students studying other subjects. They were explicitly designed to be an incentive. The Web page of the Teacher Training Agency, giving details of these inducements, is adorned with a large picture of a carrot! Conversely, these incentives implicitly acknowledge that the current funding arrangements for the majority of students not studying these subjects act as a disincentive, or are neutral in effect. The prime purpose of these funding arrangements is to tackle labour shortages in areas such as nursing and teaching and to compensate for the additional costs of lengthy training. And they have been highly effective in stimulating teacher recruitment (DfES, 2002).

Furthermore, the idea that student funding should be an incentive lies at the heart of Educational Maintenance Allowances (EMAs), available to some 16–18-year-olds.[4] EMAs are about changing student behaviour, and focus on policy outcomes. They were designed specifically as a financial incentive to improve initial access, retention, and achievement levels. Their initial evaluation confirms their effectiveness in raising average participation rates in post-16 education, especially among young men and those in urban areas (Ashworth *et al*, 2001). EMAs also have had an impact on young people's attendance patterns and achievement levels, and have encouraged some to remain in education (Legard *et al*, 2001). So, why cannot such ideas be extended to certain potential higher education students?

Both the above examples of actual policy approaches rely on grants/bursaries, rather than student loans, as incentives. In other words, the policies implicitly recognize the differential impact of different funding mechanisms on different income groups. The outcome of a policy approach, and the extent to which it has a positive, negative or neutral impact depends on the funding mechanism and the targeted socio-economic group. As research in the United States clearly demonstrates, student loans have a negative/disincentive impact on the participation of low-income groups because of concomitant student debt, but a neutral one on mid- to high-income groups. By contrast, grants have a positive outcome on the enrolment of low-income groups, and a neutral outcome for mid- to high-income groups. And tuition fees have a disincentive effect on the poor and middle-income students but no impact on high-income students (St John, 1990; McPherson and Shapiro, 1991; St John and Starkey, 1995).

Student funding in higher education could be used to stimulate participation in higher education amongst under-represented groups and to improve attainment and non-completion rates, but only if the correct policy approach or mechanism was introduced – policies predicated on the accumulation of debt may well be self-defeating. This is vital to successful outcomes. But they would be costly, which begs the question of affordability. The answer must be higher taxation.

If the level of student funding was adequate, as Cubie articulated, student funding could be used to minimize the financial risks associated with entering higher education highlighted earlier in this chapter. Similarly, it could be used to minimize the risk of failure and non-completion experienced especially among students from low-income backgrounds. If the level of student funding was sufficient, again as Cubie highlighted in his third principle, it could potentially reduce the need for low-income students to engage in term-time employment, and to experience excessive financial strain – all of which have a negative impact on student attainment and completion. The allocation of such funds would need to be based on information about student attainment and drop-out, such as that used by HEFCE in its benchmarks on non-completion. This would guarantee that funding was targeted at those most at risk.

The Dearing, Cubie and Rees reports considered it important that students should be able to choose between diverse courses, institutions, modes and location of study. Although the Dearing report identified this as one of the principles informing the development of higher education policy, it did not specifically relate this to student funding, unlike both the Cubie and Rees reports. There is now mounting evidence that the current student funding system is curtailing students' choices. For example, students are living at home with their parents because of the costs of higher education (Unite/MORI, 2002; Connor *et al*, 2001; Farr, 2001). This restricts their choice of institution and the subjects they can study, and may compromise prospective students' chances of successfully getting into higher education. However, it is students from disadvantaged backgrounds who have their choices constrained, unlike those from better-off families. For example, Forsyth and Furlong (2001) concluded that the prospects of large debts through student loans resulted in disadvantaged young people trying to minimize debt by enrolling in shorter, less advanced courses at less prestigious institutions. Knowles (2000) found that lower-income students opted for vocational rather than academic courses. So students often opt for financial security at the expense of other benefits by enrolling in less advanced, vocationally orientated, short courses run at less prestigious institutions near their parental home. Changes in student funding could reverse these trends, if it was one of the desired outcomes of a student funding system.

Thus, a student funding system that aimed to widen participation and sought to change the socio-economic mix of the student population would look very different from our current student funding system. Within the above discussion are examples of potential policy approaches, which fulfil these policy aims and outcomes. There are many other policy options, but rather than discussing these in detail, we turn to the distributive principles that could inform the actual policies.

A recent report by the IPPR (Piatt and Robinson, 2001) focuses on the allocation of resources across the whole of the post-16 sector, not just higher education. It concludes that resource allocation should be determined by the priorities set for public policy and, in particular, the priority attached to the employability/social inclusion agenda as opposed to the productivity agenda. When discussing what in essence are distributive principles it says:

> ...the most generous support should be directed to the neediest. But the definition of need must be clarified; it should not only include present need but also take into account future income.
> ...There is a compelling logic in the proposition that those who benefit in financial and personal terms from gaining a qualification should receive lower state subsidy than an individual who stands to secure a more modest return. (Piatt and Robinson, 2001: 16–17)

The report argues that the notion that the advantaged should make a greater contribution to enable the disadvantaged access to opportunities previously denied them, accords with centre-left principles. Although not specifically spelt out by the report, this means that any distributive principles used to inform student funding policies must be re-distributive and progressive in their intent, formulation and outcome.

Conclusion

It is clear that the current student funding system is not fulfilling the aims that Blunkett set out in 2000. The system neither adheres to progressive principles nor facilitates access – quite the contrary. The changes encapsulated in the 1998 reforms, in effect, were socially regressive because New Labour prioritized the expansion in higher education at the expense of widening access and increasing the representation of lower class groups whose loss of state assistance was used to fund higher education expansion across all classes.

The 1998 reforms have led to a steep rise in the financial burden of higher education for the poorest groups. Consequently, they are exposed to the greatest personal and financial risks associated with going to university. They experience the most financial hardship and pressures, and the largest debts, which together affect their chances of success. Taken together, these factors may well deter the very students New Labour wants to attract from entering higher education.

If New Labour is seriously concerned about social inclusion and changing the socio-economic mix of the student population, a far more radical approach to the student funding system is required. First of all, the system needs to be based on agreed principles and a coherent policy framework which clearly articulates the policies' aims, objectives, approach, distributive principles, and the desired outcomes of the policies. The absence of such a framework underpins the failings of the current student funding arrangements, and helps explain the contradictory nature of New Labour's policies.

Second, within this proposed policy framework, New Labour's desire to widen participation and to change the socio-economic mix of students needs to be placed at the forefront of its student funding policies so that this is the main aim and the required outcome. Then, we could move from a model of student funding which acts as disincentive (or is neutral in effect), to one which acts as an incentive, and proactively helps to stimulate demand for higher education among under-represented groups. Such an incentive model already exists for selected students such as those studying to be teachers or health care professionals. It could be extended to the majority, if we are willing to pay for it through taxation. Finally, the distributive principles informing new provisions must be redistributive and progressive in their intent, formulation and outcome.

Notes

1. There have been other strategies to widen participation such as those funded by HEFCE and initiated by HEIs, but these are not the focus of this chapter.
2. The Dearing report recommended charging tuition fees on a flat rate basis but maintaining grants for living expenses for those most in need. It is not clear why New Labour found Dearing's proposals unacceptable.
3. The sample, therefore, includes the first cohort of students affected by the introduction of tuition fees, but excludes those affected by the abolition of grants and their complete replacement with student loans, which came into force in 1999/2000.
4. There are other examples of incentives used to encourage the take-up of education and training, which raise broader funding issues, but these are beyond the bounds of this chapter. EMAs have been included here because they illustrate particularly well the incentive model of student support.

References

Ashworth, K et al (2001) Educational Maintenance Allowance: The first year, RR257, Department for Education and Employment (DfEE), London

Barclays (2001) Barclays estimate total UK student debt at £4.85 billion, press release, 24 July

Barke, M et al (2000) Students in the Labour Market: Nature, extent and implications of term-time employment among University of Northumbria undergraduates, RR 215, DfEE, London

Barr, N, and Falkingham, J (1996) Repayment Rates for Student Loans: Some sensitivity tests, Welfare State Programme, discussion Paper WSP/127, London School of Economics

Blunkett, D (2000) Modernising higher education: facing the global challenge, speech at the University of Greenwich, February 2000

Callender, C (forthcoming) Students Studying in London: An analysis of data from the student income and expenditure survey 1998/99, Greater London Authority, London

Callender, C (2001) Supplementary Memorandum Appendix 36 Higher Education: Student retention, Sixth Report, Education and Employment Committee, HC 124, HMSO, London

Callender, C and Kemp, M (2000) Changing Student Finances: Income, expenditure and the take-up of student loans among full and part-time higher education students in 1998/9, RR213, DfEE, London

Callender, C and Kempson, E (1996) Student Finances: Income, expenditure and the take-up of student loans, Policy Studies Institute, London

Connor, H et al (2001) Social Class and Higher Education: Issues affecting decisions on participation by lower social class groups, RR267, DfEE, London

Department for Education and Employment (DfEE) (1998) Higher Education for the 21st Century: Response to the Dearing report, HMSO, London

DfEE (2000) Blunkett announces major student support package to widen access and tackle hardship in higher education, DfEE press release, 25 January

Department for Education and Skills (DfES) (2001a) DfES press notice, 4 October

DfES (2001b) Key challenges of the next decade, speech by Morris at London Guildhall University, DfES, 22 October

DfES (2001c) *Student Support: Statistics of student loans for higher education in United Kingdom*, SFR 46/2001, DfEE, London, 30 November

DfES (2002) More people applying to train as maths and technology teachers, DfES press notice, 6 February

Elias, P *et al* (1999) *Moving On: Graduate careers three years after graduation*, CSU/DfEE, Manchester

Farr, M (2001) Home or away? A study of distance travelled to higher education 1994–99, *Widening Participation and Lifelong Learning*, **3** (1), pp 17–25

Ford, J, Bosworth, D and Wilson, R (1995) Part-time work and full-time education, *Studies in Higher Education*, **20** (2), 187–202

Forsyth, A and Furlong, A (2001) *Socioeconomic Disadvantage and Access to Higher Education*, Policy Press/Joseph Rowntree Foundation, Bristol

Halsey, A H (1998) Leagues apart, *Times Higher Education Supplement*, 6 February

Independent Committee of Inquiry into Student Finance (ICISF) (1999) *Student Finance: Fairness for the future*, Scottish Executive, Scotland

Independent Investigation Group on Student Hardship and Funding in Wales (IIGSHFW) (2001) *Investing in Learners: Coherence, clarity and equity for student support in Wales*, Cardiff, Wales

Knowles, J (2000) Access for few? Student funding and its impact on aspirations to enter higher education, *Widening Participation and Lifelong Learning*, **2** (1), pp 14–23

Labour Party (2001) *Ambitions for Britain*, Labour Party, London

Legard R, Woodfield, K and White, C (2001) *Staying Away or Staying On? A qualitative evaluation of the Education Maintenance Allowance*, RR 256, DfEE, London

Lucas, R, and Ralston, L, (1997) Youth, gender and part-time employment: a preliminary appraisal of student employment, *Employee Relations*, **19** (1), pp 51–66

McPherson, M and Shapiro, M (1991) *Keeping College Affordable: Government and equal opportunity*, Brookings Institution, Washington

Mortenson, T (1990) *The Impact of Increased Loan Utilization among Low Income Students*, American College Testing Program, Iowa City

Mumper, M and Vander Ark, P (1991) Evaluating the Stafford student loan program: current problems and prospects for reform, *Journal of Higher Education*, **62** (1), pp 62–78

National Audit Office (NAO) (2002a) *Widening Participation in Higher Education in England*, The Stationery Office, London

NAO (2002b) *Improving Student Achievement in English Higher Education*, HMSO, London

National Commission on Education (1993) *Learning to Succeed*, report of the Paul Hamlyn Foundation National Commission on Education, Heinemann, London

National Committee into Higher Education (NCIHE) (1997) *Higher Education in the Learning Society*, HMSO, London

Naylor, R, Smith, J and McKnight, A (2001) Sheer class? The extent and sources of variation in the UK graduate earning premium, unpublished mimeo, LSE, London

Piatt, W and Robinson, P (2001) *Opportunity for whom? Options for funding and structure of post-16 education*, IPPR, London

St John, E (1990) Price response decisions: an analysis of the high school and beyond sophomore cohort, *Research into Higher Education*, **32**, pp 141–58

St John, E and Starkey, J (1995) An alternative to net price: assessing the influence of prices and subsidies on within-year persistence, *Journal of Higher Education*, **66** (2), pp 156–86

Smith, N and Taylor, P (1999) Not for lipstick and lager: students and part-time work, *Scottish Affairs Journal*, **28** (Summer), pp 147–63

Unite/MORI (2002) *Student Living Report 2002*, Unite, Bristol

Watson, D and Bowden, R (2001) *Can We Be Equal and Excellent Too? The New labour stewardship of UK Higher education 1997–2001*, occasional paper, Education Research Centre, University of Brighton

5

Redefining Higher Education: A Case Study in Widening Participation

Patrick Ainley, Jill Jameson, Peter Jones, Dai Hall and Marc Farr

Introduction

The current government drive to widen participation in higher education is at odds with a sharp slowdown in the overall growth of student demand, increased student hardship and widespread concerns about non-completion in an era marked by the 'end of expansion and the consolidation of differentiation' amongst higher education institutions (Ainley, 1998). In practice, the great majority of unfilled places – 22,000 since 1994 (Goddard, 2001) and 8,257 in 2000–01 alone (MacLeod, 2001) – are in post-1992 universities. The earlier rapid growth of these institutions proved impossible to sustain as their traditional 'market' was eroded by competition from more prestigious universities. As a result, a process of higher education restructuring is beginning (THES, 2001). This echoes previous mergers and closures in further education (Ainley and Bailey, 1997).

Many post-1992 universities are faced with recruitment, financial and restructuring crises in a situation in which 'the university sector generally is under severe strain' to meet targets, balance finances, and maintain academic standards (Knox, 2000). Most new universities have a long-standing commitment to 'accessibility', but now have little choice but to compete ever more vigorously for non-traditional students. The educational needs of these disadvantaged students are qualitatively different from and quantitatively greater than those of traditional university entrants.

In this chapter we examine this conjunction of factors. Focused upon full-time, first degree entrants and preparation for them, we range from the 'macro' level of national higher education demand and supply conditions, through the 'meso' level of regional competition and institutional differentiation, to the 'micro' level of educational provision and the student experience. Following a brief résumé of the 'macro' level national context, we focus on a 'meso' level regional study of competition and differentiation amongst new universities in London; and a 'micro' level local examination of some level O academic programmes at one such institution, the University of Greenwich. These local programmes are aimed specifically at 'widening participation' entrants to higher education.

The national context

National participation in higher education grew dramatically during the late 1980s and early 1990s, fuelled by rising school and college staying-on and educational attainment rates, as well as by economic changes favourable to graduate employment (HEFCE, 2001: 21ff). In particular, female participation in higher education exceeded that of males since 1992–93 (HEFCE, 2001: 11–12). In spite of adverse demographic trends amongst 18–21-year-olds, the total number of students studying at British higher education institutions rose from around 1 million in 1988–89 to more than 1.5 million in 1993–94 (HEFCE, 2001: 10). Most such growth was concentrated in the new university sector for which this was a moment of growing self-confidence and optimism despite declining per capita funding (Ainley, 1994).

Since the mid-1990s, however, many of these demand-related trends have all but reversed: demographic variables have become more favourable but the key 'drivers' of demand noted above have weakened considerably (HEFCE, 2001: 21 and 25ff). Arguably, this situation has been further aggravated by recent changes to student financial arrangements. While it may be too soon to judge the overall impact of these changes on higher education participation, it is clear that student debt and hours of paid work have both increased in recent years; it also seems likely that any such impact will be felt disproportionately by those from less affluent backgrounds, who are known to be relatively debt averse (HEFCE, 2001: 37 and 60–62).

What is already clear is that, while there has been some continuing growth in postgraduate admissions, there has been almost none at undergraduate level since the mid-1990s (HEFCE, 2001: 13–14). This relates to the target first set by Tony Blair at the Labour party's annual conference in 2000 and most recently restated by Margaret Hodge as 'The Government's policy is to increase participation so that by the end of the decade, 50 per cent of 18 to 30-year-olds have the opportunity to experience higher education' (Parliamentary Review, 2002). In a national context in which 'supply has outstripped demand' for university places (Major, 2001), 'clearing' universities and higher education colleges competed heavily in 2001 to hoover up available students.

Although, in the final analysis, 'more students than ever have enrolled at British universities this autumn'(Goddard, 2001), strong competition to recruit students meant that many applicants who would formerly have gone to ex-polytechnics and higher education colleges were 'poached' by older established universities. This continues a competitive trend observed in Clearing in 2000–01, in which only four 'selecting' universities remained aloof from the desperate competition for home students (Major, 2001 and see Tables 5.1 and 5.2).

As more prestigious institutions have expanded, many new universities face an erosion of their 'traditional' recruitment markets leading to excess capacity and unfilled places.

This combination of factors is redefining the recruitment circumstances and student profile of 'new' universities in comparison with older higher education institutions. In aggregate, the former are much more heavily dependent on 'widening participation' students. In effect, this means recruiting a greater proportion of students with lower entry qualifications who require high levels of educational support, are from less privileged backgrounds and are more likely to combine study with paid work. Such students are considerably less likely to complete than those from more traditional higher education-adapted backgrounds (see for example HCSCEE, 2001). In aggregate, also, new universities are much more heavily reliant for recruitment on Clearing, the expansion of which has led some academics to speculate that 'the UK is moving towards the US-style, consumer driven higher education system' (Major, 2001; Ainley, 1994). The marked increase in recruitment through Clearing in new universities is demonstrated by a peak of 16.5 per cent of students admitted via this route in 1999 (see Table 5.2).

Table 5.1 Type of university v entry method (raw numbers), 1996–2000

Type	Clearing	Year 1996	1997	1998	1999	2000
'Federal'	N	23,089	24,592	24,365	24,254	24,795
Universities	Y	505	625	658	592	637
'New'	N	106,749	122,036	119,393	117,894	116,071
Universities	Y	12,958	17,234	16,584	18,400	16,447
'Plate-glass'	N	15,851	16,834	16,221	16,921	17,014
Universities	Y	677	759	700	711	834
'Technical'	N	18,525	20,610	19,797	20,147	21,360
Universities	Y	688	1,206	1,385	1,438	1,807
'Traditional'	N	69,265	71,810	70,188	71,900	73,737
Universities	Y	1,894	2,354	2,284	2,997	3,178
TOTAL		250,201	278,060	271,575	275,254	275,880

Data from MOSAIC, Experian Ltd

Table 5.2   Type of university v entry method (per cent), 1996–2000

Type	Clearing	Year 1996	1997	1998	1999	2000
'Federal'	N	97.9	97.5	97.4	97.6	97.5
Universities	Y	2.1	2.5	2.6	2.4	2.5
'New'	N	89.2	87.6	87.8	86.5	87.6
Universities	Y	10.8	12.4	12.2	16.5	12.4
'Plate-glass'	N	95.9	95.7	95.9	96.0	95.3
Universities	Y	4.1	4.3	4.1	4.0	4.7
'Technical'	N	96.4	94.5	96.5	96.3	92.2
Universities	Y	6.6	5.5	6.5	6.7	7.8
'Traditional'	N	97.3	96.8	96.8	96.0	95.9
Universities	Y	2.7	6.2	6.2	4.0	4.1

Data from MOSAIC, Experian Ltd

Clearing is also an important entry route for widening participation students, as the highest percentages for recruitment are among those geo-demographic categories at which widening participation initiatives are aimed (Farr, 2001). To widen participation to traditionally under-represented students in higher education could just open more places to Clearing.

Tentatively, we can construct an ideal-type 'model' of the admissions experience of widening participation students who enter new universities through Clearing. Such students may already be less 'committed' to higher education study than those for whom it had become part of an institution-alized transition from living at home to living away and from school to work following the Robbins expansion after 1963 (Ainley, 1994). Such students may be disproportionately from backgrounds where family and financial circumstances may not be conducive to living away from home. By definition, most are from family and wider socio-cultural – including educational and sometimes also ethnic – backgrounds with little or no prior experience or expectation of A level (or equivalent) success, or of entry into higher education. Indeed, many may be quite uneasy about the prospect of severing local ties in favour of a geographically distant and culturally alien institution. In addition, family responsibilities and financial circumstances may not be conducive to living away from home. Some will doubtless have applied to quite prestigious universities, albeit with varying degrees of expectation, excitement and anxiety. By contrast, self-doubts and more tangible obstacles will have constrained others to apply only to local and less 'exclusive' institutions, or even to delay their applications altogether, until their results are known.

It is this combination of factors, along with the (inevitably) modest qualifications attained by some who originally applied to more selective universities, which ultimately channels a significant proportion of widening participation students into new universities via Clearing. State school students applying late are generally more likely to gain acceptance at a local university than students applying in advance – a small but observable trend links late application to closer distance from home of final university place (Farr, 2001). It can be suggested that during the frenetic Clearing process, when decisions are taken more quickly than usual, studying closer to home is a lower-risk strategy, particularly if students are still living at home or are adults who have established their own homes.

The effect of enforced entry into Clearing on those who originally failed to meet their grades is difficult to judge. On the one hand, the experience of rejection may be damaging to the self-confidence of those for whom higher education was from the outset perceived as an uncertain and possibly ill-advised step. On the other, there may be something quite reassuring about entering a (relatively) less culturally and geographically remote higher education institution – the more so if, after all, the additional risks and other 'costs' associated with living away from home are mitigated. The accessible image that most new universities endeavour to project may well be reassuring to widening participation students in general. This sense of reassurance may be further strengthened if the peer group profile is itself more familiar than was anticipated and if living at home (combined with the possibility of maintaining established social networks and, perhaps, finding or continuing part-time work nearby) affords additional continuity with pre-university life. Educationally, however, this 'reassuring familiarity' raises some important questions, since the overall experience of 'ideal-type' widening participation students who enter new universities through Clearing is very different from students experiencing the 'total immersion' model of a 'traditional' university education.

In part, this is a question of quantitative difference: the circumstances we have depicted result in less time spent on campus and more time spent at home, travelling to and from university, socializing off campus, and working (itself compounded by the propensity for students from less affluent backgrounds to work longer hours to reduce their debts (HEFCE, 2001: 61). There is also a qualitative difference since formal and informal opportunities for intellectual transformation are greatly reduced when students are surrounded by peer group members experiencing higher education under similar conditions with school-related experiences and values remote from those associated with a university education. More probably, students' prior intellectual culture will remain largely intact with higher education reduced to an instrumental function of providing work-related credentials and skills.

Competition in the capital

Compared with the national picture, 'educational polarization' is most marked in London, at all levels of learning, becoming even more extreme at higher education level (Watson, 1999). Analysis of London new universities' most recent intake shows the emergence of a 'top' tier of Greenwich, Kingston, Hertfordshire, Middlesex and Westminster (Group 1) over a 'bottom' tier of North London, East London, London Guildhall, South Bank and Thames Valley (Group 2) (Table 5.3).

These two groups were derived using a statistical measure of the similarity of their geodemographic profiles (Spearman's Rank Coefficient). The 'top' tier attract more students from backgrounds closest in profile to those traditionally well-represented in higher education, whilst institutions such as East London and London Guildhall attract those from backgrounds traditionally under-represented who, in terms of probability, are less likely to complete the course.

Application data at the University of Greenwich shows that (for instance) in Computing and Mathematics for entry in 2001, 51 per cent of applicants to undergraduate programmes had also applied to another London new university. This figure is up from 49 per cent in 2000. Similar figures for Business Programmes were 48 per cent in 2001 and 46 per cent in 2000. According to UCAS data published in March of each year, those London new universities showing growth do so consistently year on year. Those showing decline show a continuing trend. There seems to be a strong correlation between these trends and the relative overall league table positions of these universities, though not necessarily with their ratings in the latest Research Assessment Exercise (RAE) as discussed below.

When it comes to Clearing, this pattern can be seen clearly in Tables 5.4 and 5.5. In Table 5.4, for example, the index for 'suburban semis' is 165. In other words, the universities listed under Group 1 are 1.65 times more likely to attract students from such neighbourhoods compared to the average; whereas for the category 'Council Flats' the index is 55 (Group 1 is effectively almost half as likely as the average to recruit from this group).

Table 5.3 London universities – Groups 1 and 2

Group 1	Group 2
Greenwich	North London
Kingston	Guildhall
Hertfordshire	East London
Middlesex	South Bank
Westminster	Thames Valley
City (a constant)	City (a constant)

Table 5.4   London universities Group 1 v London universities Group 2, 2000 normal route entry

MOSAIC – Normal Route	Group 1	Group 2	Per cent 1	Per cent 2	Index of 1 v 2
A High Income Families	1803	766	10.9	7.0	156
B Suburban Semis	2,119	849	12.8	7.7	165
C Blue Collar Owners	724	361	4.4	6.3	133
D Low Rise Council	809	593	4.9	5.4	90
E Council Flats	968	1,164	5.8	10.6	55
F Victorian Low Status	2,939	2,345	17.8	21.4	83
G Town Houses & Flats	1,995	1,033	12.1	9.4	128
H Stylish Singles	1,254	1,020	7.6	9.3	81
I Independent Elders	361	222	2.2	2.0	108
J Mortgaged Families	732	350	4.4	6.2	139
K Country Dwellers	528	232	6.2	2.1	151
L Institutional Areas	33	20	0.2	0.2	109
X Not Known	2,286	2,006	16.8	18.3	75
TOTAL	**16,551**	**10,961**	**100.0**	**100.0**	**100**

Table 5.5   London universities Group 1 v London universities Group 2, 2000 Clearing route entry

MOSAIC – Clearing Route	Group 1	Group 2	Per cent 1	Per cent 2	Index of 1 v 2
A High Income Families	199	111	9.2	6.5	262
B Suburban Semis	228	186	10.6	5.9	179
C Blue Collar Owners	59	54	2.7	1.7	160
D Low Rise Council	101	169	4.7	5.4	87
E Council Flats	151	468	7.0	14.9	47
F Victorian Low Status	370	830	17.2	26.4	65
G Town Houses & Flats	206	271	9.6	8.6	111
H Stylish Singles	215	360	10.0	11.4	87
I Independent Elders	43	49	2.0	1.6	128
J Mortgaged Families	87	96	4.0	6.0	133
K Country Dwellers	35	23	1.6	0.7	223
L Institutional Areas	4	6	0.2	0.2	98
X Not Known	455	526	21.1	16.7	127
TOTAL	**2,153**	**3,149**	**100.0**	**100.0**	**100**

At Clearing, the universities listed under Group 2 could be said to lose out again in that the candidates most likely to succeed are swept up by those listed under Group 1. For example, for the category 'high income families' these higher education institutions only recruit 6.5 per cent of their Clearing intake from this group, whereas Group 1 recruit 9.2 per cent from this neighbourhood type. These findings relate to reported merger negotiations between universities in Group 2.

Having focused down from the 'macro' level of national recruitment, to the 'meso' regional level of higher education polarization and mergers in London, we now examine the 'micro' level of case studies from contrasted year 0 foundation programmes for four-year extended degrees undertaken at the University of Greenwich, a post-1992 Group 1 higher education institution.

'Extended degree' programmes: a case study in widening participation

This section presents a 'micro' level case study (Yin, 1994) of two level 0 ('extended degree') programmes at the University of Greenwich targeted primarily at 'widening participation' entrants to higher education. It examines aspects of their educational provision and associated learner support, along with their student profile, performance and overall experience. In common with other new universities, Greenwich has a declared commitment to 'widening participation' (Jameson and Gill, 2001). Many such students are recruited via Clearing and are an important focus of the University's wider concerns to provide effective academic and pastoral support for student retention (Jameson, 2001). The two programmes considered are the extended combined studies programme, delivered (at the time of undertaking the research) from the University's Woolwich campus, and the extended engineering programme, delivered from the Medway campus at Chatham Maritime. These are the two largest extended degree programmes at Greenwich.

The research reported here was commissioned under the University's Institutional Learning and Teaching Strategy (Humphreys, 1999) to examine the possible contribution to enhanced student retention of effective academic and pastoral support, particularly for programmes with significant numbers of widening participation entrants. Evidence was derived from the University's retention and progression data, interviews with key staff, an anonymous student questionnaire and focus group discussions with students from the two programmes. All questionnaire, focus group and interview-based evidence gathering took place during the spring term of 2000–01.

The engineering programme evolved from an earlier HiTec course formerly delivered in a number of associate colleges. The level 0 curriculum is designed as a preparation for various three-year degree programmes, including mechanical, electrical and electronic engineering, and computer systems with software engineering. It includes all core aspects of engineering with some differentiation between 'mainstream' engineering and computer systems/software engineering students, but with a concern to provide a foundation of essential engineering and mathematical knowledge in all cases. The formal provision is supplemented by various forms of academic and pastoral support.

The combined studies programme is of more recent genesis and recruited students for the first time in 1999–2000. The curriculum includes a central core of academic and 'key' skills, a tutorial component, and a range of optional courses in (amongst other subjects) business, education, humanities, law and sociology. Success at level 0 affords entry to a variety of three-year combined and single honours programmes in these and related areas.

Both extended degree programmes are open to students whose existing qualifications are insufficient for conventional entry to higher education, along with those who wish to enter fields in which they have limited prior experience. In practice, this means a recruitment profile which bears the clear hallmark of widening participation. Tables 5.6–5.9 show aspects of the student profile for each programme. Probably least surprising are the profiles for disability (Table 5.9) and age (Table 5.6) – though it is notable that engineering includes a greater proportion of mature 'returners' to study. Rather more striking are the sex and ethnicity distributions. Table 5.7 shows, unsurprisingly, that engineering has a predominantly male intake but, less predictably, that combined studies is almost correspondingly 'feminized' in its profile. Table 5.8 reveals that both programmes, but especially combined studies, recruit a substantial proportion of ethnic minority students; in both cases predominantly of Asian or African origins, more so than (for example) from Caribbean backgrounds.

Table 5.6   Age distribution of level 0 students

	Less than 20	20–24	25–29	30+
Combined Studies	52.5	36.1	0.0	11.5
Engineering	48.1	29.6	7.4	14.8

Notes: Case study data in Tables 5.6–5.14 is from level 0 extended degree programmes at the University of Greenwich.
Source of data: student questionnaire, Spring 2001.
All indicators are expressed as a percentage of the total number of respondents who answered the relevant question.

Table 5.7   Sex distribution of level 0 students

	Females	Males
Combined Studies	77.4	22.6
Engineering	14.8	85.2

Notes: Source of data: student questionnaire, Spring 2001
All indicators are expressed as a percentage of the total number of respondents who answered the relevant question.

Table 5.8 Ethnic composition of level 0 students

	Ethnic Majority	Ethnic Minority
Combined Studies	36.3	66.6
Engineering	52.2	47.8

Notes: Source of data: student questionnaire, Spring 2001
All indicators are expressed as a percentage of the total number of respondents who answered the relevant question.
'Ethnic majority' students includes those reporting their ethnicity variously as 'white', 'British' or as being of some other European origin. 'Ethnic minority' students includes all others, including those reporting their ethnicity as 'black British'.

Table 5.9 Disability amongst level 0 students

	With Disability	Without Disability
Combined Studies	11.3	88.7
Engineering	7.7	92.3

Notes: Source of data: student questionnaire, Spring 2001
All indicators are expressed as a percentage of the total number of respondents who answered the relevant question.

Data on previous educational experiences, which could not be easily tabulated, suggest that the two intakes include students with a similar range of existing qualifications, from two A level passes (or their equivalent) to few or no formal qualifications. However, while engineering students present a mix of vocational and academic backgrounds, often with an interval of several years prior to entering higher education, the previous experiences of combined studies students are more uniformly academic and relatively recent. This latter group includes a significant number who previously failed to attain the grades required for entry into a degree programme in (for example) business, media studies or law. For these students, the extended degree programme offers a 'second chance'; in practice, however, the competition for level 1 degree places in some disciplines (especially law) is such that they may be required to achieve a minimum of (for example) 60 per cent in the cognate level 0 course, as well as an overall pass in the programme as a whole, before a level 1 place will be offered on their 'first choice' programme.

Table 5.10 shows that around half of those who registered for the 'extended' engineering programme in 1999–2000 did not successfully complete the first stage.

The programme suffered additional modest losses (those who transferred out of the University or withdrew from higher education after successfully completing the first stage) but, conversely, retained a proportion of those who did not successfully complete (but who re-registered for a level 0

Table 5.10   1999–2000 Retention and progression indicators for level 0 programmes

	Initial Cohort Size	Within-Year Non-completion	Within-Year Progression	Declined to Progress	Across-Year Progress	Across-Year Retention
Combined Studies	77	36.8	66.2	0.0	66.2	80.5
Engineering	51	49.0	51.0	7.8	46.1	51.0

Notes: All indicators are expressed as a percentage of the initial cohort size

Source of data: Information Planning and Statistics Unit, University of Greenwich.

Within-year progression is the percentage of the initial cohort that was permitted to progress at the end of the year (including those carrying limited failure).

Across-year progression is the percentage of the initial cohort that progressed to a Level 1 programme in the session following initial registration (ie without repeat or interruption), including those who progressed onto a different programme. Census date for re-registration: 30 November.

Across-year retention is the percentage of the initial cohort that had re-registered by 30 November in the session following initial registration, including those who progressed to a Level 0 programme *plus* those who remained at level 0 due to interruption or failure. Includes all those who re-registered on a different programme.

Within-year non-completion includes those who interrupted, those who withdrew (ie with no intention of returning), those who failed (with or without permission to repeat), and those unaccounted for ('nothing on record'). Reliable disaggregation of these various categories of within year non-completion is not possible.

Students who declined to progress are those who did not progress to level 1 (either of the same, or of another, programme) in the session following initial registration, despite being permitted to do so, expressed as a percentage of the initial cohort size. This measure unavoidably includes those who interrupted in the session following initial registration, but who progressed (or who plan to progress) at a later date.

Reliable identification (including reliable disaggregation) is not possible for those who declined to continue at level 0 in the session following initial re-registration, in spite of being entitled to do so (following failure or interruption).

programme). However, amongst the relatively small sub-cohort who successfully completed level 0 in 1998–99, and progressed to a level 1 engineering programme in 1999–2000, Table 5.11 reveals a very high rate of continuing success.

Extended combined studies retained and progressed a significantly higher proportion of its level 0 students in 1999–2000 compared with the 'extended' engineering programme (see Table 5.10). Nonetheless, around one-third of those who registered did not complete the stage. There are no statistics for level 1 performance (Table 5.11) as this is the first year of recruitment.

Interviews with key staff, together with student questionnaires and focus groups, shed some light on retention and progression on the two programmes. The then Head of Engineering described his School's extended programme as having 'a wide access policy' and, consequently, some 'very fragile students', who often face considerable external pressures: 'part-time students attending a full-time course with full-time jobs'. As a result, he continued, 'we lose 50 per cent, most in the first term…

Table 5.11 Level 1 retention in 1999–2000 for 1998–99 entrants to level 0 programmes

	Initial Sub-cohort Size	Within-Year Progression	Within-Year Non-completion
Combined Studies	—	—	—
Engineering	17	94.1	5.9

Notes: Within-year progression at level 1 is the percentage of the initial sub-cohort (ie those who progressed to level 1 in 1999–2000) that was permitteed to progress at the end of the year (including those carrying limited failure).

they drift away, say they will come back but never do. They fall behind and never catch up.' The programme leader for engineering argued that 'considerable academic rigour' is required, due to surveillance by professional associations. As a result, he claimed, 'we're struggling to get a quart into a pint pot'. In his view also, high attrition is inevitable but 'we'd rather have students fall down at level 0 than in year 1'. Support is variously provided from within the School and from University-wide services, such as Student Services, for study skills. There are also weekly class tutorials, timetabled surgery hours for individual academic tutoring, 'sympathetic ear' counsellors and specialist computing support. Both engineering respondents appreciated the importance of early intervention but in the words of the then Head of School, staffing is 'very tight' and, as a result, follow-up is often 'too late'.

The programme leader for extended combined studies likened her level 0 curriculum and the approach as a whole to that of a US community college foundation programme: that is, skills-oriented with some subject-specific content. This contrasts with the engineering programme, where skills are mainly 'bolted on' to the central subject content. In common with the engineering programme, however, timetabled group tutorials and academic 'office' hours are available for all students with additional support from Student Services. There is some diversity of approach within the range of subject options offered with, for example, law and business appearing to replicate the content-centred approach of engineering, more so than education, humanities or sociology. These differences were said to be reflected in contrasting failure rates between subjects, during 1999–2000.

Tables 5.12–5.14, based on the questionnaire responses, show that students on the combined studies programme evaluated their academic and pastoral support more favourably than their counterparts in engineering. These differences of view were largely confirmed by student focus groups. The combined studies group generally welcomed its programme as an alternative to further A-level study and as an induction to higher education. Some had maintained their original subject preference (especially in the case of prospective law students) and hoped to use the 'extended' year to access it. Others appreciated the opportunity to explore new areas and to keep their options open for a further year. By contrast, most engineering students felt they were on a 'crash course' which only the 'fittest' would 'survive'.

This case study of two extended programmes suggests that contrasting conceptions of curriculum design and student support are in operation. The combined studies programme emphasizes 'nurturing' and skills development, while engineering is more heavily content based. The contrast between these two approaches should not be overstated, however: nurturing and skills development are not absent from the engineering programme, while some individual courses within the combined studies programme are more strongly content centred. Moreover, differences in the retention experiences of these programmes cannot be easily and directly related to their conceptions of curriculum design and student support; other factors, for example, the students' own backgrounds and circumstances, are also significant. Furthermore, these differing approaches are embedded in the wider academic cultures associated with their respective disciplines (see Becher and Huber, 1990). The engineering

Table 5.12   Student evaluation of the induction programme

	Number of Responses	% Helpful	% Adequate	% Not Helpful
Combined Studies	60	75.0	25.0	0.0
Engineering	26	38.5	42.3	19.2

Table 5.13   Student evaluation of academic feedback and support

	Number of Responses	% Well Supported	% Adequately Supported	% Not Well Supported
Combined Studies	60	41.7	45.0	16.3
Engineering	27	0.0	31.5	68.5

Table 5.14   Student evaluation of 'pastoral' support

	Number of Responses	% Well Supported	% Adequately Supported	% Well Supported	% Support Not Needed
Combined Studies	60	36.7	35.0	5.0	26.3
Engineering	24	25.0	14.6	46.8	16.7

curriculum is subject to the influence and requirements of professional body accreditors. For these reasons, fundamental curriculum change will not easily be achieved.

This case study is unable to provide conclusive evidence with which to judge the longer-term efficacy of 'nurturing' vis-à-vis alternative approaches to curriculum design and student support. The previous year's cohort of successful engineering students, whose very high level 1 progression was noted, is clearly too small a sample for any meaningful inferences to be drawn. Concerns have also been expressed about the possible creation of a 'dependency culture', if students are excessively 'nurtured', which may engender problems if and when high levels of support are subsequently withdrawn. On balance, however, it seems difficult to dispute the value of a 'nurturing' approach and equally difficult to see why, given the necessary resources, such a model of enhanced student support could not be adopted in a variety of circumstances.

It should be pointed out, though, that most entrants to higher education will encounter lower levels of student support compared with their former school or college and with a much less 'supervisory' approach from tutors. For some, this contrast in their immediate educational environment is accompanied by a significant falling away of parental involvement, in both study itself and in 'personal maintenance'. The need to take term-time work is likely to be another complicating factor, which may differ (at least in extent) from previous experiences in school/college. On top of all this is the need to adjust to the distinctive academic culture of higher education: what to do in lectures; how to use a university library; how to write acceptable essays without plagiarizing; what kind of relationship to establish with tutors and so on. Successful students therefore need to be self-motivating, self-disciplined, personally and socially skilled, academically acculturated for higher education and excellent organizers of their time and money, etc. For 'widening participation' students, who are typically less affluent and from families and communities with little prior experience of higher education, many of these adjustments are likely to present considerably more difficulties and conflicts, compared to 'traditional' university entrants. This is why effective academic and pastoral support assumes such importance under widening participation.

Conclusion

Today just under one-third (32 per cent plus) of young people aged under 21 domiciled in the UK continue their participation in education to some form of higher education. This can be compared with a participation rate of 12 per cent in 1979, and around 2 per cent prior to the Second World War (Tonks, 1999). Approximately two-thirds remain in school or further education from age 16–18. At this stage, more students drop out from school sixth forms (though not from sixth-form colleges) than from further education, or rather, many 16–18-year-olds move from sixth form to further education (Ainley *et al*, 2001). Non-completion in further education as in higher education is widely recognized to be closely associated with student poverty (Martinez and Munday, 1998). The loss of grants and introduction of fees means that for most students working their way through their programmes of study, education without the certainty of a future career is combined with part-time, casual jobs. This combination of education with 'McJobs' – convenient, uniformed, efficient, unskilled low-paying jobs, the work equivalent of 'fast food' (Ritzer, 2000) – not only makes it harder for students to complete their studies, but detracts from the personal meaning of their university experience. Higher education as a whole may now have lost some of the significance it once had for an elite minority of students. It is less prized by today's students for its biographical significance than for the necessity of gaining qualifications to enter or secure core employment with prospects of permanency and progression.

This is the reality of the medium (one-third), not mass (more than half), participation higher education system created by the 1992 Further and Higher Education Act (Scott, 1995). The Departmental Review of Higher Education announced by Estelle Morris on 23 October is an admission that the Blair/Blunkett 50 per cent participation target cannot be met without 'redefining higher education', as Morris announced the purpose of the Review in October 2001. Simultaneously, Morris proclaimed the abolition of Individual Learning Accounts for students and trainees in the new Learning and Skills Sector. Funding for higher education students is already being reviewed by the DfES. If specialist further education colleges, already designated as 'Centres of Vocational Excellence', are to be turned into higher education institutions through links to local universities, and former polytechnics are given various 'missions' to provide courses linked to specific employment (ie turned into further education colleges), some new form of funding has to be found for all the 'extra' higher education students this will create. Universities UK has indicated that the extra money needed to meet the targets is of the order of £14.36 billion (Thomson, 2001), but even this would not address wider further/higher education issues such as the need for 'non-advanced further education' provided outside the Centres of Vocational Excellence.

As indicated earlier, the HEFCE's paper (2001) shows students spurning new universities leading to recruitment crises at several institutions. As a result, the Council argues that the MASN (maximum number of students set by the Council for each university and higher education college it funds) 'should be abolished'. This would open higher education to a free market in student places and allow the Russell Group of elite universities to privatize themselves by introducing full cost fees. Research funding would also be concentrated in this 'Ivy League' even more than it is already if the suggestion (reported in the same issue of the sector's house journal) by Sir

Howard Newby, HEFCE's Chief Executive, is implemented – namely to suspend the Council's expensive and bureaucratic RAE.

This further concentration of research funding will relegate those universities and colleges not in the Russell Group to 'teaching only' institutions. Along with the RAE, another bureaucratic rigmarole is also being challenged following the resignation of the head of the Quality Assurance Agency (QAA). QAA's assessment of teaching quality supposedly influences student applications and thus substitutes for free market choice. Lack of government support for QAA points towards a totally Americanized system in which the binary line will be redrawn between state universities and their associated (further education) community colleges and the 'Ivy League' where courses will cost more. This will enhance an elite system for the few, where – as a rule of thumb – the older the university, the younger, whiter and more affluent the students it will attract, combined with a mass system for the many. The 'Ivy League' of selecting and researching universities dominates the competition for students in the Poaching and Clearing wars that are the national context for the local case studies that have been described.

Acknowledgements

UCAS and Experian Ltd provided data analysed at the Universities of Greenwich and Lancaster and by Experian Ltd.

References

Ainley, P (1994) *Degrees of Difference: Higher education in the 1990s*, Lawrence and Wishart, London

Ainley, P (1998) The end of expansion and the consolidation of differentiation in English higher education, *Teaching in Higher Education*, **3** (2), pp 143–56

Ainley, P and Bailey, B (1997) *The Business of Learning: Staff and student experiences of further education in the 1990s*, Cassell, London

Ainley, P *et al* (2001) Progression in and from further education: some problems for an integrated system of lifelong learning, in *What progress are we making with Lifelong Learning? The evidence from research*, ed F Coffield, University of Newcastle upon Tyne

Becher, T and Huber, L (1990) Editorial, *European Journal of Education* (Special Issue on Disciplinary Cultures), **25**, pp 235–40

Farr, M (2001) Home or Away: A study of distance travelled to higher education, *Journal of Widening Participation and Lifelong Learning*, March, University of Staffordshire

Goddard, A (2001) Great news for Hodge as enrolments soar, *Times Higher Education Supplement*, 12 October

Higher Education Funding Council for England (HEFCE) (2001) *Supply and Demand in Higher Education*, HEFCE, Bristol

House of Commons Select Committee on Education and Employment (2001) *Higher Education: Student retention, Sixth Report*, HC 124. Available at: http://www.publications.parliament.uk/pa/cm200001/cmselect/cmeduemp/124/12403/htm

Humphreys, J (1999) *Institutional Learning and Teaching Strategy*, paper presented to the Learning and Teaching Committee, University of Greenwich

Jameson, J (2001) *Towards a University Retention Strategy*, paper presented to Academic Council, University of Greenwich

Jameson, J and Gill, I (2001) *Strategy for Widening Participation*, paper submitted to HEFCE, July 2001, University of Greenwich

Knox, T (2000) Let them decide how good they want to be, *Times Higher Education Supplement*, 8 September

Macleod, D (2001) Bums on seats row, *Guardian*, 27 November

Major, E (2001) It's your call... course supply has now outstripped demand and it's a student buyers' market, *Guardian*, 14 August

Martinez, P and Munday, F (1998) *9,000 Voices: Student persistence and drop-out in further education*, Further Education Development Agency (FEDA), London

Parliamentary Review (2002) 16, Session 2001–02, 11–15/2/02, 11 February

Ritzer, G (2000) *The McDonaldization of Society*, Sage, London

Scott, P (1995) *The Meanings of Mass Higher Education*, Open University Press and Society for Research into Higher Education, Buckingham

THES (2001) Leader: Mergers mean bigger, but not always better, *Times Higher Education Supplement*, 19 January

Thomson, A (2001) £15 billion needed to hit targets, *Times Higher Education Supplement*, 30 November

Tonks, D (1999) Access to UK higher education, 1991–98: using geodemographics, *Widening Participation and Lifelong Learning*, **1** (2), August, http://www.staffs.ac.uk/journal/art-1.htm

Watson, J (1999) *An Education Audit for London*, Focus Central London TEC, London

Yin, R K (1994) *Case Study Research: Design and methods*, 2nd edition, Sage, London

6

| Higher Education: A Risky Business |

Louise Archer, Carole Leathwood and Merryn Hutchings

Introduction

As contributors to this book reiterate, 'widening participation' remains a key concern within British higher educational policy since the transformation from an 'elite' to a 'mass' higher education system has done little to affect low participation levels among particular, disadvantaged social groups. Recruitment of 'working class' students is especially low (NCIHE, 1997), and has been identified as one of the last access frontiers (Woodrow, 2000). But relatively little is known about the views of working class 'non-participants' and their reasons for not going to university.

There are various views as to why working class groups do not participate equally in higher education. Some previous research and policy discourses suggest that working class groups tend not to participate because of a 'poverty of aspiration' (CVCP, 1998) embedded within habit, culture and professional or peer expectation (Robertson and Hillman, 1997). Government rhetoric, in particular, positions higher education participation as a 'rational' choice for economic, personal and social reasons. Such approaches tend to assume that in higher education participation is naturally desirable and that non-participant working class groups experience a 'deficit' (in knowledge, aspiration, etc) that hinders their access. Such broad-brush approaches also fail to take account of differences in participation rates between different working class groups, for example in terms of ethnicity and gender.

Although they are the focus of much public and policy discourse, relatively little is known about what 'non-participant' working class groups of people think about higher education and how they understand the (im)possibility and (un)desirability of participation in higher education. This chapter attempts to address some of these concerns by exploring the views of ethnically diverse, working class men and women who are mainly 'non-participants' in higher education. It will be argued that due to unequal risks and costs associated with participation for working class groups, 'non-participation' can often be viewed as a rational, pragmatic strategy of risk avoidance, rather than a lack of aspiration or talent.

The research study

This chapter draws on data collected from a larger project, Social Class and Widening Participation in Higher Education, a two-year research project, funded by the University of North London, to investigate the barriers to higher education participation among British working class groups. This project used focus group discussions to examine the views of 118 'non-participant' working class people aged 16–30 living in North and East London[1] and 85 higher education students (in their first term of their first year in a post-1992, inner city university)[2] in addition to a national MORI survey of 1,200 'working class' respondents.[3]

For the practical purposes of identifying potential working class respondents for this study, we drew on a broad range of indicators including occupation (of respondent and/or parents), previous family experience of higher education and fee remission for higher education students.[4] However, definitions of social class are inherently problematic. For example, conceptualizations of social class that rest primarily upon economic factors and employment status have been criticized for making gendered assumptions, for treating class groupings as homogeneous, and for failing to adequately account for the changed industrial and labour scene at the start of the 21st century (Walkerdine, Lucey and Melody, 1999). Social class is changing, fluid and subjectively experienced (Walkerdine, 1990; Skeggs, 1997; Reay, 1999; Zmroczek, 1999), and is clearly located within enduring structural constraints and inequalities (Mahony and Zmroczek, 1997). In addition to gendered, classed relationships, attention has been drawn to the importance of 'race' and ethnicity within social class. As Franklin (1999) stresses, there are differences in black and white class structures, whilst Reynolds argues that 'many black women in Britain identify 'race as the starting point of any self-definition' (Reynolds 1997: 10). Reynolds (1997) further insists that 'to be a black working-class woman in Britain is construed as meaning something entirely different to being a white working-class woman in Britain' (1997: 14–15).

Our own theoretical stance (Archer, Leathwood and Hutchings, 2001) is one which, like many others, conceptualizes identity as fluid, shifting and 'becoming' (Alexander, 1996), rather than 'achieved', static or fixed. At the same time, structural inequalities of 'race', class and gender are never complete or absolute. They are both material and discursive, shifting and socially/historically constructed, and they are differently constructed and enacted across time and context for different individuals and groups. These structures are, however, stubbornly durable, and continually reproduced, albeit variously and differently, within a network of multiple, unequal power relations. They also generate and may be met by resistance, and we see identities and inequalities as recursively linked (Mama, 1995).

Risk and higher education participation

Risk emerged as an important, central theme running throughout respondents' accounts within our research. As Beck (1992) argues, risks are unevenly distributed within society and this uneven distribution works to reproduce and perpetuate class inequalities. Positions of privilege enable the purchasing of protection from risk, whereas disadvantaged positions carry the greatest threats and risks:

> The history of risk distribution shows that, like wealth, risks adhere to the class pattern, only inversely: wealth accumulates at the top, risks at the bottom. To that extent, risks only seem to *strengthen*, not to abolish, the class society. Poverty attracts an unfortunate abundance of risks. By contrast, the wealthy (in income, power or education) can *purchase* safety and freedom from risk. (Beck, 1992: 35)

In this research study, respondents' stories reinforced the argument that working class groups occupy a structurally more 'risky' position and are more prone to experiencing disadvantages that restrict ability to participate in education. In other words, the (economic, social and personal) risks and costs of participation are higher for working class students (Archer and Hutchings, 2000; Hutchings and Archer, 2001).

Working class students and non-participants alike recognized that participation in higher education entails considerable social and economic risks, costs, financial hardship and insecurity, and all with no guarantees of success. Non-participant respondents did recognize the potential benefits of obtaining a degree, but many felt themselves to be in positions where going to university would be 'impossible' due to financial, personal and cultural constraints. Perceptions of the highly risky, costly and uncertain nature of higher education participation spanned across application, participation and graduate employment prospects. It was widely agreed that debt is riskier for working class groups, and respondents highlighted the diverse, but very real, possibilities of failure (drawing upon their own experiences of educational failure) and the diverse social and economic consequences of failure for themselves and their families. In the face of these risks, we would suggest that for many respondents non-participation could be identified as a pragmatic and rational way of managing risk by 'sticking to what you know'. For example, non-participant men compared the security of continued paid employment with the gamble of a long period of study, and many chose to stay with the former.

Knowledge, information and cultural capital

For many non-participant respondents, going to university was a 'non-choice'; it had simply never entered into their choice/decision-making horizons. The MORI survey revealed that 59 per cent of the sample had no plans ever to go to university, and almost half of all respondents (49 per cent) had never thought about doing a degree (this figure rose to 60 per cent among social class E interviewees). Within the focus groups it became evident that few working class respondents had a family history of higher education participation to support and guide them through the process of application and entry. As a result, many non-participants (and also, retrospectively, some students) reported that they knew relatively little about how to apply to university, what it might be like there or what studying in higher education might cost and entail (see Hutchings and Archer, 2001). Working class students in our study reported that knowing someone who had been to university was a very important factor influencing their decision to apply. This personal contact not only introduced university into respondents' horizons of choice and made it seem 'achievable', but provided an important source of information, support and advice.

It has been argued that working class families are highly disadvantaged within the higher education process, as compared to middle class applicants, due to inequalities in the social and cultural capital and resources that potential students are able to draw upon (Reay, 1998). Research has shown that students in further education are given less information about higher education than those in schools (Roberts and Allen, 1997). In our study, 44 per cent of respondents in the MORI survey reported that they had received no information at all about higher education from school or college. Furthermore, working class and minority ethnic students tend to receive less help and advice relating to higher education application from their schools than middle class students (Reay, 1998).

Issues of advice and information are particularly crucial due to differential, classed use of particular information sources. Work by Ball and Vincent (1998) distinguished between 'cold', formal knowledge and 'hot', grapevine knowledge. They found a wide mistrust of particular 'official' sources of information among working class families and a heavy reliance upon 'hot' or grapevine knowledge. Working class non-participants in our study also largely distrusted official government, LEA and higher education sources of information. These were regarded as biased and only representing institutional or governmental interests; for example, some non-participant women argued that 'they need to get as many people in the college as they can' and 'they just want people to come because they get money for that'.

In contrast, informal, 'hot' local knowledge was used more heavily, being regarded as more useful and reliable. Further education respondents were also highly critical of the careers advice they received from independent, 'professional' careers advisers, who (it was perceived) did not know them or hold their interests at heart. In comparison, working class higher education students narrated the importance of having had trusted friends or family members who encouraged them through entry routes and provided an important motivation to apply for university or college. For example, one of the young women in further education said, 'I just heard some girls [at the bus stop] saying 'Gateway College'... I just, I just heard 'Gateway' and I went to the operator and got the number and prospectus and I came here.'

Hierarchy of universities

Most non-participant and participant respondents had an idea that there were important differences in status, resources and accessibility between universities. Most were also aware that only certain (less prestigious) universities are accessible for working class students and that these carry reduced chances of success in the job market afterwards. 'Dream' universities were those which are 'nice looking', had 'grass', were further away and guaranteed better graduate jobs: 'It didn't even look like a uni, it was wow! And like you got grass out there... and it's so posh and that, I liked it' (Eve, 18, black female, further education student).

Some minority ethnic respondents also mentioned that these 'better' universities tended to be dominated by white students, although some black women were motivated to try to access such institutions 'to prove a point'. But generally, access to these institutions was considered to be the domain of middle class students who had the necessary money, status and whose families were able to 'plan ahead'. In comparison, working class respondents recognized that a mixture of social and financial factors (family responsibilities, cost of transport, need to carry on in paid employment) necessitate 'keeping close' (Pugsley, 1998) and attending a 'local' university. Local universities were talked about as grey, concrete, 'sad' and more likely to be attended by working class and minority ethnic students (Hutchings and Archer, 2001).

This perceived hierarchy of institutions, and the differential (lower) employability associated with degrees from 'less prestigious' institutions, operated as a powerful discourse against participation among non-participant respondents. Many of these respondents also identified the current shift to mass higher education as a barrier to participation because it was felt to have resulted in an 'over-crowded' graduate job market. In this, it was felt that working class graduates (having attended 'second rate' universities and having achieved lower qualifications as a result of juggling work, financial and social pressures) would be the first to be 'squeezed out'. The consequences of being 'overqualified' and unable to get a graduate job were identified as depression, increased family poverty and lost time, money and employment prospects.

Social and identity risks

Government rhetoric suggests that educational participation is rational, desirable and valuable at a number of levels (national, social and personal) and can bring about desirable and positive changes for disadvantaged social groups (DfEE, 1998). Data from this study suggest, however, that among working class respondents, reasons for non-participation were often grounded in discourses of identity (class, gender and race/ethnicity) and emotion. These views related to visions of the higher education system as 'other', largely unknown and alien. The importance of attending to issues of identity and inequality when considering issues around social class has also been highlighted by Mahony and Zmroczek (1997), who stress that social class both structures people's lives and is reconstituted by them.

Several non-participant and student respondents identified a risk of 'changing' class identity as a result of participation in higher education. Higher education was largely perceived to be a middle class, 'snobby' system in which working class students were disadvantaged and 'different'. Indeed, 45 per cent of the MORI sample agreed that 'the student image is not for me'. Some focus group respondents also anticipated, or recounted, being intimidated by middle class students and by 'big and scary' universities. Independent of whether respondents personally expressed a wish to go to university or not, 'students' were widely represented as middle class (and white) and therefore 'different' to oneself. Images of (middle class) students were largely negative, with students positioned as 'lacking common sense', 'immature' and as socially inadequate. This latter view was particularly prevalent amongst white respondents. Many respondents shared a view of university student life as characterized by 'drinking and partying', but this stereotype was generally regarded as negative due to the risks of alcoholism and debt associated with a culture of 'cheap drink'.

However, as other writers have noted, there was a pervasive theme of ambiguity and tension between 'leaving' and 'holding on to' working class identities within respondents' talk (Lawler, 1999; Reay, 1997). Both non-participants and participants talked about the value of 'not changing' (ie to not become middle class as a result of going to university). This echoes hooks' (1994) argument that the process of engagement with education can involve a 'betrayal' of one's working class origins. Many respondents talked about the value of holding on to 'working class' characteristics such as 'common sense' in comparison to the middle class preoccupation with academic knowledge. Indeed, some non-participants explicitly argued against the value of getting a degree because it was only 'paperwork', as compared to the 'real life' value of common sense in the workplace. As various other researchers have written, educational success was often positioned as oppositional to working class identities, and this was clearly grounded within respondents' own experiences of educational failure and 'spoiled' learning identities.

Gendered identities also provided a key site for resistance, particularly amongst male respondents, where education was not valued as a 'manly' option. The majority of non-participant men conceptualized participation in higher education negatively because it would involve a potential risk and loss of 'strong', 'responsible' masculine status, power and identity. Moreover, their talk often revealed the men's reluctance to give up their 'local' everyday powerful identities as working class men in order to enter a middle class (men's) world of higher education, in which they would be disadvantaged.

The form of the resistant masculine identities voiced varied between men from different ethnic backgrounds. For example, many of the white working class non-participant men constructed 'traditional' masculine identities grounded in manual work ('chippies', 'sparkies' and 'labourers'). These identities were generally valued and respected in contrast to 'imma-ture' and 'soft' students. Masculine identities were defined through paid work, rendering study 'unthinkable' (Cohen, 1988) and unnecessary (Archer *et al*, 2001a). In comparison, many black (mostly Caribbean) young men constructed 'cool' black masculine identities. These identities centred around work, style, clothes, cars and heterosexuality, which Majors (1992) has termed 'Cool Pose'. These young men resisted higher education participation as incompatible with maintaining the symbols of autonomous black masculinity. As Drew said: 'Now I'm living on my jays, yes, I've got a car to look after. I've got my yard to look after. I can't be going to uni' (Drew, 21, black Caribbean shop assistant).

A number of Bangladeshi and Asian young men, however, suggested that whilst they valued the ideal of going to university, participation was impos-sible due to their financial and domestic responsibilities as male 'breadwin-ners' within their families:

> Since leaving school more or less, financially I have to be responsible for my family because I am the oldest... It is a kind of pressure knowing that you are expected to take care of your parents and the rest of the family. (Shahid, 22, Bangladeshi, cashier)

> The motive was to finish secondary school, go to work straight away, earn the money, give it to Mum – they would send it off to Bangladesh to help family etcetera, etcetera. (Selim, 24, Bangladeshi, administrative worker)

The women's accounts, however, drew heavily upon notions of the rela-tionship between higher education and 'respectable', or acceptable, working class femininity. Propensity to participate appeared to relate to the extent to which women respondents could negotiate a 'fit' (or not) between these two competing demands. For some of the white young women, middle class student femininity was unattractive, undesirable and resisted. For example, Vicky berated some girls who had gone away to university and 'changed': 'A couple of girls I know... they come back and they look like grungers... it's not the way they went' (Vicky, 18, white British further education student).

But it was notable that women generally tended to report the main sources of discouragement and disapproval as coming from their families. We have discussed this elsewhere (eg Archer *et al*, 2001b; Hutchings *et al*, 2000; Leathwood *et al*, 2001), drawing upon theories of class envy, mobility and resistance in relation to discourses around 'respectable' femininity (eg Lawler, 2000; Reay, 1996a, b, 1997; Skeggs, 1997; Walkerdine, 1990). This disapproval was experienced by younger and older white women and occasionally by older black women:

> Where I'm from, I'm from Manchester, and the area is just very sort of working class. I had these dreams above my station you know, sort of to go to London and do a degree. It was all very sort of *(acts indignation, disapproval)* well like, 'What is this not good enough for you?' So I've had to deal with a lot of my family, none of them into education at all, not even stepped onto the A level ladder, just gone you know straight from school and what not. And it's really been shunned, I've really been shunned for coming here actually. But I'm smoothing it over and hopefully I'll prove to them that it's not a bad thing me going away. I can go back and put something in maybe. Not that I want to go back there! *(laughs)* It's, it is really difficult to come down here. Especially when parents, they don't understand at all, you know, you sort of explain why you want to do it and they're like 'Yeah but you've got a job, you've got all these things', all these physical objects that you have, computers, a car, whatever. And they think it's great and you, you know, your mind wants something else. And that's very difficult to sort out. (Sally, 22, white English student)

With her phrase 'I had these dreams above my station', Sally articulated a theme that ran through several of the white women's accounts: that she knew 'her place' in society, and that a desire to move beyond that was somehow illegitimate, especially for women. She also experienced some guilt at leaving: *'I can go back and put something in maybe'*, although she is clear that she does not want 'to go back there'. Hatton also describes the guilt she experiences as 'a working-class girl gone wrong' and said, 'I became a stranger in my own family' (Hatton, 1999: 214). Sally, as the 'good' daughter, wanted to avoid this, to smooth it over and hopefully persuade her family that her going away would not be 'a bad thing'. The contradictions between wanting to escape from, whilst at the same time preserve, working class identities are apparent here (Lawler, 1999). Another white woman in the study explained how her parents had compared her choice to enter higher education negatively with that of her cousin who had got a good husband and a house. Gendered and raced assumptions about what is appropriate and respectable (Skeggs, 1997) for white working class women come through in these accounts.

Black women in the study did not report this kind of resistance from parents, nor the same kinds of dilemmas about leaving their working class identities behind. It may be that, as Reynolds states, 'many black women in Britain identify 'race' as the starting point of any self definition' (Reynolds, 1997: 10), and that this supersedes class identities. At the same time, Mirza's identification of a strong commitment to education amongst second-generation Caribbean people, the belief in meritocracy, and definitions of femininity which incorporate female autonomy and women taking part in paid work, are also likely to come into play (Mirza, 1995). This does not mean, though, that the black women received only encouragement. One older black woman spoke about the resistance she faced from others because she was a mother, whilst Grace found that:

> I think, I think for me work were the ones that were quite negative about me going. 'Cos I'd been at work for like three years with the same people and I think what they felt was that I felt I was so much better than they… I dunno, it was like I was trying to attain to a level that was not achievable for me. But my parents were really pleased. And they supported me as much as they can. (Grace, 26, African Caribbean student)

However, Janita (an Asian higher education student) received not only support from her parents, but an unequivocal expectation that she would go to university: 'No, my parents sent me to uni! It was like "You're going!" That was it! (*laughter*)' (Janita, 19, Pakistani student).

Issues of 'race', ethnicity and racism were raised by a number of respondents as impacting upon the likelihood of participation or non-participation. The ethnic composition of different universities was talked about by both minority ethnic and white respondents as potentially disadvantageous and risky (Archer and Hutchings, 2000). Some black respondents recounted their experiences of racist teachers and their fears that white university staff may also 'mark them down'. Black women in particular talked about their family's efforts to counter teachers' low aspirations for their daughters, for example confronting teachers to allow their daughters to be entered for higher-level examinations and to apply to university. Similar findings are reported in the work of Mirza (1992). A few ethnic minority respondents suggested that racism hinders their prospects within the job market. In comparison, a few white non-participant women used discourses of 'modern racism' (Billig *et al*, 1988; Wetherell and Potter, 1992) to argue that they would be at risk (in terms of personal safety and academically) within institutions that are 'dominated' by minority ethnic groups. These women talked about how 'a lot of white people don't want/like to mix' and suggested that 'widening participation' may actually work against their own interests. This can be interpreted as an example of Cohen's (1988) assertion that 'the working-class "goes racist" when or wherever the presence of immigrants or ethnic minorities threatens to expose the ideological structures which it has erected to protect itself from recognising its real conditions of subordination' (1988: 34).

Issues of age were also raised as entailing risks of 'not belonging' and feeling out of place socially and academically. Mature students were more likely to report receiving disapproval and discouragement from friends and family for being 'irresponsible' in their wishes to return to study. A long period out of education was viewed as increasing the danger of 'looking stupid' at university and reliving previous educational failures. Mature respondents were particularly likely to perceive the entry routes back to higher education as being too long and difficult. All these identity risks raise questions in terms of ownership and 'belonging' for working class students in relation to academic cultures (Read *et al*, forthcoming).

Financial and economic risks

The financial risks of higher education participation were mainly understood by working class non-participants as highly important in mediating participation. Money was viewed as giving (middle class) people a 'chance' to participate, but (lack of it) constrained working class participation. Participation was perceived as completely impossible by/for those people on state benefits. Issues around finance, and the need for working class students to engage in paid employment throughout university study, were seen as significant barriers and risks to participation. These views contrast with official rhetoric around the economic returns of participation:

> The economic benefits to individuals from participating in higher education are probably the most significant factor affecting demand... These private rates of return, were they to be well known by potential students... would be likely to stimulate high levels of demand for higher education. (NCIHE, 1997)

The impenetrability of the loans and fees system constituted a considerable barrier to participation. Systems of support keep changing, the regulations are hard to decipher, and there are no 'joined up' support mechanisms. Students we interviewed were receiving and paying differential amounts in relation to loans and fees due to confusing and often inaccessible information. As Stella, a first-year student, said, the financial help booklet 'was like reading something in video manual language'.

Respondents largely lacked knowledge of what the financial costs of higher education study might be and estimates of the potential costs varied wildly. The relationship between fees and loans was also seen as confusing: 'You're going to university and you've got to take out a loan to pay these people your tuition fees, you're in debt of a thousand pounds every term' (Chantelle, 17, black Caribbean further education student).

The loans were also widely perceived as inadequate to cover the costs of living and studying, particularly in London: 'You still have to go and get a job though, 'cos that [the loan] ain't gonna last you' (Justine, 17, white further education student).

Loans also carried the risk of debt, to which non-participants were particularly averse ('You're going to be in debt practically for the rest of your life'). These issues provided strong reasons for not participating: 'I know people [who] got As in their A levels and they're not going to university 'cos they can't afford it' (Reka, 17, Asian female, further education student).

Respondents' limited access to information about fees/loans and finance was compounded by a distrust of 'official' sources of information and by cultural discourses that regarded the government's wider educational agenda as clearly rooted within national economic reasons. Many respondents appeared to be sceptical of the educational system as a whole. For example, they regarded routes designed to widen access as 'money-making' schemes. 'It's a complete and utter rip-off, education. The older you get... the more money they get off you' (Jodie, 18, white female, unemployed). 'They would be after your money, not how brainy you are' (Laura, white female, 30, bank worker).

Issues around finance also cross-cut with many other themes, such as retention and the risk of 'dropping out'. Many students identified that they were particularly at risk of 'dropping out' due to financial difficulties. Single mothers and those students previously on benefits were also particularly at risk.

Academic risks

The majority of respondents felt that they would be at risk academically at university, for various reasons. Mostly, academic risks were explicitly related to the financial risks (having to earn money would reduce their opportunities to do academic work) and to entry routes (vocational qualifications and access routes were seen as a less good preparation than other qualifications). The majority of non-participants were unclear about what entry qualifications are required for university, but it was widely assumed that whatever these were, they would be higher than the ones they personally held. As Aimee and Laura (both white women, not in education) said:

> Interviewer: What sort of qualifications do you think you need to get onto a degree course?
>
> Aimee: Quite a lot. Ones higher than I have.
>
> Laura: Higher than Einstein.

The MORI survey also revealed that only 32 per cent of respondents thought that they had grades or qualifications that would allow them to go to university, and this figure fell to 17 per cent among social class E. Where focus group respondents had knowledge of alternative entry routes, the legitimacy of these was often questioned.

> My cousins and my sister... they thought BTEC was a cartoon character or something. That's the truth! My Mum and Dad and uncles don't recognize BTEC as a qualification. (Asad, 20, Pakistani further education student)

> You're not going to get in there [university] with a GNVQ are you? (Patrick, 18, black further education student)

Both higher education participants and non-participants thought that the qualifications they held (such as GNVQ, BTEC, Access courses) were regarded less highly than A levels. It was also argued that within universities, working class students with 'non-traditional' qualifications are 'labelled' and/or unprepared

> At the end of the day... they're looking for A level students. GNVQ, the whole lot of it, they're glamorized. Yes, they want A levels, they want As and Bs and if you haven't got it, you might get in... but you're going to be labelled. (Michelle, 16, black, not in education)

Respondents thus suggested that they might feel marked out by their 'different' qualifications that would make failure in higher education more likely.

Academic risks also related to the hierarchy of universities and concerns about the level of ability of other students. Failure was seen as a real possibility, and was particularly threatening for working class students who had encountered family opposition. However, the risks of failing were also located within a pervasive view that study/education is boring and something that would have to be endured (rather than being undertaken for its intrinsic interest, as suggested by, for example, the Robbins report (HMSO, 1963).

> [Education]'s boring. No one sits here telling us that... it's going to be thrilling, it's going to be a buzz, it's going to be like a drug where you're going to want more and more and more. I don't get that impression at all. (Jodie, 27, white, unemployed)

Many non-participant respondents were employed in occupations from which it is difficult to accumulate the forms of accreditation that are currently recognized as routes for entry to higher education. Mechanisms that do recognize more diverse forms of potential and life experiences, such as APEL (Accreditation of Prior Experiential Learning), remain marginalized within the higher education system and thus offer limited potential for widening participation.

Conclusion

Higher education remains 'a risky business' for many working class non-participants, and these risks are differently constructed and experienced by different working class groups. If these risks are to be mitigated, and widening participation amongst working class groups is to be facilitated, action is needed on many different levels, including by government, universities and schools.

At the time of writing, some policy initiatives have been instigated in this area. The Government appears to have recognized that the abolition of student grants and the introduction of fees and loans may be deterring some people from applying to university, and a review of student finance is under way. Some of the academic risks may be mitigated for future potential students if recent and proposed developments to the post-16 curricula result in greater parity of esteem for vocational and academic qualifications. Widening participation projects which result in stronger links between schools, colleges and universities may go some way towards improving access to information about higher education for working class young people, and perhaps reducing the impression that university is 'other' to their experiences and lives.

Some developments, however, are not so positive. As Gewirtz (2000) has identified, some current policies are at risk of further 'solidifying' hierarchies in education, and discussions under way to create a separate and elite tier of research universities (THES, 2001) risk further exacerbating class divisions in higher education participation. Differential funding of institutions, and the persistence of class-based variations in the economic, social and cultural capital of students, point to the need for far more radical challenges to structural inequalities in society if widening participation initiatives are to be truly successful. Social justice will be achieved only when all young people, whatever their class or cultural background, have an equal opportunity to go to university. Such an opportunity will only exist when continuing in education becomes part of the repertoire of acceptable and 'normal' things to do in every section of society. And for this to happen, both government and universities need to review their policies.

Notes

1. Overall, roughly equal numbers of men and women took part in the non-participants' discussion groups. Approximately one-third of the sample self-identified as 'black' (Black African, Black Caribbean, Black-Other), one third 'Asian' (Pakistani, Bangladeshi, Indian and Asian-Mixed) and one-third 'white' (white British, white Italian and white Turkish). Ten groups were recruited within further education, predominantly from Basic Skills courses with unlikely immediate progression to higher education (eg NVQ level 1). Six further groups were recruited from the general public using a professional firm. These groups all

comprised respondents aged 16–30 who were working class non-participants, and groups were structured according to gender and ethnicity (single sex groups of African Caribbean, white and Bangladeshi respondents).

2. A total of 17 focus group discussions and interviews were conducted with a total of 85 new first year undergraduates at an inner-city, post-1992 university. Respondents were recruited from a range of courses from across the faculties. Of these respondents, 51 were women and 34 were men. Approximately 30 per cent of respondents could be identified as 'white British', 20 per cent as Asian, 20 per cent as black and 27 per cent were from other (mainly white European) backgrounds.

3. Questions were administered through the MORI Omnibus survey to adults from social classes C1, C2, D and E, aged 16–30 years, living in England or Wales. Questions were asked over three survey sweeps and a total of 1,278 respondents were successfully targeted. Of these respondents, 56 per cent were female and 44 per cent male. 91 per cent of respondents were white and 9 per cent from ethnic minorities. Overall, 17 per cent of the sample had been/were at university, 17 per cent expressed possible plans to apply and 59 per cent did not plan to go to university at all.

4. It is not possible to assign individuals to specific social class groups. Respondents filled in a form indicating their own and their parents' employment. However, more detail would be needed to allocate to a class. Some parents were unemployed, and their class category is therefore ambiguous. However, the range of parental and personal occupations fall within the lower socio-economic groups.

References

Alexander, C (1996) *The Art of Being Black: The creation of black British youth identities*, Oxford University Press

Archer, L and Hutchings, M (2000) 'Bettering yourself': discourses of risk, cost and benefit in ethnically diverse, young working-class non-participants' constructions of higher education, *British Journal of Sociology of Education*, **21** (4), pp 555–74

Archer, L, Leathwood, C and Hutchings, M (2001a) Engaging with commonality and difference: theoretical tensions in the analysis of working class women's educational discourses, *International Studies in Sociology of Education*, **11** (1)

Archer, L, Pratt, S and Phillips, D (2001b) Working class men's constructions of masculinity and negotiations of (non) participation in education, *Gender and Education*, **13** (4), pp 431–49

Ball, S J and Vincent, C (1998) 'I heard it on the grapevine': 'hot' knowledge and schools choice, *British Journal of Sociology of Education*, **19**, pp 377–400

Beck, U (1992) *Risk Society: Towards a new modernity*, Sage, Newbury, CA

Billig, M *et al* (1988) *Ideological Dilemmas: A social psychology of everyday thinking*, Sage, London

Cohen, P (1988) The perversions of inheritance: studies in the making of multi-racist Britain, in *Multi-Racist Britain*, ed P C H S Bains, Macmillan, London

CVCP (1998) *From Elitism to Inclusion: Good practice in widening access to higher education*, Main report, CVCP, London

DfEE (1998) *Higher Education for the 21st Century: Response to the Dearing Report*, DfEE, London

Franklin, A (1999) Personal reflections from the margins: an interface with race, class, nation and gender, in *Women and Social Class: International feminist perspectives*, ed P Z Mahoney, UCL Press, London

Gewirtz, S (2000) *Cloning the Blairs: The reconstruction of working-class families in Labour's education policy discourse*, Centre for Public Policy Research Annual Seminar, 12 July 2000, King's College, London

Hatton, E J (1999) Questioning correspondence: an Australian woman's account of the effects of social mobility on subjective class consciousness, in *Women and Social Class: International feminist perspectives*, ed P Z Mahony, UCL Press, London

HMSO (1963) *Higher Education: Report of a Committee (Chairman: Lord Robbins)*, Cmnd 2154, HMSO, London

hooks, b (1994) *Teaching to Transgress: Education as the practice of freedom*, Routledge, London

Hutchings, M and Archer, L (2001) Higher than Einstein: constructions of going to university among working class non-participants, *Research Papers in Education*, **16** (1), pp 69–91

Hutchings, M, Archer, L and Leathwood, C (2000) Above my station? Gender, race and class in women's discourses of higher education, ESREA Access Network Conference, University of Barcelona, 25–26 September 2000

Lawler, S (1999) Getting out and getting away: women's narratives of class mobility, *Feminist Review*, **63**, pp 3–23

Lawler, S (2000) Escape and escapism: representing working class women, in *Cultural Studies and the Working Class: Subject to change*, ed ISM, Cassell, London

Leathwood, C, Archer, L and Hutchings, M (2000) The influence of class, 'race' and gender in working class women's negotiations of participation in higher education, in *Gender and Education Conference*, Institute of Education, London

Mahony, P and Zmroczek, C (eds) (1997) *Class Matters: 'Working class' women's perspectives on social class*, Taylor and Francis, London

Majors, R B (1992) *Cool Pose: The dilemmas of black manhood in America*, Lexington Books, New York

Mama, A (1995) *Beyond the Masks: Race, gender and subjectivity*, Routledge, London

Mirza, H (1992) *Young, Female and Black*, Routledge, London

Mirza, H S (1995) Some ethical dilemmas in fieldwork: feminist and anti-racist methodologies, in *Antiracism, Culture and Social Justice in Education*, ed M G B Troyna, Trentham, Stoke-on-Trent

NCIHE (1997) *Higher Education in the Learning Society*, HMSO, London

Pugsley, L (1998) Throwing your brains at it: higher education, markets and choice, *International Studies in Sociology of Education*, **8** (1), pp 71–90

Read, B, Archer, L and Leathwood, C (forthcoming) Challenging cultures? Student conceptions of 'belonging' and 'isolation' at a post-1992 university, *Studies in Higher Education*, **28** (3)

Reay, D (1996a) Dealing with difficult differences: reflexivity and social class in feminist research, *Feminism and Psychology*, **6**, pp 443–56

Reay, D (1996b) Insider perspectives or stealing the words out of women's mouths: interpretation in the research process, *Feminist Review*, **53**, pp 57–73

Reay, D (1997) The double-bind of the 'working class' feminist academic: the success of failure or the failure of success? in *Class Matters: 'Working class' women's perspectives on social class*, ed P Z Mahony, Taylor and Francis, London

Reay, D (1999) Class acts: educational involvement and psycho-sociological class processes, *Feminism and Psychology*, **9** (1), pp 89–106

Reay, D and Ball, S J (1998) 'Making their minds up': family dynamics of school choice, *British Educational Research Journal*, **24** (4), pp 431–48

Reynolds, T (1997) Class matters, 'race' matters, gender matters, in *Class Matters: 'Working class' women's perspectives on social class*, ed P Z Mahony, Taylor and Francis, London

Roberts, D and Allen, A (1997) *Young Applicants' Perceptions of Higher Education*, Heist, Leeds

Robertson, D and Hillman, J (1997) *Widening Participation in Higher Education for Students from Lower Socio-Economic Groups and Students with Disabilities*, Report 5, NCIHE, The Stationery Office, London

Skeggs, B (1997) *Formations of Class and Gender: Becoming respectable*, Sage, London

THES (2001) 23 November, p 1

Walkerdine, V (1990) *Schoolgirl Fictions*, Verso, London/New York

Walkerdine, V, Lucey, H and Melody, J (1999) Class, attainment and sexuality in late twentieth-century Britain, in *Women and Social Class: International feminist perspectives*, ed P Z Mahony, UCL Press, London

Wetherell, M and Potter, J (1992) *Mapping the Language of Racism: Discourse and the legitimation of exploitation*, Harvester Wheatsheaf, London

Woodrow, M (2000) Class – the last frontier, *The Lecturer*

Zmroczek, C (1999) Class, gender and ethnicity: snapshots of a mixed heritage, in *Women and Social Class: International feminist perspectives*, ed P Z Mahony, UCL Press, London

7

Widening Participation: The Place of Mature Students

Alison Fuller

Introduction

In recent years, policy making in the UK higher education sector has been preoccupied with how the system can be expanded to address two broad imperatives. The first relates to the perceived national economic need for an increase in the supply of people with higher-level knowledge and skills. The second relates to the 'social inclusion agenda', promoted by the current Labour government, which seeks to widen participation in higher education by traditionally under-represented groups. Prior to the period of expansion in the 1980s and 1990s, higher education was primarily considered as a route for the minority academic elite. This population was relatively homogeneous as students were mainly aged 18–21, were male, white, from middle or upper social classes, entered university with good A level grades, and studied full-time (McNair, 1993). Although young people's participation has increased to over 30 per cent, with take up by young women growing particularly strongly, there are still major concerns (as has been pointed out elsewhere in this book) that those from lower socio-economic groups and from certain ethnic backgrounds are still seriously under-represented. I suggest in this chapter that, ironically, the policy debate about widening participation has too often limited its focus to the proportion of young people taking up higher education. Whilst this concern is clearly important, it fails to high-light the massive growth in take up of higher education by mature students over the past 20 plus years.

The injection of adults (students aged 21 and over) into higher educa-tion served to diversify the age profile of the traditional student popula-tion. In addition, mature students have other diversifying effects in that they are more likely than their younger peers to enter university without conventional entry level qualifications (A levels), to be from lower socio-economic groups, to study on part-time courses, and to study at sub-degree level.

I recognize that an explanation for rising adult take up requires a range of perspectives on changing patterns of participation, including the influence of policy and funding arrangements on the availability of opportunities. In this chapter I want to focus on the growth in importance of higher education for adults themselves, and to provide perspectives that help explain why increasing numbers have been pursuing courses in higher education over the past 20 or so years. I want to suggest that such an explanation should include an analysis of the changing relationship between individual and society. In particular, I wish to distinguish between the approach taken here, which locates individuals in their socio-economic context, and that taken by successive UK governments, which conceives the individual in isolation. Keep (1997) has developed a particularly cogent critique of the individualism apparent in government policy.

This chapter is organized in four sections. The first provides a statistical account of the rise in mature student participation in higher education institutions and recent patterns of take up. The statistics I present include data on participants' characteristics as well as on their mode of attendance and level of study. The second section examines credentialist and labour market explanations for the rise in adults' participation in higher education level courses and qualifications. I outline previous sociological approaches (Dore, 1974; Collins, 1979), which perceive increasing take up of educational qualifications by young people as an outcome of institutional change and increasing bureaucratization. I argue that such analyses are relevant to understanding recent trends in adults' participation if they are combined with an account of recent labour market and skill trends.

Section three suggests that in addition to credentialist and labour market explanations, an understanding of wider social changes is required to make sense of rises in adults' take up of higher education. In this regard, I argue that the reflexive modernization thesis (Beck, 1992; Beck, Giddens and Lash, 1994; Giddens, 1990, 1991, 1994) is helpful, first, in its conception of individual and institutional change as mutually transformative, and second, by identifying the implications of social change, such as the availability of new opportunities and uncertainties, for the course of individual biographies. Of central relevance to the reflexive modernization perspective is the idea that new areas of activity are opening up to more people as an (unintended) effect of the changing relationship between individual and society. I suggest that the rise in adults' participation in higher education provides one illustration of this phenomenon. The chapter concludes by reminding policy makers of the challenge of widening participation in higher education and cautioning them against an over preoccupation with young people.

Mature student statistics

First, and to locate current figures in an historical context, I wish to high-light the dramatic increase in participation of mature students in higher education over the past 30 years. The number of adults taking up courses leading to higher education level qualifications in further and higher education institutions rose from 255,000 in 1970 to nearly 1.5 million in 1998–99, an increase of about 425 per cent (Fuller, 2000a). Table 7.1 provides an overview of changes in the participation of under-21s and mature student groups in higher education since 1966. It indicates that the percentage increase for the population of over-21s was considerably higher than that for the under-21 age group. The under-21s remained in the majority throughout the period presented in the table, although as a proportion of the total student population the group declined from 83 per cent of the total in 1966 to 67 per cent in 1992.

More recent statistics (see Table 7.2) show that the majority of students in the contemporary higher education population are aged 21 or over. The figures in Table 7.1 are also interesting in that they indicate that the number and proportion of mature students has been rising strongly since the 1980s, which was before the removal of the binary divide between universities and polytechnics in the UK. Following this change, expansion has been even more substantial (Uden, 1996).

Tables 7.2 and 7.3 present figures on the composition of the contemporary student population by age, mode of attendance, level of study and gender. They provide evidence of how important, in numerical terms, the mature student population has become to higher education institutions and indicate that studying on part-time courses and on 'other undergraduate' level programmes are the modal types of participation engaged in by older mature students (aged 25 plus).

Table 7.2 confirms the significance of the mature student population to higher education institutions. It focuses on patterns of participation by

Table 7.1   First-year full-time and sandwich undergraduates in higher education in the UK by age

Academic Year Beginning				Thousands				
	1966	1970	1975	1979	1982	1987	1992	% Change 1966–92
Men and Women								
Under-21	87.6	102.6	107.4	107.9	136.4	138.6	220.9	**152%**
21+	17.7	27.3	31.4	34.1	39.3	47.8	107.7	**508%**
TOTAL	105.3	129.9	138.8	142.0	175.8	186.4	328.6	**212%**

Source: Compiled from DES Statistical Bulletin 12/80, Table One and DE Statistical Bulletin 13/94, Table 3

Table 7.2 Students at UK higher education institutions by level of study, mode of study, age and by all years, 1998–99

All Years	TOTAL	Postgraduate	First Degree	Other Undergraduate
Full-time/ Sandwich				
21–24	**342,956**	64,047	242,376	36,533
25 and over	**239,736**	80,905	121,411	37,420
21 and over	**582,692**	144,952	363,787	73,953
All ages[1]	**1,179,264**	146,376	908,332	124,565
Part-time				
21–24	**51,787**	13,461	15,341	22,985
25 and over	**547,800**	201,038	72,462	274,300
21 and over	**599,587**	214,499	87,803	297,285
All ages[1]	**626,812**	217,591	93,435	315,786
All Modes				
21–24	**399,677**	82,339	257,787	59,551
25 and over	**822,209**	316,437	194,006	311,766
21 and over	**1,221,886**	398,776	451,793	371,317
All ages	**1,845,757**	403,340	1,001,983	440,434

Source: Derived from Table 3, Higher Education Statistics for the UK 1998/99 (HESA, 2000)

age, mode of attendance and level of study. Overall, it shows that there was a total of 1,845,757 students of all ages studying on undergraduate and postgraduate courses in 1998–99. Of these, 66 per cent were aged over 21 and 45 per cent were aged 25 or over. The figures indicate that nearly half of those participating in full-time or sandwich courses are mature and the older mature student group accounts for around one-fifth of this population. The table indicates that the bulk of the older mature student population is participating on part-time courses. The table shows that 87 per cent of the total part-time population is 25 or over. Just under two thirds of the 25 plus age group studying part-time are undertaking courses at first degree or other undergraduate level.

Table 7.2 also shows that participation in first degrees accounts for over half of all take up in higher education institutions, and participation in courses at 'other undergraduate' level comprises around a quarter of all participation in higher education institutions. The vast majority of those studying at 'other undergraduate' level are 25 plus.

Table 7.3 focuses in more detail on participation in part-time undergraduate provision in higher education institutions by level of study, age and gender.

Women comprise the majority of the mature, part-time student population. Of all students studying on part-time courses at higher education

Table 7.3 All undergraduate part-time students in UK by level of study, age group and gender analysed by all years, 1998–99

All Years	TOTAL	First Degree	Other Undergraduate[1]
Under 21	**15,503**	**5,246**	**10,257**
Female	6,941	2,006	4,935
Male	8,562	3,240	5,322
21–24	**38,326**	**15,341**	**22,985**
Female	20,056	6,886	13,170
Male	18,270	8,455	9,815
25 and over	**346,762**	**72,462**	**274,300**
Female	213,169	45,811	167,358
Male	133,593	26,651	106,942
All ages	**409,221**	**93,435**	**315,786**
Female	245,797	54,944	190,853
Male	163,424	38,491	124,933

[1] Other undergraduate includes Diploma of Higher Education (DipHE), Certificate of Higher Education (CertHE), foundation courses at higher education level, HNC/D, professional qualifications at undergraduate level, other undergraduate diplomas and certificates.

Source: Derived from Table 3, Higher Education Statistics for the UK 1998/99 (HESA 2000)

institutions 60 per cent are female. Of all those students who are aged 25 or over, 61 per cent are female. It is important to note that most of the mature student undergraduate population is studying for 'other undergraduate' qualifications rather than for first degrees. In this regard, four out of five mature students aged 25 plus were studying on 'other undergraduate' courses. The HESA also reports that 63 per cent of all first year part-time undergraduate students are aged 30 or over and that most of this population (64 per cent) is studying on 'other undergraduate' programmes (HESA, 2000: Table 1f).

The increase in take up of courses in higher education institutions by older students is not only important for numerical reasons but also because the growth in take up of full-time and particularly part-time courses at higher education level by mature students has served to diversify the traditional student population described in the Introduction. The diversifying effect of the rise in older participants has been noted: 'The change in age profile has led to greater diversity among the student body. The influx of mature students has brought about more women, more black students and more students without the standard A level entry qualifications in to the system' (McGivney, 1996: 7).

Research undertaken for the National Committee of Inquiry into Higher Education (NCIHE, 1997) showed that mature entrants to higher education were more likely to be from lower socio-economic groups (III and below) than young entrants. Around a third of entrants aged over 25 were from socio-economic groups IIIm (manual occupations), IV and V compared with a quarter of 18–20-year-olds in the same groups. Similarly, a survey of the characteristics of higher education students found that those aged 26 plus were more likely to come from lower socio-economic groups than their younger (19 and under) counterparts (Hogarth *et al*, 1997). The same survey investigated the level of entry qualifications held by young and mature students. It found that 41 per cent of those aged 26 and over possessed A levels on entry to higher education compared with 92 per cent of those aged 19 or less.

In summary, the statistical picture highlights the following points:

- There has been a dramatic increase in take up of higher education by mature students over the past 20 plus years.
- In recent years there has been a large increase in take up by older adults (25 plus).
- The vast majority of those studying on part-time courses are mature (25 plus).
- Most of those studying at 'other undergraduate' level are over 25.
- The majority of those studying part-time and at other undergraduate level are 30 plus.
- The majority of mature students studying part-time are female.
- Mature students aged over 25 are more likely than their younger peers to come from lower socio-economic backgrounds and to enter higher education without A levels.

Rising take up, credentialism and labour market change

In this section, I consider the socio-economic context which underlies increases in adult participation in higher education. I outline the main 'credentialist' approaches to explaining the growth in importance of educational participation and qualifications. The main previous sociological approaches perceived increasing take up as an outcome of institutional change (Dore, 1976; Collins, 1979). Dore and Collins drew on a Weberian understanding of the modernization process which essentially conceived the increasing bureaucratization of society as the principal driver of social change and action (Fuller, 2001). Although differing in their concerns and the countries in which they conducted research, Collins' and Dore's accounts both related the growth in importance of educational qualifications to the process of industrialization and the development of a modern labour market characterized, particularly after the Second World War, by the rise of the public sector, large corporations and rigidly divided forms of work organization. Under this scenario, young people with 'good' educational qualifications improved their chances of gaining secure, well paid jobs in the expanding white collar, managerial and technical areas of employment. Dore (1976) identified the problem of credential inflation and under-employment which occurs when the stock of 'modern jobs' fails to keep step with the level of qualified people leaving the education system. Both Collins and Dore argued that educational qualifications were used as selection devices and were critical of this usage because they believed that high-level qualifications were not needed for the majority of jobs. Seen from this perspective, it was, therefore, unfair to allocate occupational opportunities to individuals on the basis of educational qualifications. Neither writer focused on individuals and the meanings they ascribe to participation or qualifying.

During the post-war period there were also unskilled and semi-skilled employment options available, particularly in manufacturing and process industries, for those without or with few qualifications. Early explanations for the growth in importance of qualifications could safely assume that adults had no need to qualify or re-qualify later in life because they were already slotted into a static labour market where there was no demand for higher level qualifications, or where they had fulfilled the relevant requirements for qualifications as young people. Until the last 20 years or so, the economic, social and industrial conditions did not exist for adults in countries such as the UK and the United States to pursue qualifications in mid-life (Fuller, 1999). One of the questions raised in this chapter, then, is to what extent credentialist perspectives can account for recent rises in adults' take up of higher-level qualifications in the UK, a trend which, as we saw earlier in this chapter, emerged and then intensified after Collins' (1979) and Dore's (1976) work was published.

During the 20 years since Dore's (1976) and Collins' (1979) analyses were published, patterns of employment and consumption have altered dramatically (Reich, 1991). The demise of primary industries; the decline of manufacturing and the associated rise in male unemployment, combined with the emergence of new sectors based on micro-electronic, information and communication technologies; the growth of the service sector and, relatedly, part-time and temporary employment are some of the well-documented features of change (see for example Reich, 1991; Aronowitz and Di Fazio, 1994). Hutton (1995) has argued that fresh social and economic divisions have emerged from the past two decades of technological, economic and political shifts, and that new relationships have developed between the labour force and employers. Drawing on the work of economist J K Galbraith, Hutton proposes that the UK is a 30:30:40 society. He describes the difference between the 30 per cent of the adult population that is extremely disadvantaged, particularly through unemployment or minimal part-time work, the 30 per cent that is 'marginalised' because of being recently self-employed or working in insecure jobs with no 'formal employment protection', and the '40 per cent whose market power has increased since 1979' (Hutton, 1995: 106–08). Those in the last group are categorized as 'privileged' and include people in full-time permanent employment or who have been employed for more than two years.

The above characterization of the contemporary British labour market can be partly explained by structural changes in the economy. These include a reduction in the manufacturing sector's share of GDP from 34 per cent in 1970 to just over 20 per cent in 1994, and a rise in the share of financial and business services from 12 per cent of GDP in 1970 to about 20 per cent in 1994 (DTI, 1995). Such trends have intensified in the late 1990s (DfEE, 1998) and into the new century as slowdown in manufacturing even in sectors such as telecommunications is adversely affecting jobs. The decline of manufacturing has had a major effect on jobs, which in this sector have traditionally been male, full-time and permanent. In contrast, the growth in the service sector is associated with 'contracting out' and related increases in part-time and temporary work (DTI, 1995). In the UK, employment in manufacturing reduced by 33 per cent between 1980 and 1992 (DTI, 1995). Currently the manufacturing sector only accounts for one-fifth of the total UK economy.

Such changes in the structure of employment have implications for skills levels (see for example DfEE 1998; Brown, Green and Lauder, 2001; Green, 2000; Felstead, Ashton and Green, 2000, 2001; Gregory, Zissimos and Greenhalgh, 2001). The research by Gregory and her colleagues is particularly interesting because it shows that changing patterns of consumption and related changes in patterns of employment had significant implications for skills during the 1980s (as well as in the 1990s). The researchers conclude, 'A broad summary would identify the growth of consumption as the main source of the rise in skilled employment, with technological change as the main destroyer of low-skill jobs' (Gregory, Zissimos and Greenhalgh, 2001: 36–37).

The recent pace and scope of employment-related change has helped to create a context in which many people's lived experience, as well as their perceptions, of labour market and skill trends are characterized by a mix of uncertainty and opportunity. By 'pace of change' I am thinking particularly of the sorts of technological innovations occurring over the past 20 years or so, which have enabled more to be produced by fewer people and which have facilitated the emergence of the global economy (Reich, 1991). By 'scope of change' I have in mind the implications of globalization for employment including the facility now available to multi-national corporations to (re) locate their production and other aspects of their business (for example research and development) so creating, losing and displacing jobs across countries and continents.

The proportion of young people under 25 currently progressing to higher education has risen to 40 per cent (Carvel, 1999). It follows that older adults looking to return to the labour market or to change occupations have to compete with an increasingly well qualified young workforce for the limited supply of 'good' jobs, as well as repositioning themselves due to industrial change. Recent economic and technological trends and the rising participation of young people in post-compulsory education have fuelled credential inflation (Wolf, 1997) and extended the role qualifications have traditionally played in the selection of job applicants. If recipients and users (including employers) of qualifications value academic and general qualifications, then the growth in importance of gaining higher-level qualifications to people across the age range is reinforced. I would argue that the increase in take up of higher education level courses by mature students over the past 20 or so years is indicative, at least in part, of adults' demand for the higher-level knowledge and skills which might help them compete for places in the privileged 40 per cent of employees identified by Hutton.

Historically, and until recently unlike their full-time peers, those taking up part-time higher education courses have not had their tuition fees paid from public funds (Fuller, 2000b). I suggest that where the individual has paid tuition fees from his or her own resources, it is likely to be an indicator of two things: first, individual demand; second, the strong link between employment and the student's financial ability to return to study. In relation to the concerns of this chapter, the first point relating the individual's payment of fees to demand is particularly relevant in that it highlights the issue of individual choice. In some cases adults may be self-funding their participation in part-time higher education to help them change careers or employers. In other instances it may be the case that employees feel obliged to participate in higher education by the competitive employment climate in which they are operating (Schuller, Raffe and Clark, 1997). The statistics appear to confirm the findings of studies that most students on part-time courses in higher education are economically active (Callender, 1997; Brennan *et al*, 1999). The recent survey of part-time students conducted by Brennan and colleagues found that around 83 per cent of respondents were in work 'before, during and after their studies'. The vast majority of these were in full-time employment. Recent HESA figures (2000) show that two-thirds of older mature students (aged 30 plus) are paying the fees for their part-time undergraduate courses from their own resources (Fuller, 2000b). The employed status of so many part-time students helps to explain why a large proportion of them can fund their own studies.

Rising take up, reflexive modernization and social change

I suggest that in addition to the above economic and labour market factors, an understanding of wider social change is also required to make sense of the growth in importance of higher education to adults. The reflexive modernization thesis (Beck, 1992, 1994; Giddens, 1990, 1991, 1994) is helpful, first, in its conception of individual and institutional change as mutually transformative and, second, by identifying the consequences of social change for people's lives. Of central relevance to the reflexive modernization perspective is the idea that new areas of activity have become available to more people as an (unintended) effect of the changing relationship between individual and society. I would argue that the rise in adults' participation in higher education over the past 20 years or so is illustrative of this point.

I have discussed the reflexive modernization thesis in detail elsewhere (Fuller, 1999), identifying how it consists of two interrelated dimensions, a novel (non-deterministic) way of understanding social change and a description of the conditions which underlie contemporary experience. In this chapter, I want to focus on those aspects of the thesis which identify the relevance of the reflexive modernization perspective to changes in the scope and character of individual decision making. An important theme in Giddens' work is his elaboration of the cultural shift that has taken place from what he refers to as 'traditional' to 'post-traditional society' and the implications of this for how individuals experience their personal, domestic and working lives. He asserts that 'in post-traditional contexts, we have no choice but to choose how to be and how to act' (Giddens, 1994: 75). Giddens argues that, under contemporary conditions, individuals are aware that there are multiple ways in which life course and styles can be developed, even if some perceive their *real* choices as limited. For Giddens, the association of the contemporary period with uncertainty as well as opportunity is expressed particularly through the process of detraditionalization, the negative connotations of which are balanced by increasing 'lifestyle opportunities' which the exposing of tradition to interrogation and re-constitution enables.

For Beck (1992), key themes are the production of risk and the process of individualization. He is particularly interested in the phenomenological effect of living in the risk society in terms of how people think and make decisions in everyday life. As Archer and her colleagues point out in Chapter 6, risks are unevenly distributed throughout the population with some groups 'carrying the greatest threats and risks'. Both Beck and Giddens agree that living against a backdrop of uncertainty and multiple choices (whether real or illusory) promotes counterfactual thinking as some adults try to calculate the pros and cons of particular actions. This insight is underpinned by awareness that knowledge is revisable and that actions will inevitably have unintended consequences. For Beck, Giddens and Lash (1994), the changing relationship between individual and society facilitated by the 'freeing of agency from structure' places more emphasis on individuals and their ability to relate reflexively to institutional change.

Following the perspective of the reflexive modernization thesis, processes such as detraditionalization are making it less likely for successive generations to follow in the footsteps of their parents. This is at least partly because new areas of activity have been opened up to individual decisions as a feature of an increasingly reflexive relationship between individual and society. In the past, decisions about an individual's life course were largely influenced by his or her birth characteristics. Ascriptive attributes such as gender, race and social class largely determined future domestic and occupational roles. From this viewpoint, decision making in pre/early modern eras might be conceptualized as 'traditional' in that there was no, or little, role for individualized decisions about issues such as 'career'. In contrast the reflexivity characteristic of the relationship between agency and structure (as conceived by the reflexive modernization thesis) points to the break-up and re-formation of social solidarities along new dimensions. One consequence of this is that more areas are opening up to individual decision making. Giddens observes:

> In modern social life, the notion of lifestyle takes on a particular significance. The more tradition loses its hold, and the more daily life is reconstituted in terms of the dialectical interplay of the local and the global, the more individuals are forced to negotiate lifestyle choices among a diversity of options (Giddens, 1991: 5).

Beck and Giddens are also interested in the consequences of social change for individual biography and have adopted a narrative view of identity formation to conceptualize how people make sense of social change in terms of their own experience. Of particular relevance is Beck's discussion of 'individualization' (1992). He highlights the concept of individualization as a social process, and as a feature of contemporary society in which collective ties are breaking down and individual isolation is increasing. Beck illustrates his point by discussing institutional changes to the family and the implications of these for individual identity and biography. He asserts that in the contemporary era, 'each person lives through several family lives as well as non-familiar forms of life depending on the life phase and *for that very reason* lives more and more his/her *own biography*' (Beck, 1992: 115, original emphasis).

In some similarity, Giddens makes connections between his understanding of social change and its consequences for identity and what he calls the 'reflexive project of the self'. Giddens defines this as 'the process whereby self-identity is constituted by the reflexive ordering of self-narratives' (1991: 244). He states, 'The construction of the self as a *reflexive project*, [is] an elemental part of the reflexivity of modernity; an individual must find her or his identity amid the strategies and options provided by abstract systems' (Giddens, 1990: 124, original emphasis).

I suggest that the aspects of the reflexive modernization approach to social change identified above are relevant to understanding changes in people's behaviour, of which the rise in adults' take up of higher education provides one illustration. In my view, Giddens' analysis of the erosion of tradition as a guide for action means that people's life courses may differ in significant respects (for example in terms of family relationships, working patterns and educational participation) from those of previous generations and it sheds light on why increasing numbers of adults, from various backgrounds, are seeking new ways, such as combining work and higher-level learning, to respond to the uncertainties and opportunities characteristic of contemporary life. Field (2000) goes further in that he links what he calls the 'silent explosion' in lifelong learning to the explanations of social change and the conditions under which we live offered by Beck and Giddens.

The relevance of the reflexive modernization thesis to explaining why increasing numbers of adults have been participating in higher education has been explored by considering the perspectives and motivations of mature students themselves (Fuller, 1999). In this study, I conducted in-depth one-to-one interviews with 10 mature students in their 30s and 40s (eight of whom studied part-time) who were completing or had recently completed first degrees. The interviews were wide ranging but elicited individuals' perspectives on themes germane to this chapter including why they had returned to study and the meanings of their experiences. In summary, interviewees explained their participation as an effect of two broad areas of their contemporary experience. First, it was interpreted as illustrative of the expansion of areas of activity in which they could exercise choice and make decisions which they perceived would facilitate personal growth. This was contrasted with the limited scope for individual decision making their parents had experienced and which they, themselves, had experienced as young people. Second, participation in higher education and the attainment of higher-level qualifications was seen as a resource which could help them respond to labour market changes such as increasing demand for higher-level skills and qualifications.

In this and the previous section, I have used two different theoretical perspectives (credentialism and reflexive modernization) to shed light on why adults' take up of higher education has been increasing over the past 20 years or so. I have also sketched out the relevance of the changing structure of employment and skill trends to explaining this trend. In terms of understanding social change and its relevance to the growing importance of higher-level qualifications to adults, I would argue that ideas garnered from the reflexive modernization thesis build usefully on the institutional explanations advanced by Collins (1979) and Dore (1976). In my view, the dynamic of reflexivity is particularly salient as it enables us to conceptualize the relationship between institutional and individual change as mutually transformative and enables us to take a more active view of individual agency and identity formation. This approach contrasts with the credentialist perspective which conceives institutional change as driving individual behaviour and which, therefore, explains rising individual demand for educational qualifications as resulting (solely) from increasing bureaucratization. From this standpoint, the individual is conceptualized as passive and is assumed to act (only) in response to structural change and in order to gain or maintain status. I would argue that making connections between the changing relationship between individual and society and new patterns of participation serves to deepen our understanding of why more adults in mid-life are taking up courses in higher education.

Conclusion

In this chapter I have used quantitative data, and contextual and theoretical perspectives to describe and shed light on the growth in take up of higher education by adults. The discussion concludes by reminding policy makers of the challenge of widening participation in higher education and cautioning them against an over-preoccupation with young people. The statistical account provided earlier in the paper shows the extent and pattern of older student take up of higher education and indicates how this group helps fulfil the Government's aim of achieving a more diverse student population, particularly with regard to age, sub-degree level and part-time study. The theoretical and contextual perspectives offered in sections two and three help illuminate why adult participation has risen, and why it is likely to remain strong and could grow further if the availability of opportunities were extended to the whole population. However, the levelling off in applications for places witnessed over the past couple of years includes mature as well as younger students (Crace, 1999). It is clear that if the government is to meet its targets for expansion it must find ways of easing the financial burden studying imposes on most students. There are signs in recent pronouncements from the Education Secretary that the government is now willing to review its recent strategy towards tuition fees for full-time students, who, as we have seen from the statistics, are mostly young. However, it is not clear whether this rethink includes tuition fees for the mostly older students studying on part-time courses. It should. Given that most part-time students pay their tuition fees out of their own resources, there are strong grounds for arguing that many on low incomes, or in temporary or insecure jobs, are being deterred from participation. Increasing the ability of these groups to take up higher education would facilitate the attainment of government targets on higher education take up, encourage lifelong learning and make headway in the political mission to increase social inclusion.

Expanding take up of higher education by disadvantaged populations remains a serious problem for policy makers pursuing a 'social inclusion agenda'. It is unclear as yet whether simply adding another sub-degree level qualification, the foundation degree, will help, since the majority of mature students are already pursuing courses at this level. A more effective strategy for expanding part-time, adult take up may be to increase the number and geographical spread of institutions dedicated to providing courses designed to be studied part time. The examples of the Open University and Birkbeck, which between them provide courses to one-third of the part-time undergraduate population (HESA, 2000), indicate that such dedicated institutions seem best placed to attract older mature students.

References

Aronowitz, S and Di Fazio, W (1994) *The Jobless Future, Sci-Tech and the Dogma of Work*, University of Minnesota, London

Beck, U (1992) *Risk Society: Towards a new modernity*, Sage, London

Beck, U, Giddens, A and Lash S (1994) *Reflexive Modernisation: Politics, tradition and aesthetics in the modern social order*, Polity Press, Cambridge

Brennan, J *et al* (1999) *Part-time Students and Employment: Report of A Survey of Students, Graduates and Diplomates*, QSC, The Open University, London

Brown, P, Green, A and Lauder, H (2001) *High Skills*, Oxford University Press, Oxford

Callender, C (1997) *Full and Part-time Students in Higher Education: Their experiences and expectations*, Report 2, National Committee of Inquiry into Higher Education (NCIHE), London

Carvel, J (1999) Blair's revolution for learning: plan for huge rise in university numbers, *Guardian*, 8 March

Collins, R (1979) *The Credential Society: An Historical Sociology of Education and Stratification*, Academic Press, New York

Crace, J (1999) Older and wiser? *Guardian Higher*, 20 April

Department for Education, *Statistical Bulletin*, 13/94, HMSO, London

Department for Education and Employment (DfEE) (1998) *Labour Market and Skills Trends 1997/1998*, DfEE, Sheffield

Department for Trade and Industry (DTI) (1995) *Competitiveness: Forging ahead*, Cmnd 2867, HMSO, London

Department of Education and Science, *Statistical Bulletin*, 12/80, HMSO, London

Dore, R (1974) *The Diploma Disease: Education, qualification and development*, George Allen and Unwin, London

Felstead, A, Ashton, D and Green, F (2000) Are Britain's workplace skills becoming more unequal? *Cambridge Journal of Economics*, **24**, pp 709–27

Felstead, A, Ashton, D and Green, F (2001) Paying the price for flexibility? Training, skills and non-standard jobs in Britain, *International Journal of Employment Studies*, **9** (1), pp 25–60

Field, J (2000) *Lifelong Learning and the New Educational Order*, Trentham Books, Stoke-on-Trent

Fuller, A (1999) Qualifications, adults and social change: a theoretical and empirical examination of the growth of qualifications taken by adults in the last 20+ years, unpublished PhD dissertation, Institute of Education, London

Fuller, A (2000a) *Mature Students and Participation in Higher Education*, paper presented at the Progression to Higher Education Conference: Issues and Possibilities, Institute of Education, 7 December

Fuller, A (2000b) Developing capability: part-time higher and lifelong learning, in *Policies, Politics and The Future of Lifelong Learning*, ed A Hodgson, Kogan Page, London

Fuller, A (2001) Credentialism, adults and part-time higher education in the United Kingdom: an account of rising take up and some implications for policy, *Journal of Education Policy*, **16** (3), pp 233–48

Giddens, A (1990) *The Consequences of Modernity*, Polity Press, Cambridge

Giddens, A (1991) *Modernity and Self-identity: Self and society in the late modern age*, Polity Press, Cambridge

Giddens, A (1994) Living in a post-traditional society: towards a theory of reflexive modernisation, in U Beck, A Giddens and S Lash, *Reflexive Modernisation: Politics, tradition and aesthetics in the modern social order*, Polity Press, Cambridge.

Green, A (2000) Education, globalisation and the nation state, in the lecture series The Learning Society and the Knowledge Economy sponsored by NACETT, Autumn, NTET 35

Gregory, M, Zissimos, B and Greenhalgh, C (2001) Jobs for the skilled: how technology, trade, and domestic demand changed the structure of UK employment, 1979–1990, Oxford Economic Papers, **53**, pp 20–46

Higher Education Statistics Agency (2000) *Students in Higher Education Institutions* 1998/99 HESA, Cheltenham

Hogarth *et al* (1997*) The Participation of Non-traditional Students in Higher Education*, HEFC Research Series, Institute for Employment Research, Warwick

Hutton, W (1995) *The State We're In*, Jonathan Cape, London

Keep, E (1997) There's no such thing as society...: some problems with an individual approach to creating a learning society, *Journal of Education Policy*, **12** (6), pp 457–71.

McGivney, V (1996) *Staying or Leaving the Course: Non-completion and retention of mature students in further and higher education*, NIACE, Leicester

McNair, S (1993) *An Adult Higher Education: A vision*, NIACE, Leicester

National Committee of Inquiry into Higher Education (NCIHE) (1997) *Higher Education in the Learning Society, Main Report*, NCIHE, London

Reich, R B (1991) *The Work of Nations: Preparing ourselves for 21st century capitalism*, Simon and Schuster, London

Schuller, T, Raffe, D and Clark, I (1997) Part-time higher education and the student–employer relationship, *Journal of Education and Work*, **10** (3), pp 225–36

Uden, T (1996) *Widening Participation: Routes to a learning society – a policy discussion paper*, Leicester, NIACE

Wolf, A (1997) Growth stocks and lemons: diplomas in the English market place 1976–96, *Assessment in Education: Principles, policy and practice*, **4** (1), pp 33–50

8

The Applications Process: Developing an Admissions Curriculum

Anna Paczuska

Introduction

There are now more routes into higher education than ever before. There is also more information available about the various routes, about higher education admissions procedures, courses, combinations of courses and qualifications. The need for comprehensive information and guidance for students about different progression opportunities is widely acknowledged. Accordingly, the research and preparation that full-time students are encouraged to undertake before completing their application forms for the Universities and Colleges Admissions Service (UCAS) is increasing. Indeed, many post-16 institutions have formalized the preparation for the UCAS application process into year-long courses for their students. Such courses may be timetabled into the official school or college curriculum or else make up significant elements of the tutorial support offered to students.

Preparation for applying to higher education is not confined to information giving. Students are also encouraged to develop their skills in research and self-presentation in order to prepare their applications thoroughly. On some programmes the skills development element is considered significant enough to warrant accreditation and many Access courses award formal credit to students for the skills displayed by them in researching and completing their UCAS forms (for example College of North West London, 2000).

Despite differing institutional settings, the overall structure of the support is often similar and influenced by the stages of the UCAS admissions process itself (London College of Printing, 1998; Southwark College, 2001; Epsom and Ewell High School, 1999; Futures, 2001). Students applying to higher education are encouraged to learn about UCAS and about the stages of the admissions process as a way of making an application to higher education. This applications process is presented as a series of stages that students have to go through and that have to be learnt about before they are attempted. This preparation for the UCAS application effectively comprises an admissions 'curriculum'. As with the rest of the school or college curriculum, what is learnt and the knowledge available to students cannot be entirely defined by the formal content of the curriculum. Rather, it depends on a complex interplay of the ideas, perceptions and attitudes students bring with them and the context in which they learn as well as the more explicitly defined aspects of the curriculum content.

This chapter develops the idea of an admissions 'curriculum' as distinct from mere access to information and facts about the admissions and applications processes. Such a 'curriculum' is a central element in the admissions process to higher education and is the arena in which many of the tensions and contradictions relating to entry to higher education are played out. An admissions curriculum may be used simply to transmit existing dominant cultural assumptions about higher education, which tend to reproduce existing patterns of progression, or, as I argue in this chapter, it can attempt to challenge traditional assumptions about higher education. Good practice in curriculum design and the identification of clear aims and objectives and the promotion of reflexive self awareness offer an opportunity to develop an admissions curriculum that particularly aims to support wider participation.

UCAS and access to information

What students learn about applications and admissions to university is largely framed by the work of UCAS, the UK clearing-house for university admissions. UCAS is itself a product of the way the British higher education system has evolved (Maclaren, 2001). UCAS evolved from UCCA the clearing-house for 'old' universities which was founded in 1961. From a system which originally formalized the concept of the admissions process for elite institutions it grew into a system which 'was standardized, centralized, acted as a watchdog and also provided a systematic base for statistics to monitor trends and to help plan policy and provision' (Bligh, Thomas and McNay, 1999). A parallel system, the Polytechnics Central Admissions System (PCAS), was set up in 1985. In 1993, following the ending of the binary line between universities and polytechnics, PCAS and UCCA merged to form UCAS. Today UCAS acts as a clearing-house for applications to some 261 higher education institutions. The figure for institutions in UCAS is expected to increase as the provision of higher education courses in further education colleges expands.

UCAS is more than just a clearing system. It is also an organization that collects, processes and distributes information and statistics about university admissions. It has a well developed policy of enabling students to be as fully informed as possible about the decisions they need to make and gives access to the information they need in order to make a successful application to university. UCAS promotes what is essentially an 'equal rights' approach to university admissions where facts about admissions are constantly being collected and distributed to potential applicants in order to enable maximum awareness of all the different possibilities open to students and how students may access them. The same information is available to all. It is up to the individual student to make the best use of it.

The commitment is ongoing. A recent attempt to achieve greater transparency in admissions by UCAS is the development of admissions criteria profiles (ACPs). This initiative aims to make clear the 'hidden criteria' for entry to subjects where academic as well as non-academic criteria need to be fulfilled. The initiative is intended to address entry to 'high demand' subjects in particular but applies to all subjects and routes. Each subject or programme will present its formal entry requirements together with an indication of the other qualities sought and how they may be evidenced by an applicant.

The attempt to promote equal opportunities for admissions to higher education does not mean UCAS necessarily tries to make all admissions procedures conform to the same pattern. UCAS has developed advice, information and systems to cater for diversity with the British higher education system: 'UCAS even considered at the level of mechanism and structure, has in recent years exhibited a tendency to respond to, and support diversity rather than making everything fit the same pattern' (Maclaren, 2001). There are separate systems for full-time undergraduates, nurses and midwives, graduate teacher training students and social workers – all with different application dates and timetables. There are also separate arrangements for art and design students as well as long-standing special arrangements that cater for college interviews for Oxford and Cambridge colleges.

The UCAS arrangements are essentially meritocratic. Although it might appear 'fair', the meritocratic, equal rights approach is limited in its capacity to widen participation because it largely ignores social and cultural inequalities that are produced and maintained outside of education. The approach overlooks the implicit acceptance of the cultural assumptions on which the British university applications system is based such as the selectivity of higher education, its elitism and the assumed superiority of academic qualifications. Any admissions curriculum based on this equal rights approach in turn reflects these elements.

Another perhaps more immediate issue for students applying through UCAS is the sheer volume of material available. A recent survey found that 68 per cent of students would have liked more information to contribute to the decision-making process when applying to higher education (Connor and Dewson, 2001). While lack of information can be an issue for many students, too much information can also be problematic. The same report concluded that although there is a great deal of information available, much of it is excessively detailed and not sufficiently tailored to personal circumstances. The report pointed out that the value of the information is greatly increased if the information is communicated personally to a student. Careers advisers generally provide the raw information but the one-to-one contact and advice often comes from other staff and teachers involved with the student in a wider role.

Advice and guidance as curriculum

So, in many institutions the need to prepare and provide support for students completing the UCAS application form has been developed into a formal programme of topics to be covered. There may also be accompanying course handbooks which contain a summary of content as well as references for further reading and sources of information (for example Southwark College, 2001). Handbooks may include an introduction from a teacher explaining the purpose of the programme and why it is important (for example Epsom and Ewell High School, 1999). Topics that make up the content of such admissions courses are often similar and reflect information issued centrally by UCAS such as:

- The benefits of higher education.
- Researching courses and institutions.
- The UCAS form, how to present yourself effectively, how to complete the form.
- Finance.
- Interviews, making a choice, holding offers.
- Clearing.
- Gap year and study abroad.

The programme may be full and complex, yet, because the overall structure is so clearly influenced by the stages of the UCAS admissions process itself – an example of what has been called 'curriculum as fact' (Young, 1998: 23), the content is largely taken for granted as obvious. Such an admissions curriculum partly enables students to acquire concepts and understandings that will help them in completing their UCAS applications by teaching them how to present their achievements in a way that admissions staff value. At the same time, like the UCAS system that frames it, it implicitly passes on certain values about higher education to applicants – values that universities themselves transmit through the UCAS process, such as:

- The selectivity of higher education (universities 'choose' from a pool of suitably qualified applicants).

- The exclusiveness of certain universities (indicated by demanding academic entry requirements).
- Traditional values about academic and vocational knowledge (Access and vocational qualifications are not acceptable, or not as acceptable, as entry qualifications to all universities).

The formal content of the curriculum, however, encourages applicants to research and gather information about different courses and different universities and to learn how to present their achievements to match university entry criteria. For the conscientious student there's a daunting amount of research to be done. Sources of information are plentiful, as the Southwark College guide to making an application explains:

You can find out more about different Degree subjects by:
Talking to your tutor
Using the Student Advice Centre resources
Using the Internet
Booking a Careers and Education Guidance Interview
Going to university open days
Getting university prospectuses
Talking to people you know who have been to university.

This research process can be both arduous and time consuming. Consider for example the time necessary to fulfil this Action Plan recommended to the students at Southwark College:

Research Action Plan
1. Ring up at least 10 universities and get a prospectus sent to you, by July.
2. Visit at least two open days, by October, and go to the college HE Fair.
3. Book yourself a Careers and Education Guidance interview, by September.
4. Spend at least five hours in the Student Advice centre finding out what information there is, by October.
5. Ring up the student union for at least two universities to get more information, by October.
6. Talk to your tutor about what [he or she] would recommend, by October.
7. Get the DfEE leaflet on 'Financial Support for Students in Higher Education' by October.
8. Find out about the careers you are interested in and what qualifications they require, by September.
9. Find out what arrangements your Local Education Authority makes for students applying for Financial Support in HE, by Christmas.

The information gained is all potentially useful but can it justify the time spent in gaining it? And how does a student then select relevant facts from all the information? The assumption is that students need all this information because it enables them to make informed choices. Research indicates otherwise. The UCAS system and many careers advisers follow a rational plan in designing access to advice and information. However, patterns of decision making by students are rarely based on an orderly evaluation of all the facts but are 'very different from the technically rational assumptions of much current policy' (Hodkinson,1995). For example, visiting universities is not often the basis for making decisions about them. Students tend to visit individual universities only after they have received or even accepted their offers as a way of confirming their choices (Ball, David and Reay, 2001).This indicates that decision making is not based on researching choices in the way we might expect.

Tutors also often stress the financial benefits of gaining a degree. Typically potential students are assured that their employment prospects and earnings will increase after graduation: 'Graduates in general usually have a wider career choice compared with those who complete their studies at 18. The vacancy picture is normally better as are graduate salaries especially over the long term' (Futures, 2001).

As Hodkinson points out, such arguments presume that young people will make rational decisions based on considering the facts:

> From this perspective good decision making takes the young person through a series of logical stages... the inevitable focus of decision making, when seen from this perspective, is the making of the 'correct' career decision as a preliminary to the next stage of education and/or training. From this point of view, careers education and guidance are essential to increase the chances of such a correct decision, mainly by providing correct information and giving help in how to make a decision. (Hodkinson, 1995: 4)

But content is not the sole determinant of what students learn. What students learn from any curriculum depends on what they know already. What learners bring with them to a learning event, including past experiences, perceptions and understandings, is central to the way their learning occurs:

> The characteristics and aspiration of the learner are the most important factors in the learning process. The response of the learners to a new experience is determined significantly by past experiences which have contributed to the ways in which the learner perceives the world. The way one person reacts to a given situation will not be the same as others and this becomes more obvious when learners from diverse backgrounds work together. (Boud, Keogh and Walker, 1987: 21)

The same factual content and the same curriculum result in different outcomes for different students from different backgrounds. This means the knowledge gained from an admissions 'curriculum' may depend on a number of possible factors which might include:

- Students' existing knowledge and understanding of higher education.
- What students have achieved already (and how student achievement is judged by their tutors).

- What students are studying and how their tutors (and other students) regard the possible outcomes of their current studies.
- How tutors regard the courses and institutions students want to apply for.
- How much time students spend on work in relation to the admissions process.

Cultural capital

The ideas of Bourdieu and Passeron (1977) help to explain how a range of social and cultural and economic elements influence the outcomes of learning for an individual. Learning is not a socially neutral process dependent simply on students' formal ability to absorb the knowledge they are presented with in the curriculum. Bourdieu and Passeron developed the concepts of social, economic and cultural capitals and used these to show how social advantage and disadvantage are produced and maintained.

Bourdieu's argument (1978) was that schools do not generally enable students to acquire certain types of cultural capital, yet, paradoxically, this is essentially what is needed to succeed in school. Achievement and success in school are judged on values that relate to the social, economic and cultural capitals of dominant or powerful groups, and these capitals are largely produced, and reproduced, outside the classroom. There is a strong relationship between success in school and possession of the right sort of cultural capital. This provides a dilemma for widening participation. Those who lack the values and capitals associated with the dominant group find it more difficult to gain the necessary cultural capital to succeed in education through education alone. Yet schools operate as if *all* pupils possess the attributes of the dominant group and those who lack the linguistic and cultural competences associated with dominant groups are denied educational success:

> Educational underachievement of working class children is not the result of their deficits of ability, but should be understood in relation to middle class cultural privilege and class cultural discrimination, the cultural violence of arbitrarily defining thinkable cultural distinctions. (Gamarnikow and Green, 1999)

Bourdieu developed the concept of 'habitus' to explain how individuals are influenced by their background and environment. Habitus is an idea that expresses how individuals perceive and understand their past and their present. 'Habitus operates at a subconscious level and so is beyond introspective scrutiny or control by the will' (Tett, 2000). Although habitus operates at a subconscious level it is not immutable. Tett explains how Bourdieu argued that habitus 'is no more fixed than the practices it helps to structure', so although it is subconscious, it is dynamic and capable of change. It is part of the process which determines the way cultural and social inequalities are transmitted and reproduced, but may itself change as circumstances and possibilities relating to specific groups change.

Taking these ideas into account, how can we develop an admissions curriculum appropriate to supporting an increasing diversity of applicants through the UCAS process? Research shows student choice is an increasingly complex process. We also know that much of the present information-giving assumes a traditional linear progression pattern, based on progression patterns for 18-year-old students who go straight to university from school. We also know that this pattern is no longer the only one and the linear pattern is based on assumptions about cultural capital that not all students posess. As described elsewhere in this book, progression patterns for 'new' students who account for the expansion in numbers of higher education students may include changes of direction and gaps between different stages of education, the result of a complex balancing act between personal, social and financial considerations.

The complexity of higher education

The issues surrounding the development of an admissions curriculum for widening participation are further complicated by the changing context for higher education itself. The tensions inherent in the current change from an elite to a mass system of higher education affect how we see higher education and influence how we look at what's available in higher education. As Peter Scott points out (Scott, 2001), the British higher education system that applicants are being encouraged to access contains features of not one but two systems. On the one hand there is the traditional elite system largely accessed by those with lots of the right sort of cultural capital, which is highly selective, with its close personal relationships between staff and students, close connections between research and teaching and which is valued, among other things, for its scarcity. On the other hand there is the mass system, which caters for large numbers in the former polytechnics, admits students with a diversity of profiles on entry, may be more impersonal because of sheer numbers and is also the site of innovation in curriculum content, assessment and modes of delivery.

Scott speculates whether the balance between 'old' and 'new' can be maintained overall. For those developing and delivering an admissions curriculum the tension between old and new offers contradictory sets of values and presents a problem of how to identify the overall issues for students. The rise of the QAA and the increasing focus on quality in the student experience should in theory provide a unified approach for viewing the higher education landscape. As Scott points out, however, the values that are used to judge the student experience relate not to the whole system but largely to the elite section of it as 'old criteria are used to measure new aspirations'. This puts 'new' at a disadvantage compared to 'old' as new is judged by the values of old. Old ideas about what is valuable about higher education – or what Scott calls the 'reworking of traditional assumptions about academic intimacy, ultimately embodied in the ideal of the Oxford traditional system' – clash with the reality of 'new' higher education. For some this means the traditional model is wrong and 'seems truly out of place in a truly mass system' (Scott, 2001: 194). For others league tables confirm the 'superiority' of the old.

These contradictions that underpin the values put on provision in different universities echo the contradictions inherent in government widening participation policy itself. On the one hand the Government promotes wider participation and social inclusion. On the other hand it lauds progression to 'elite' institutions and, therefore, implicitly underplays the achievements of students who progress to former polytechnics. This under-valuing permeates the criteria used to draw up league tables for education institutions. We can only speculate how it spills over into the attitudes of the teachers and career advisers.

This creates a complex and confusing framework for any admissions curriculum. The university system is in flux and with it the value put on different kinds of knowledge as represented by different qualifications, skills and abilities. As Michael Young has pointed out (Young, 1998), the content of a curriculum, whether overt or implicit, is heavily influenced by what officially counts as knowledge and what people in power (education-alists, politicians, employers) decide is useful and valuable knowledge at any particular time. In admissions terms 'valuable' knowledge is tradition-ally 'academic' knowledge and knowledge related to cultural capital. It influences:

- how applicants and their tutors view their chances of success in relation to different institutions (depending on what academic qualifications are required for entry);
- the structure of the applications form (traditionally this concentrated on enabling students to present academic achievements);
- the criteria for selection of applicants (which focus largely on academic ability);
- the opinions of admissions tutors (which, research shows, mainly focus on formal academic achievement);
- the information made available to applicants about the admissions process (which stresses formal academic qualifications).

The publication of skills and other criteria for entry and the development of complementary routes to higher education which emphasize skills beyond the academic do not sit easily alongside the traditional values placed on academic knowledge. The information that applicants gain about the applications process is interpreted against this background of tensions and contradictions.

Just as the choices facing students are complex, so too are the choices for their advisers. Policy imperatives and funding regimes encourage tutors and institutions to progress the maximum possible numbers of students to higher education. At the same time some progression is clearly valued above others – the value reinforced by league tables. Does this affect how staff value different student achievements? Does it affect the advice students are given? Does it support a curriculum to promote wider participation?

UCAS and widening participation

Given the complexity relating to the application process, several points present themselves. The first concerns UCAS and the availability of information about entry to university. Given that traditionally the criteria for academic success and for admission to university have been implicit rather than explicit and based on the values of socially dominant groups, the impulse to encourage students to research and analyse as much information as they can is a good one. It is not sufficient, however, and, developed in isolation, leads to students being confronted with baffling amounts of information. The sheer amount of information produced by UCAS, and increasingly by other research bodies, is vast. There are numerous handbooks for students, handbooks for tutors, handbooks for parents, Web sites, videos, help lines and advice sessions. These lay out the detail and requirements of the admissions process and can be helpful – they also in themselves constitute an alternative admissions curriculum. At the practical level, however, the information is complex and the complexity increases as the available amount of information increases. For some students this can be overwhelming. For example, students quoted in a recent report commented, 'they just throw the information at you' (Connor and Dewson, 2001).

As already mentioned, the approach also implicitly accepts the 'selectivity' of higher education, which is itself based on ideas of academic meritocracy rooted in ideas of 'intelligence' and 'merit' that are associated with particular social groups. Although statistics produced by UCAS and more general admissions research focus attention on 'exclusionary practices' by higher education, an acknowledgement that admissions procedures are dominated by cultural practices that favour socially dominant groups above others, the main concern of the UCAS approach is to enable access to information. This largely bypasses the inherent inequalities that are maintained through the transmission of cultural capital by social mechanisms outside of education. Students say personal advice is important but what information should be selected? How should it be presented? What information would be most useful to traditionally excluded groups? Is information all that is needed?

Much has been written about the need to be clear at the outset about the overall purposes of a curriculum rather than beginning with curriculum content (see for example Gosling and Moon, 2001). The use of learning outcomes, rather than content (or information), as the starting point for curriculum design can promote more clarity about the issues and also make the issues more visible for students. It begins by asking the question 'What outcomes might be desirable?' Curriculum design is then about developing provision to enable students to achieve those outcomes. So what outcomes should an admissions curriculum be promoting?

The general assumption behind existing admissions curricula seems to be that students should want to progress to higher education (see Chapter 6) and should therefore work towards completing a UCAS application form and hand it in on time. To achieve this, however, students are expected to undertake a number of activities. Such activities might involve a range of expected outcomes: knowledge outcomes (the gaining of factual knowledge), process outcomes (reflecting on the options and analysing the issues), personal outcomes (in terms of making choices based on personal preferences and skills).Within this breadth of possible outcomes, which is important? Which would best help an individual to make choices? Which will best promote progression from non-traditional students?

One way to answer these questions is to ask those who have a stake in the process – they might include students, tutors, higher education admissions tutors and parents – what they think the outcomes should be. Learning outcomes identified through such a consultation process might point to a number of different purposes for learning within an admissions curriculum. These could provide the basis for designing flexible provision to enable students to explicitly choose or identify their own learning outcomes (Fenwick and Paczuska, 1996).

We might also consider which curriculum elements in particular may promote wider participation. It may not be possible to overcome structural inequalities but what might be possible is to develop students' understanding of the possibilities and opportunities available to them and to see themselves as 'suitable for higher education' even where their traditional self image or 'habitus' has been to exclude such possibilities. Changing self-perceptions, which have been internalized and work at a subconscious level, is no easy matter. Tett (2000) describes the idea of 'promoting self-knowledge' through cultivating 'reflexive self-narratives' among students to enable them to challenge their 'habitus' and predispositions. She argues that how people describe their experiences reflects the ways in which they construct their (gendered) identities. She suggests 'reflexive self-narratives' can help challenge assumptions students have about their about identities and suggests that if students can share their own reflexive stories about their lives, 'this can become an important resource for re-presenting their experiences for more self aware interrogation'.

What is effective for challenging gendered assumptions is also potentially useful to challenge cultural assumptions. This can be done as a basis for developing an admissions curriculum that specifically promotes reflection on students' experiences of education. This reflection becomes part of a strategy to challenge internalized assumptions about the relationship between 'non-traditional' students and higher education. It is not easy to design a curriculum that will develop reflexivity among younger students, as attempts to develop a model of assessing prior experiential learning (APEL) suitable for post-16 students have shown (Paczuska, 1992). It is, however, important to acknowledge that while access to information is important as part of the strategy to promote wider participation, on its own it is not enough. It is also important to find ways to challenge the 'taken for granted' assumptions that leave 'non-traditional' students at the mercy of the instinctive and subconsciously learned behaviours that work against their progression to higher education. An approach that incorporates a reflective and self-aware examination of the contradictions and tensions associated with progression potentially offers a basis for developing an admissions curriculum that supports progression for those who have traditionally been excluded.

References

Ball, S, David, M and Reay, D (2001) *An Exploration of the Processes Involved in Students' Choice of Higher Education*, ESRC Final Project Report, London

Bligh, D, Thomas, H and McNay, I (1999) *Understanding Higher Education: An introduction for parents, staff, employers and students*, Intellect Books, Bristol

Bloomer, M and Hodkinson, P (2000) The complexity and unpredictability of young people's learning careers, *Education and Training*, **42** (2), pp 68–74

Boud, D, Keogh, R and Walker, D (1987) *Reflection: Turning experience into learning*, Kogan Page, London

Bourdieu, P (1978) Cultural reproduction and social reproduction, in *Power and Ideology in Education*, eds J Karabel and A Halsey, Oxford University Press, New York

Bourdieu, P and Passeron, J-C (1977) *Reproduction in Education, Society and Culture*, Sage, London

College of North West London (2000) *Access to Science, Computing and Mathematics*, course submissions document to LOCN, London

Connor, H and Dewson, S (2001) Social class and higher education: issues affecting decisions on participation by lower social class groups, in *Opportunity for Whom?* eds W Piatt and P Robinson, IPPR, London

Epsom and Ewell High School (1999) *Higher Education Guide: 2000 Entry*

Fenwick, A and Paczuska, A (1996) An integrated approach to learning outcomes, paper to Changing Assessment to Improve Learning Conference, University of Northumbria

Futures (2001) *Directions into Higher Education: A guide for students who are considering entry to higher education in 2002*, Central Information Unit, London

Gamarnikow, E and Green, A (1999) Developing social capital: dilemmas, possibilities and limitations in education, in *Tackling Disaffection and Social Exclusion*, ed A Hayton, Kogan Page, London

Gosling, D and Moon, J (2001) *How to Use Learning Outcomes and Assessment Criteria*, SEEC, London

Hodkinson, P (1995) How young people make career decisions, *Education and Training*, **37** (8), pp 3–8

London College of Printing (1998) *Applying to Higher Education 1999 Entry: Tutors Guide*

Maclaren, A (2001) The admissions system: expansion, inclusion and the demands of diversity, in *The State of UK Higher Education: Managing change and diversity*, eds D Warner and D Palfreyman, Open University Press, Buckingham

Paczuska, A (1992) *APEL, Progression and Records of Achievement*, Report of the TVEI Access to Higher Education Project, Division of Continuing Education, South Bank University, London

Piatt, W and Robinson, P (2001) *Opportunity for Whom?* IPPR, London

Scott, P (2001) Conclusion: triumph or retreat, in *The State of UK Higher Education: Managing change and diversity*, eds D Warner and D Palfreyman, Open University Press, Buckingham

Southwark College (2001) *UCAS Handbook for Students*

Tett, L (2000) 'I'm working class and proud of it': gendered experiences of non-traditional participants in higher education, *Gender and Education*, **12** (2), pp 183–94

Young, M F D (1998) *The Curriculum of the Future*, Falmer Press, London

9

Higher Education Provision and the Change to a Mass System

Ruth Farwell

Introduction

At the start of the 21st century Peter Scott, Vice Chancellor of Kingston University, wrote about Britain's move to a mass higher education system in his aptly entitled chapter 'Triumph or retreat' (Scott, 2001a). He described this mass system as retaining 'many of the admirable qualities of an elite system'. Scott believes that Britain is possibly unique in attempting to increase participation in higher education through a system that retains 'traditional academic attributes in nearly all institutions, and not just in a segregated elite sector'. He regards this 'experiment' as a success. He also poses a question: 'Is Britain's elite-mass system capable of further extension and reform without damaging its essential academic culture?' Scott finds no compelling evidence to suggest that the successful experiment cannot be sustained.

I would argue that if we are to widen participation still further then there is compelling evidence that current systems for organizing higher education must change. True, increased participation has, to a great extent, taken place without loss of what the academic community holds dear – the traditional academic curriculum is one example. But how much more can participation increase without a shift change in the system? Increasing numbers of undergraduates, including 'new' students without a family tradition of higher education, cause us to review our provision and support services. More radically there is an emerging agenda which calls for a redefinition of the purposes of higher education and offers cultural as well as economic arguments for change and expansion (Scott, 2001b).

The government's target of one in two 18–30-year-olds progressing to higher education is laudable in terms of social justice and economic growth. However, as Sir David Watson, Vice Chancellor of the University of Brighton and chair of the Universities UK longer-term strategy group, stated, 'the sector needs to reach students with non-traditional qualifications in order to achieve the government's participation target' (Watson, 2001b). If we are to attract 'new' learners into higher education how will this impact on higher education provision?

So far the widening participation agenda has influenced provision very little. Debate about the content of higher education and the provision itself has been largely polarized between those who defend the status of 'traditional' academic knowledge and others who advocate an employability agenda. Barnett outlines the issue as follows:

> In the former situation – call it epistemic supremacy – definitions of knowledge were formed by the academic 'tribes and territories', and these reciprocally served to define the nature of higher education (as an initiation into the conversations of the academics); and that form of higher education was assumed to have a benefit to society, even if diffuse. Now we are moving to a situation in which the wider society is defining for higher education the forms of knowledge and being it deems valuable; and these in turn are serving to frame the character of higher education. (Barnett, 1994: 93)

Neither of these approaches seriously take account of the student view of the curriculum in terms of content or delivery. Further, although we clearly need to consider what kind of courses would 'tempt' new learners to higher education we also have to think beyond the immediate need to recruit. Apart from a few academic specialists in the area, such as Peter Scott, Ronald Barnett and Michael Young, the curriculum debate is rarely centred on a serious exploration of what kind of curriculum would rise to the challenges of the 21st century or whose interests should be reflected in the curriculum and in the way higher education provision is organized.

How far have we moved?

There is no doubt that even though higher education has clung to many of its traditional values, the last 30 years has been a period of massive change. The number of participating students is one example. In 1971 there were just 176,000 students in 45 universities. By the turn of the century the numbers of students in higher education were more than ten times that with 1.8 million students in the system (Scott, 2001a).

What is taught in higher education has also changed to a certain extent and the subjects now on offer at degree level are different. For example, no one would argue that computing is not a bona fide degree level subject, but that was not the case in the 1960s. In addition, over the last 25 years training for certain professions, which was formerly undertaken outside of universities, has become the province of higher education. Professions allied to medicine and teaching are examples. This has naturally led to changes in participation levels and to the groups represented in higher education. Now that all trainee nurses are included in higher education and many of those originally trained before nursing was a higher education qualification are upgrading their professional qualification in universities, it is hardly surprising that numbers participating have increased.

New subjects and the increase in the numbers of higher education students have contributed to a general impression that British higher education is a massive success story in terms of increasing participation and changing the profile of students entering higher education. These successes, however, mask significant differential participation rates between different social classes. Increased participation has largely been from the professional and middle classes. Any young person who is a child of parents in the professional or middle classes, who has appropriate qualifications and who wants to progress to university, will do so. True, the participation rate of those from social class V (unskilled) has doubled in the last 10 years, but they still have not increased their share of the student population (NAO, 2002a). As Watson has said: 'The sector still reinforces social polarisation. Supply has met demand for the middle classes and those who are well-qualified but only a small impression has been made on social groups IIIm (skilled manual), IV (partly skilled) and V (unskilled)' (Watson, 2001a).

Those from the lower socio-economic groups who have entered higher education tend, as Scott says, 'to be concentrated in the newer and less prestigious institutions' (Scott, 2001a). Forecasting recruitment difficulties for some institutions in summer 2001, Watson noted that 'the institutions that attract students from lower socio-economic groups are the ones that are suffering the market effect' (Watson, 2001a). These institutions, he said, were experiencing difficulties with recruitment because other, more prestigious universities were 'choosing students who, in the past, they might not have chosen'.

Most of the institutions affected by under-recruitment in 2001 were former polytechnics, many situated in large urban conurbations. These same institutions had been in the vanguard of widening participation and recruited the 'first wave' of new learners in the 1980s and 1990s. Now they are failing to attract the very students that have been the mainstay of their work – that is, 'new' students from lower socio-economic backgrounds. In order to survive, some of these institutions will now have to place themselves in the forefront of what might be termed the 'second wave' of widening participation. How will higher education relate to this second wave? In order to answer this question it is worth reflecting on how higher education responded to the 'first wave' of 'new' learners.

The elite system and the first wave of 'new' students

Higher education may have moved towards a mass system in terms of numbers but it still retains many features of an elite system that remain embedded in the provision. Scott (2001a) argues that the higher education system 'reveals the perhaps surprising persistence of traditional academic patterns'. These vestiges of the elite system hold back progress on opening up the sector still further to 'new' learners, or make it more difficult to think creatively about retaining those who make up the groups of the new learners. For Scott this indicates that 'too little attention has been paid to the system bias against innovation' (Scott, 2001b). There are several areas in the organization and delivery of higher education which exemplify the tensions between traditional patterns and the more flexible approaches.

Modular courses

Much of the academic debate in the 1980s and early 1990s focused on the rights and wrongs of reorganizing university courses as modular programmes. Those opposed claimed that modularity permits students to 'pick and mix' but with a consequential loss of academic coherence in students' programmes. Conversely, those who were pro-modularity argued that modular courses afforded students more control over their own learning. First, students are able to choose (within reason) their programmes and, second, modularity can allow students to study at a pace that suits their circumstances.

Yet despite the benefits for 'non-traditional' learners of flexible and modularized learning programmes that can be tailored to a variety of needs, traditional patterns of provision persist. Although most universities now claim to have unitized or modular systems, the perceived benefits to learners are not evident. In spite of the apparent focus on enabling 'new' learners to progress to higher education, the biggest expansion in higher education in recent times has been in full-time undergraduate provision. Over the same period the 'new' students who actually managed to progress to higher education have increasingly taken up more part-time paid employment at the same time as undertaking their studies (Brennan *et al*, 1999; Callender, 1997). This is most evident among students from the lower socio-economic groups, from ethnic minorities and from mature students. These students, who made up the 'first wave of widening participation, are precisely those students who might benefit from being able to vary their rate of study from the norm. Yet for the most part the academic provision, even in new universities, has not allowed them to do so. Students who wish to study fewer than the amount of units equivalent to full-time study will find that university administration systems will not in practice allow them the choice that is theoretically theirs. Full-time is still the dominant mode of study; although part-time study increased, the proportion overall of part-time students declined from 38 per cent to 33 per cent during the six-year-period up to 1993/94 because growth in full-time study was faster (HEFCE, 2001a).

Completion

A further issue is the ability of certain types of students to complete their courses. A number of factors make completion difficult for 'new' students, many of whom are older and may have family responsibilities or part-time jobs. Their ability to complete is not solely about their academic ability but is also linked to their social circumstances and to the complexity of factors that impact on their lives. But, at the same time as the Government is urging the higher education sector to widen participation, so institutions are being judged on an outdated notion of what constitutes successful completion. The institutions with the lowest completion rates are likely to be new universities that have the highest populations of 'new' students. Such institutions appear at the bottom of the league for completion, implying that they are somehow 'unsuccessful', 'failing' or attracting 'poor-quality' students. But failure is not necessarily the issue here; rather it is the way that characteristics of the elite system have been used to define the criteria with which to judge the whole sector, including those universities with a majority of 'new' students. The yardstick of completion rates cannot capture the positive achievements of 'new' students as it is based on narrow notions of mode of attendance which apply to the elite system.

The funding council's performance indicators for completion are predicated on a traditional model of a student in higher education – one who progresses directly from school or college (perhaps after a gap year) and enrols on an Honours degree which is normally completed in three years. A student who does not complete his or her degree in this standard amount of time is automatically seen as a non-completion based on current criteria. Included among the so called 'failures' are all those students who gain academic credit or a qualification lower than the one they originally intended or who do not complete a full year of study having enrolled as a full-time student and subsequently switched to part-time study. For these students their achievements are positive. Many intend to return to study at a later date and add more credit to their portfolio or just want to take longer to complete. The HEFCE indicators on efficiency themselves reinforce this picture as they show the institutions where completion of an Honours degree in more than three years is not unusual, and these are usually the institutions normally associated with widening participation. Regrettably, though, this is generally seen as an element of poor performance by the institution rather than a positive means of assisting learners to complete. The funding council's system for measuring completion cannot credit the achievements of 'new' learners who by their criteria have 'failed' to complete. The real 'failure', it might be argued, is the funding council's inability to put in place a system robust enough to measure a wide range of achievement. In the current system non-completion is synonymous with wastage. Are the new learners of the 'second wave' to continue to be judged in the same way as those in the 'first wave'? Or can higher education put in place systems which credit all student learning and do not label as 'waste' or 'failure' those who do not complete their degrees through three years' full-time study?

Students' changing skills profile

A further issue is the way that higher education responded to the changing skills profile of 'new' students. Within higher education changes lower down the system are often seen as having a negative effect on higher education's ability to support students on their university programmes. For example, from the higher education perspective, innovations in the 14–19 curriculum and qualifications system are widely viewed as producing students under-prepared for higher education study. Those in higher education who take this view argue that changes lower down the system are the cause of undergraduate under-achievement.

The mathematics curriculum is an example of one way in which the changing attributes of the students impacted on higher education provision. In the 1990s students coming to higher education after having successfully studied (new) GCSE – and then A level – mathematics courses were increasingly regarded by higher education as not adequately prepared for the (traditional) degree curriculum in mathematics. Rather than acknowledging that students had different skills as a result of their new post-16 studies, higher education assumed the students were lacking. Thus the four year maths degree was born (LMS, 1992). This enabled students with new skills to achieve the outcomes of the old three-year Honours degree by studying for an extra year. A sensible response would be for both further and higher education to work together in partnership to achieve curriculum matching to enable students to progress successfully.

Standards and admissions

The general unwillingness of higher education to change its provision also means prospective higher education students from Access courses continue to be viewed with suspicion. This is still the case despite the rigorous accreditation procedures that have been developed for courses delivered by Open College Networks, themselves strictly reviewed by the Quality Assurance Agency (QAA). Ironically this suspicion of the non-traditional is often found in subjects still in their infancy in higher education, such as nurse education, which are often fiercely protective of their new-found 'academic' status. Gatekeepers in these subject areas may adhere more rigidly to traditional values about what a student in higher education should possess on entry than those in more established disciplines. Gatekeepers in areas that wish to assert their new-found higher education status may well be deterred from more flexible admissions procedures and other innovative approaches because they are concerned about accusations of lowering standards.

Subjects and content

Innovative approaches to the curriculum have in the past met with derision and accusations of 'dumbing down' from within and without the higher education community. For example, Chris Woodhead, while still Chief Inspector of Schools, referred to media studies and certain other new degree courses as 'vacuous'. Woodhead's comments were timed to hit the media just when A level results were about to be made available to anxious students hoping to get the grades to progress to higher education – some to study those same 'vacuous subjects'. Certainly some of the courses criticized by Woodhead were precisely those in greatest demand by students. But media studies is not a discipline 'invented' to cater for the whims of empty-headed students. Rather it marks the growth of a new area of intellectual endeavour with its foundations in new approaches to interpreting and critiquing popular culture as represented in new media. The academic lights of media studies, such as Barthes and Derrida, could be regarded as complex – or even difficult to access – but their work could hardly be judged 'vacuous' as in Woodhead's designation.

The issue of what is a 'real' subject for study at university level continues to be used to imply that new subjects, often offered first at 'new' universities, are in some way inferior to traditional areas of study. Recently, in the round of party conferences in October 2001, Roderick Floud, Rector of London Guildhall University and President of Universities UK, argued that new vocational subjects (and the institutions that offer them) are just as valid as traditional ones: 'What is the difference between an institution that educates lawyers, accountants, doctors... and one that educates businessmen, artists and designers? Really, are they any different? They are all vocational. They all incorporate... a high level of intellectual achievement' (Floud, 2001).

It is worth remembering Floud was speaking nearly 10 years after the binary divide had been removed but even after 10 years of a unified, mass system some of higher education is not comfortable with new provision.

The fear of change

As we have seen, the higher education system is not over-eager to shed traditional attitudes, embrace change and accommodate new learners. Attempts to diversify the higher education curriculum have had very little impact. Traditional values are still evident and are supported by those who criticize higher education for diversifying and 'dumbing down'. Changes where they have occurred – for example new or different subjects taught at degree level – have had to be fiercely defended. Diversity has not had an easy ride and it seems is often regarded as detracting from, rather than adding value to, higher education.

Why has there been such entrenchment and reluctance to change higher education curriculum and organization? Perhaps it was in part because, at around the same time as expansion occurred, there were also other pressures on higher education. Accountability and external inspection of quality were high on the politicians' agenda and became a key focus of institutional development. The quality inspection process was introduced in the early 1990s and went through a number of earlier methodologies but by the middle of the 1990s had settled down – for a while at least – with teaching quality assessment, or subject review, and institutional audit. For the purposes of this discussion, subject review perhaps is the most important. All courses in higher education institutions, and in some further education colleges where higher education provision is offered, were 'inspected' in the relevant subject review by peers, and more recently under the organization of the QAA. It is worth noting that although subject review has generated much hostility among higher education staff, there were no explicit external reference points for this process of inspection. The judgement is made against the aims and objectives of the subject provision itself, which is set by the institution that offered it.

The quality debate, which caused outrage among academics with accompanying claims that institutional autonomy and academic freedom were being threatened, was provoked further by the requirement for 'benchmark' standards for higher education provision proposed by the QAA. It was proposed that standards would be defined for each subject area and include a set of outcomes for all undergraduate honours degrees in that subject. The curriculum had to provide students with the opportunity to meet the outcomes. Assessment had to measure whether students have met the outcomes. The assessment process had to be robust in its ability to reflect adequately students' differential achievements. This innovation sparked rumours that a national curriculum for higher education was in the offing.

The benchmark monster turned out to be toothless. The result of the process of generating benchmark statements was, for the majority of subjects, a set of bland outcomes that could be satisfied by almost any degree course in the land – at least at the level of subject knowledge. But the real fear behind the opposition to benchmark standards was the loss of autonomy that it seemed to herald. Benchmarks appeared to be yet more evidence, especially when accompanied by New Labour's widening partici- pation agenda, that higher education institutions, while still expected to be centres of academic excellence, would no longer be autonomous and would be expected to conform to agreed standards in the same way as publicly funded schools and colleges. The opposition to outcomes included resis- tance to the possible imposition of the use of 'competences' to assess students' skills and the potential for the growth of a 'tick box' culture for higher education apparently heralded by the introduction of national voca- tional qualifications (NVQs) into other education sectors. Writing of the relationship between the professions and higher education, Jessup stated:

> It would seem necessary to create qualifications which assess the knowledge required to underpin and extend competent performance, directly in relation to performance. It is suggested that this should occur even if the knowledge is assessed separately as apart of an academic discipline. (Jessup, 1991: 127)

Contributing to the spectre of NVQs for higher education was the develop- ing focus on students' skill development and on the principle that degree courses should prepare graduates for the workplace. A view was emerging that degree courses were not adequately providing graduates with the skills that they needed in the workplace and that higher education should focus more on the skills that graduates gain on their courses (see for example UDACE, 1991). In the 1990s surveys of what employers wanted in gradu- ates, what skills they, as graduates, were expected to have, showed that graduates were lacking in the skills employers want. Benchmark state- ments in part responded to this and refer to the transferable skills employ- ers say they want as well as subject-specific knowledge and skills, which describe communication skills, team working, IT skills, etc. QAA now requires each course to publish a 'programme specification' which has to make explicit the skills students are expected to acquire while on a particu- lar programme. While the benchmark statements are in no way a national curriculum, they do mark a process of introducing more external reference points against which the higher education curriculum is judged. Undoubtedly the higher education sector is not as autonomous as it once was. It has fought hard (and won) against some attempts to introduce constraining factors on the curriculum – for example, look at any of the QAA subject benchmark statements – but autonomy about what is taught has been eroded.

Changes in higher education

There are some indicators that higher education is taking on some of the attributes of further education. Because of economic factors students are now much more inclined to study at local institutions. Indeed, some students even spend some of their higher education career in a further education college. By 2000 there were more students studying higher education in a further education college than there were in higher education in total three decades previously (Scott, 2001a). There are strong policy steers which encourage higher education institutions to serve their local communities and work in partnership with further education colleges. The funding council, HEFCE, introduced a range of funded initiatives to promote such partnership (including HEFCE, 1999, 2001b, 2001c). Alongside this comes the pressure to increase the 'professionalism' of academic staff by 'training' staff to teach, providing staff development in learning and teaching and the establishment of the Institute of Learning and Teaching (ILT). The idea that teaching staff in higher education should be 'reflective practitioners' would have been anathema not that long ago. It is true that in some degree courses in the past (teacher and nurse training, for example), students were expected to engage in reflective practice, but it was not a phrase typically associated with university lecturers, at least as far as their teaching practice was concerned. There is resistance across the sector to the ILT as it is not clear what the benefits of membership are and indeed the most recent round of elections to the ILT council have been fought on a ticket of reforming the ILT.

This is all highly central to the debate around widening participation. There was less general reluctance to embrace the cultural changes among the former polytechnics. They were used to external validation of courses through CNAA and external inspection by HM Inspectorate. Skills development and academic staff training had already become accepted practice in many former polytechnics. The 'elite' old universities and the civic universities have been the sites for the strongest opposition to institutional and subject review. A glance through the headline articles during the late summer of 2001 indicates just the extent of the opposition against the QAA from the Russell Group in particular (THES, September 2001). This polarization of response to change between sectors contributes to the problem. The apparent willingness of former polytechnics to embrace change may signal loss of 'quality' in higher education for some. Yet despite embracing change and successfully implementing widening participation to accommodate the 'new' learners, the same institutions still come bottom of the government-inspired league tables, whilst the elite institutions, those that have changed least, occupy all the top places. This issue is explored in more depth in Chapter 5. Small wonder many staff in the former polytechnics are also moved to resist change when they are judged by criteria which imply that tradition equals 'quality'.

This resistance is fuelled the more that 'new' universities move to teaching and learning provision which echoes that of the further education sector. Yet there are good arguments why change should be supported.

Choosing the future

Strategies developed to date for organization and delivery of courses in higher education have not been entirely successful in widening participation – nor in retaining students once recruited. We are still a long way off the target of 50 per cent participation by 2010. The increase in students taking level 3 courses in schools and colleges is bottoming out. If we look at the conventional routes into higher education, it is apparent that these alone are not going to deliver the increases needed to hit the target. To fuel a 'second wave' of widening participation we need to attract students from groups that have not traditionally participated in higher education, most importantly the students from lower socio-economic groups that other initiatives have failed to reach.

This will occur against a background of increasing competition between institutions. The need to meet government widening participation targets means students who might have been recruited to some of the institutions with the 'most progressive social missions' are now being courted by the more prestigious universities. Market forces are at work – and are working against some of the institutions that were in the vanguard of widening participation. As Watson (2001b) has argued, 'issues of sector organisation are becoming more intense, especially in conurbations such as London, where the universities with the most progressive social missions are beginning to look like market failures'. In the past, 'new' universities might have been protected against loss of their traditional intake by the Maximum Aggregate Student Number (MASN) imposed by HEFCE which put a cap on the numbers of full-time home and EU undergraduate students any institution could recruit. The abolition of MASN in 2002 means institutions wishing to expand may do so without limit, in theory, leaving other institutions to under-recruit unless they can stimulate new demand.

Many institutions are faced with a difficult future, and higher education as a whole is faced with change. Clearly some institutions must face immediate change if they are to survive. These are most likely to be those who received the first wave of new learners. To maintain their student population they will have to innovate to attract those learners who have not been enticed by higher education so far. Other universities, the elite institutions, will also be faced with change when, as a result of changing recruitment patterns, they find themselves with a different student profile from the one they have had in the past. It will be interesting to see how retention rates hold up as they accept students different from their past intakes.

While changes to admissions and academic organization have begun, the higher education curriculum has been that part of the system most resistant to change. We should be thinking about changing the higher education curriculum to attract different groups and to retain those we have struggled to recruit. We also need to think about the kind of curriculum that will equip students for a changing future.

The innovations in teaching and learning that schools and further education colleges have developed are a potentially liberating force for higher education. Some universities are liaising with local schools and colleges to facilitate progression through curriculum matching (see Chapters 13 and 17). The funding council is pinning its hopes on progression partnerships to achieve the necessary expansion of higher education to meet the 50 per cent target (HEFCE, 2001c). Effective local partnership can enable progression and can also be a starting point for acknowledging a wider purpose for higher education than that provided by the traditional academic curriculum.

Young reflects on the relationship between sociology of education and the emergence of mass schooling. He remarks that

> The problems associated with mass schooling cannot... be dealt with by improvements in schooling alone... The failure of schools to give a high priority to the conditions for learning is not just a problem of school improvement. It can only be overcome in a learning society which privileges learning relationships in all spheres and sectors of society. (Young, 1999)

He goes on to say that although 'schools claim something of a monopoly over young people's learning, they remain far from being effective learning organisations themselves'. He likens the situation in schools with that in universities which have had 'a similar near monopoly over knowledge production and yet they find it increasingly difficult to respond to the knowledge demands of modern societies' (Young, 1999).

How can higher education change its provision, and in particular its curriculum, to respond to the knowledge demands of modern societies? What kind of curriculum would attract students with different relationships to mainstream knowledge? Who should be involved in deciding the content? Should we expect students to fit with the demands of universities as they are – the 'come and get it' model (Acland *et al*, 2002) – or should we be promoting dialogue about learner needs and student support? Or more radically, should we be moving towards provision that reflects both learner needs and also wider social, moral and ethical concerns? How can we ensure provision responds to change? We have to answer these questions if we are to survive. We could learn from the last 30 years and acknowledge that learning and knowledge for a modern society will not necessarily fit into the traditional elite package of higher education.

Acknowledgement

Many thanks to Anna Paczuska and Annette Hayton for their help and suggestions on this chapter.

References

Acland, T *et al* (2002) Change the institution or change the student: exploring tensions for widening participation, in *Challenging Social Exclusion in HE and FE*, Report of FACE Annual Conference 2001, Southampton Institute

Barnett, R (1994) *The Limits of Competence: Knowledge, higher education and society*, SRHE/Open University Press, Buckingham

Brennan, J *et al* (1999) *Part-time Students and Employment: Report of a survey of students, graduates and diplomates*, QSC, The Open University, London

Callender, C (1997) *Full and Part-time Students in Higher Education: Their experiences and expectations, Report 2, National Committee of Inquiry into Higher Education*, NCIHE, London

Floud R (2001), quoted in Tories: it's full steam ahead, *Times Higher Education Supplement*, 12 October

HEFCE (1999) *Reach-out to Business and the Community Fund*, consultation document, HEFCE 99/40

HEFCE (2001a) *Supply and Demand in Higher Education*, consultation document, HEFCE 01/62

HEFCE (2001b) *Higher Education Active Community Fund*

HEFCE (2001c) *Partnerships for Progression*, consultation document HEFCE 01/73

Jessup, G (1991) *Outcomes: The emerging model of education and training*, Falmer Press, London

London Mathematical Society (LMS) and Royal Statistical Society (1992) *The future for honours degree courses in mathematics*, LMS, London

National Audit Office (NAO) (2002a) *Widening Participation in Higher Education in England*, HMSO, London

NAO (2002b) *Improving student achievement in English higher education*, HMSO, London

Scott, P (2001a) Triumph or retreat, in *The State of UK Higher Education: Managing change and diversity*, eds D Warner and D Palfreyman, Open University Press, Buckingham

Scott, P (2001b) High wire, *Guardian Education*, 4 December

THES (2001) Russell elite go for the jugular of ailing QAA, Times Higher Education Supplement, 21 September

UDACE (1991) *What Can Graduates Do?* A consultative document, UDACE, Leicester

Watson, D (2001a) quoted in Crisis as 8,000 places unfilled, *Times Higher Education Supplement*, 29 June

Watson, D (2001b) quoted in No A levels? No problem… *Times Higher Education Supplement*, 7 September

Yorke, M (2001) Outside benchmark expectations? Variation in non-completion rates in English higher education, *Journal of Higher Education Policy and Management*, **23** (2), pp 147–58

Young, M (1999) *The Curriculum of the Future*, Falmer Press, London

Part 2

Developing Strategies for Widening Participation

10

A Framework for Institutional Change

Margo Blythman and Susan Orr

Introduction

History is littered with failed attempts to achieve institutional change. Our own position is that we are committed to develop new organizational forms and innovative ways of working that promote social justice. In the area of equality of opportunity it is particularly difficult to make change happen. So why is it so very hard?

Partly it is difficult because institutions do not exist in a vacuum. Issues of national policy and social structures are outlined in Part One of this book. However, we also have to examine actual institution experience and the focus of this chapter is on issues in implementing institutional change. Our view is that it is necessary to analyse the institution one is working in from a micropolitical angle (Ball, 1991; Ball and Goodson, 1985; Blase, 1991; Gronn, 1986; Hargreaves, 1994). This involves the operation of power, diverse and conflicting goals within the organization, different (and possibly conflicting) educational and social value positions and diverse personal and professional interests. In analysing the organization, therefore, we need to identify where power lies, how it operates and where there is 'space' for action. Foucault (1998) argues that this space always exists since competing discourses can produce space to manoeuvre in any power relationship. In this chapter we relate micropolitical analysis to the case studies which follow in subsequent chapters. We do this under the following six headings:

- Key players and their motivations.
- Institutional cultures.
- Resistance.
- Institutional structures.
- Resources.
- Forming alliances.

Key players and their motivations

For successful innovation a key priority is the identification of key players. These are likely to be the senior managers (or a key and powerful senior manager), middle managers, leaders of the innovation, in this case access and participation strategies, and lecturers who are in general affected by the innovation. We then need to identify these people's motivation in relation to the innovation, which is likely to be based on values and material interests connected to their own personal identity. In the case of widening participation does the motivation come from commitment to some educational or social value, a resource imperative, fashion or a bureaucratic need to keep the 'rules'? In Chapter 11, Angela Fenwick, whose project aims to increase participation in medicine by under-represented groups, points out that the Council of Heads of Medical Schools requested all medical schools to look at equal opportunity issues and come up with an action plan. Such 'requests' exemplify an apparent voluntary action which, in practice, becomes an externally imposed rule. So for institutions is the motivation authentic or compliant; in other words, is it genuine or is it lip service? If there is some strong institutional management desire to widen participation, does it come from considerations of equity and social justice or from a position that this is the only space left to 'grow the business', like a supermarket moving into a disadvantaged area because there are no sites left in 'nice' middle class suburbs? Fenwick identifies that at her university it was important that under-represented groups were funded by additional places rather than 'depriving' traditional high academic achievers of their places.

Another aspect of institutional motivation is 'administrative convenience' (Hargreaves, 1983). An illustration of this is another example described by Fenwick, provided by the university raising its entry qualifications for medicine to escape from the administratively messy position of carrying many UCAS 'insurance offers' and therefore finding it difficult to predict student numbers.

Any hope of change and successful introduction of innovation has to recognize the interplay of such factors. At its simplest, a finance director is unlikely to be convinced by an appeal to values of social justice and an over-worked lecturer is unlikely to be convinced by an argument about the need of the institution to increase income. With resource managers we need to use the language of accountancy; with lecturers the language of pedagogy and social justice may be more effective (though we recognize that, of course, there may be exceptions).

Institutional cultures

The culture (or cultures) of institutions differ. The 'official' culture can vary from being openly committed to widening participation as a central mission, through being an 'entrepreneurial' university, to being a 'centre of excellence' – from inclusion to elitism. Or all three may collide. Fenwick outlines the tension between her university's image as an internationally renowned research university with high entry qualifications and the desire to make entry easier for students from disadvantaged backgrounds. She also argues that a traditional research university is unlikely to have prioritized developing relationships with local schools and colleges since it does not see itself as having a local focus.

Below the official culture of an institution there often lies the unofficial management culture which, in the current climate, is usually a reflection of financial pressures the institution is facing. One public face of this can be 'don't bring me problems; bring me solutions', which mainly operates as a euphemism for 'solve the problem with no additional resources'. This can lead to unintended consequences and is described by Dinsdale in Chapter 16. In her project to give voice to widening participation students, particularly around higher education progression, she found that guidance provided by higher education institutions has become 'partial and competitive'. It is perceived as such by potential students and so becomes counter-productive. This is despite a discourse of impartiality at official mission level.

Additionally there will be numerous sub-cultures and alternative cultures operating within institutions which, in any particular situation, may be as powerful as or even more powerful than the management culture. It is important to be aware of competing and contradictory cultures within the institution and possibly within the senior management. Any senior management is likely to be struggling with a number of issues. Beckett, who argues for high-quality higher education advice and guidance in the sixth form, points out in Chapter 14 that it cannot be assumed that management recognition of an issue ensures that it becomes a management priority. In Chapter 17, Harding, in her account of a Sussex cross-sector collaborative project, identifies the problem of relying on managers for dissemination of information, even for an officially approved project. From the other end of the spectrum, Dinsdale identifies the issue of student voices within the organizational culture and the extent to which student voices have any power.

Resistance

We also have resistance to change. In some cases this is simply due to a lack of understanding that can be resolved. In Chapter 13 Lawley examines the benefits of 'compact' schemes. They identify how some compact staff were resistant to new types of students because of their lack of information about changes in qualifications and the curriculum in each other's sectors. Harding explains that some higher education staff had difficulty in designing activities for year 10 pupils on a visit since they had limited knowledge of that level of work. However, sometimes opposition goes deeper. Are those who resist motivated by values or resources? In other words, are they more inclined to a 'sorting' rather than developmental model of higher education, seeing the role of higher education as being to measure and exclude rather than create talent in a more inclusive way (Dore, 1997)? Or does their reluctance come from a pedagogic value that resists expansion of student numbers because it decreases their valued opportunities for small group and one-to-one teaching? Or is it simply resistance to an initiative that staff see as being yet more work?

In Chapter 12 Jeffrey outlines various forms of resistance met by the black student mentoring project including a clash of values over the best way to deal with disadvantage in black communities. Another tension in the case study came from the fact that the project was exclusively for black students, which some staff found problematic. Fenwick points out that at her university it was important to avoid any hint of 'lowering standards' if the project was to have a positive reception. In his case study on Access (see Chapter 15), Carey indicates the importance of higher education being both willing and able to adapt its cultural values and practices to meet more complex student needs.

Another source of resistance comes, as Fenwick points out, from staff in institutions where individual professional status comes from research output rather than access and progression initiatives. Initiatives based on value conflict or clashes of material interest are a source of particular difficulty. As Dinsdale comments, practicalities are easier to change than attitudes and Lawley identifies the difficulties in trying to get staff to think 'outside the box'. If thinking outside the box also creates an interest or value conflict, perhaps we have to settle for working around resistance.

Of course, for any individual and situation more than one motivational factor may be operating within the same person or group and around the same issues. Any sense that one individual is totally on board or totally resistant, or that any particular part of the initiative is met with complete commitment, compliance or resistance, would be an over-simplification. It is important to avoid an over-simplified classification of individuals or even patterns of behaviour. We are likely to find frequently what Bowe, Ball and Gold (1992) call the tension between 'service and survival'; in other words, tensions between budget requirements and educational values. Jeffrey cites the loss of opportunities for visits and cultural activities as the funding for his project dried up.

An additional complexity in a number of the case studies is that the project involved more than one institution across schools, further and higher education. Lawley outlines the difficulties coming from initially very different ways of working and sectors' annual work cycles as well as incompatibility in data systems. Dinsdale and Beckett foreground the historical lack of communication and understanding between institutions in different sectors and Fenwick and Lawley highlight confusion around qualifications. There is also the more fundamental issue, outlined by Carey, of persuading higher education to change to meet the needs of the more diverse student population rather than attempting to mould the students to fit existing practices.

Institutional structures

The structure of the organization and how to build structural alliances is important. This starts with identifying the extent to which formal structures have real power. Is a particular committee, or the academic board, really a powerful decision-making body or does it rubber stamp decisions agreed elsewhere? If so, then where are the decisions made, or deliberately not made (Morley, 2000)? How do you get access to this grouping? Dinsdale achieved this when she identified the importance, in her situation, of the Admissions Committee and was invited to become a member. What is the role of the formal senior management team meetings in relation to an initiative? Is there one key powerful senior manager? Howard Jeffrey attributes importance to the support for the black student mentoring project from the then principal. Where should the initiative be located structurally to be most effective and have the greatest chance of being more than lip service? High-profile structural location and relationships can give a project symbolic power. Lawley points out the advantages of inviting key partner institutions to join the university's Board of Governors. Jeffrey identifies the value of significant media publicity, association with well-known multi-national corporations and government figures, and symbolic awards such as the Queen's Anniversary prize and scholarships.

Some structural problems can be easily resolved, as Fenwick illustrates, through provision of bursaries and access to halls of residence. Dinsdale describes practical improvements such as crèche facilities at open days, earlier provision of timetables and improved information, all of which make her institution more accessible to students with family responsibilities. Other problems require longer-term structural solutions. We noted above the importance of identifying where decisions are made and how to have input to the decision-making process. Local situations vary and there may be reasons to locate widening participation projects in the marketing unit, with student services or within the main academic structures. In each case the location will affect the power to achieve the aims. Beckett argues for the importance of having key posts in support of access and progression, such as a higher education adviser, in the formal structure of schools and colleges. He also argues for the importance of this post having appropriate status and time.

Resources

This leads on to an analysis of the role of resources, including time, money and physical space (locations, both structural and physical, send out a message about power). The resources needed vary. Beckett identifies the importance of administrative support and an information resource base as well as a key post in his situation. We need to identify what resources are required, who controls them, what pressures the resource managers are under and what their main motivation is likely to be. Any innovation requires ways of accessing various types of resource. In some cases we have to recognize and work within a situation of very limited resources but, as Dinsdale illustrates, it may be possible to come up with low-cost and sustainable improvements.

A common problem is the temporary nature of a resource and the difficulty of achieving continuation. Much has been written on the problems of one-off project funding (Kennedy, 1997). It may be useful as a way of getting started and there are some clear advantages. Jeffrey identifies the independence of mission and thinking that external funding allows, and Lawley points out that being a special project gives clear objectives to be monitored. In the longer term, however, the often more difficult role of embedding in an annual budget has to be managed, as Jeffrey illustrates. An analysis, therefore, has to include not only how to get the resource but also how to keep it and ensure that it is embedded in core funding. Harding identifies a related issue with external projects, which is their short-term nature. This leads to short-term and part-time employment patterns for project officers. If a longer term aim is met by a series of short-term projects this leads to the project infrastructure and project team having to be 'constantly reinvented and re-formed' which is 'time-consuming and energy-sapping'. It also means that longer-term strategies like the Sussex Coastal Highway are never fully evaluated for their long-term effectiveness. At institutional level both Jeffrey and Harding indicate that embedding with core funding is often difficult to achieve. Dinsdale makes the point that time limited projects tend to be on the periphery of the institution, or, as Jeffrey states, they are 'bolted on' rather than integrated into main structures.

Forming alliances

Success is likely to require structural (and cultural) alliances with other parts of an institution. The importance of wide alliances should not be ignored and Jeffrey indicates that, in retrospect, the project would have benefited from a wider network of support rather than simply relying on the albeit very strong support of the principal. Beckett points out that the development of networks and alliances, especially across institutions, 'demand[s] time and a pro-active approach' and Dinsdale indicates the importance of these alliances being real rather than formal. Effective alliances between sectors, Carey argues, enable the introduction of curriculum changes, flexible provision and new pedagogic and assessment methods.

It is useful to note the key success factors in building alliances. These are likely to be an understanding of the values and job pressures (in particular, time) of potential allies and a recognition that cooperation is a two-way process and that building up a reputation as reliable and providing a high-quality service is likely to make you a preferred partner. This is a route to 'joined up thinking'.

Learning from the school sector

Of course, none of this is easy. There is an extensive literature on trying to achieve organizational change, with a significant strand devoted to the application of this theory to educational institutions. Morrison (1998) provides a thorough account of this and of its impact on education including, amongst other things, the influence of Japanese quality models, organization theory, key theories of leadership and the impact of post-modern conceptions of the world. In the education sector the extensive school improvement literature is an attempt to achieve change in the compulsory sector. This literature is often ignored, consciously or unconsciously, by those trying to achieve change in further and higher education. This may indicate a failure to realize how much post-16 education has to learn from ideas developed in the compulsory sector.

The school improvement literature is well outlined and critiqued by Harris and Bennett (2001). A seminal work grappling with the problem of educational change is Fullan (2001), which argues that successful implementation of change depends on a number of factors. The first of these is the characteristics of the change including clarity, need, practicality and complexity. A second factor is 'the social conditions of change', the local situation and its constraints and opportunities. The third factor is the role of external policies and pressures. Fullan also outlines problems in achieving continuation. These include achieving pro-active participation and a sense of ownership by the participants, the need for changes at both behavioural and normative level and the necessity of achieving the correct balance of pressure and support in pushing forward on the initiative.

Bascia and Hargreaves, again writing from the school sector, offer another perspective which they call the 'darker side' of education reform (Bascia and Hargreaves, 2000: 3), which impacts on the lives of those participating both willingly and unwillingly. For Bascia and Hargreaves the main question is 'Why does educational reform so often fail?' (2000: 4). They suggest two main reasons. The first is a failure to understand the complexity of the role of educators and the second is a failure to recognize the importance of external structural factors and the way they shape and inhibit efforts at reform.

Bowe, Ball and Gold (1992) identify two key flaws in many attempts to achieve change. The first is having a single change focus, which militates against joined up thinking, and the second is neglect of institutional history, thus failing to recognize micropolitical factors. They point out that change is rarely achieved without conflict and is seldom politically neutral; some interests are advanced by it and others damaged. Equally, innovations are interpreted and responded to according to the diverse interests and outlook of those involved. There are a number of examples of this in the case studies that follow. Sometimes change comes from above and sometimes from below but both are hard to achieve.

The 'problem' with equal opportunities

Widening participation is the latest signifier in higher education for the concept that has also been known as equal opportunities, equality of opportunity or social justice. It acknowledges that there are social groups that have been denied access to certain benefits of society. These groups, often thought of as 'the disadvantaged', are mainly groups excluded on the basis of class or ethnicity. There is still exclusion based on gender but this is reflected in the pattern of entry to different subject areas rather than entry *per se*. Problems of inclusion faced by students with disabilities still persist. We have to recognize that moves to combat social exclusion touch very deep values and material interests. Such moves challenge, at a fundamental level, the way institutions, and all those within them, operate. Equal opportunities also challenges established social power relationships and therefore vested interests. It is worth remembering that this is not new and a brief glance at some of the 1980s and early 1990s initiatives show the various approaches that were taken.

One strand failed to problematize introducing radical change. A Commission for Racial Equality (CRE) manual on further education and equality (1995) lists as its key points the following:

> Equality of Opportunity needs to be built into a college's strategic plans, mission statements and charters. It should be monitored thoroughly and systematically so that achievements can be identified and shortfalls remedied.
>
> Equal Opportunity initiatives should be led by senior management, with imagination and commitment and given the highest profile.
>
> Successful pursuit of equality of opportunity will enhance the performance of the college as a whole. (CRE/EOC, 1995: 7)

In the quotations above there is no suggestion that implementation may face barriers.

Another strand, an example of which is Managing the Delivery of Guidance in Colleges Appendix 2 (FEU, 1994), acknowledges that implementation needs to recognize *external* influences such as national policy, financial imperatives for both students and institutions, the role of a performance indicator culture and the part played by other key players, but it offers little on factors inside the institution. An earlier strand, arguably coming before the arrival of new public management (Deem, 1998) and exemplified in an ILEA guide to its anti-sexist policy (ILEA, 1985), appreciates more of the difficulties. This indicates, in particular, the need for discussion in order for participants to achieve ownership, but goes on to a standard linear model of developing a policy/planning implementation/action plan (later ones included monitoring). These are all aimed at change from above. When we look at change from below (ILEA, 1990), the difficulties begin to emerge in a way that many of us will recognize. Karahali, in her introduction, comments to those working in this area:

> I hope you do not get so sucked in by a system that needs a named person for each area ie the institutional sexism that leaves you feeling isolated and personally responsible, to a greater or lesser extent, for this institutional sexism in your college and wear yourself into the ground trying to fight it. (ILEA, 1990: 2)

More than ten years later this still resonates. We know all this yet we still find it very hard to make change happen.

Micropolitics

We need to go back to micropolitics to help us understand the best way to proceed. Morley (1999: 2) describes a micropolitical perspective as recognizing 'control and conflict as essential and contradictory bases of organizational life'. Ball (1994) sees this control and conflict as happening at all levels within an organization and also at national policy levels. Micropolitics at institutional level may be 'replaying a larger scale scenario of educational politics's and 'Teachers' careers, institutional micropolitics and state power and policies are all intertwined in a complex process of changes in patterns of control, relationships and values' (Ball, 1994: 64).

McInnis (2000) argues that changes in teaching and assessment methods and more diverse student bodies can create pressures for lecturers which undermine fundamental work motivation, and that these are experienced differently according to stage in career, type of institution and discipline. These pressures are usually a result of the rapid expansion of higher education, declining resource and the development of new public management (Ozga, 1998; Deem, 1998). This is related to the marketization of higher education both as a major export industry and as the vehicle for ensuring international competitiveness (Lafferty and Fleming, 2000), and a consequent crisis in university identity and resultant reformulation of academic professionalism (Marginson, 2000). Wilmott (1995) relates these pressures to the commodification of academic labour resulting from political and economic pressure to tighten the link between capitalist values and the organization of academic labour.

Ball (1987) identifies key micropolitical concepts as including power, goal diversity, ideological disputation, conflict, interests, political activity and control. He also identifies as a key issue the extent to which micropolitical activity is conscious or intuitive, strategic or short term, advancing group or individual interests, led by material interests or values and dependent on the particular situation. Both Ball (1987) and Blase (1991) emphasize that the institutional level interacts in a dialectical way with the level of national structural and cultural factors.

The role of power

Micropolitical analysis, although including many concepts (see above), is essentially about power. We have suggested tools to analyse why some innovations work and others fail. Power is a complex concept. Hoyle (1982) distinguishes between power based on authority and power based on influence. He argues the importance of the latter in any micropolitical analysis:

> Influence differs from authority in having a number of sources in the organisation, in being embedded in the actual relationships between groups rather than located in an abstract legal source, and it is not 'fixed' but is variable and operates through bargaining, manipulation, exchange and so forth. (Hoyle, 1982: 90)

We take a Foucauldian position. Foucault argues that 'we must construct an analysis of power that no longer takes law as a model and a code' (Foucault, 1998: 90). In institutions we cannot assume that in practice power lies where it is supposed to lie according to formal codes. Observation of how governing bodies in many further education colleges operate, with a lack of real authority, evidences this. Instead power now operates by techniques of 'normalization' in a multiplicity of relationships and as a process which 'through ceaseless struggle and confrontations, transforms, strengthens and reverses them' (1998: 92) with disjunctions and contradictions. Normalization establishes a particular view of the world as normal and allows those dissenting to be labelled as 'dinosaurs' and regarded as in some way refusing to recognize what is portrayed as reality. One of the key methods of 'normalizing' the views of those with power is through discourse, the language they use. The language takes on an apparent neutrality that is difficult to challenge while actually supporting a deeply politicized position. This is what for Foucault is discourse that normalizes the regime of power. Shore and Selwyn (1998) have analysed management discourse in relation to the marketization of higher education including terms such as 'cost effectiveness', 'value for money', 'efficiency', 'performance review' and 'performance related pay'. It would be easy for those of us who are practitioners to develop similar lists around the two great 'normalizing' ideas of standards and financial imperatives.

Foucault also argues that power is mobile and there is no easy distinction between those with and without power (Foucault, 1998: 94). Power struggles happen everywhere and both change and move since 'where there is power there is resistance', which may also be mobile and transitory (1998: 95–96). This means that there is always space to operate micropolitically since there are always competing discourses. Shore and Wright (2000) argue that one form of resistance is to re-appropriate key words and develop alternative meanings for them.

Motivation

The other crucial factor is the motivation of those with power, whose support is necessary for implementation. We have argued above that motivation might come from values, individual or institutional self-interest or compliance. Maguire (2001) identifies the role of both personal identity and the ideological dimension in relation to inner city teachers from working class backgrounds. Trowler (1998) argues that the values of academics in higher education are an important factor in the social processes on policy implementation in the academy and that managerialism often fails to recognize this. It is sometimes argued that we need to settle for a large degree of compliance, that many of those involved will cooperate because they have to or it is in their interest to appear to give support. In the short term this may work but the danger is that when the person driving the innovation moves on, the roots are not there and the project withers.

Conclusion

To achieve successful and embedded innovation we need to recognize the motivational factors of all concerned. We also need to understand the official and unofficial cultures that are operating, know where power lies structurally, have a way of accessing resources of all kinds, as well as understand the different discourses and use them. Additionally we need to form structural alliances across the institution. For example, any attempt by marketing and school liaison units to bring in students from groups traditionally excluded is unlikely to have any long-term success if the support systems are not in place and the curriculum and teaching and assessment methods do not adjust in recognition of the changing student body – a form of Biggs' (1996) constructive alignment. Finally we need to recognize that time is a tight resource and we should not plan to use up other people's. None of this is easy but it offers a route to genuine long-term increase in access and participation.

References

Ball, S J (1987) *The Micropolitics of the School*, Routledge, London

Ball, S J (1991) Power, conflict, micropolitics and all that! in *Doing Educational Research*, ed G Walford, Routledge, London

Ball, S J (1994) *Educational Reform: A critical and post-structural approach*, Open University Press, Buckingham

Ball, S J and Goodson, I (1985) *Teachers' Lives and Careers*, Falmer Press, London

Bascia, N and Hargreaves, A (2000) *The Sharp Edge of Educational Change*, London: Routledge Falmer, London

Biggs, J (1996) Enhancing teaching through constructive alignment, *Higher Education*, **32**, pp 347–64

Blase, J (1991) The micropolitical perspective, in *The Politics of Life in Schools: Power, conflict, and cooperation*, ed J Blase, Sage, London

Bowe, R, Ball, S J, with Gold, A (1992) *Reforming Education and Changing Schools*, Routledge, London

Commission for Racial Equality/Equal Opportunities Commission (CRE/EOC) (1995) *Further Education and Equality: A manager's manual*, CRE, London

Deem, R (1998) 'New managerialism' and higher education: the management of performances and cultures in the universities in the United Kingdom, *International Studies in the Sociology of Education*, **8** (1), pp 47–70

Dore, R (1997) *The Diploma Disease*, Institute of Education, London

FEU (1994) *Managing the Delivery of Guidance in Colleges*, FEU/ED, London

Foucault, M (1998) *The Will to Knowledge: The history of sexuality*, Penguin, London

Fullan, M (2001) *The New Meaning of Educational Change* (3rd edition), Routledge Falmer, London

Gronn, P (1986) Politics, power and the management of schools, in *The World Yearbook of Education 1986: The management of schools*, ed E Hoyle, Kogan Page, London

Hargreaves, A (1983) The politics of administrative convenience, in *Contemporary Education Policy*, eds J Ahier and M Flude, Croom Helm, London

Hargreaves, A (1994) *Changing Teachers, Changing Times*, Cassell, London

Harris, A and Bennett, N (2001) *School Effectiveness and School Improvement*, Continuum, London

Hoyle, E (1982) Micropolitics of educational organisations, *Educational Management and Administration*, **10**, pp 87–98

ILEA (1985) *Implementing the ILEA's Anti-Sexist Policy: A guide for colleges of further education*, ILEA, London

ILEA (1990) *Working the System: Gender equality work in further education colleges*, ILEA, London

Kennedy, H (1997) *Learning Works: Widening participation in further education*, Coventry, FEFC

Lafferty, G and Fleming, G (2000) The restructuring of academic work in Australia: power, management and gender, *British Journal of Sociology of Education*, **21** (2), pp 257–67

Maguire, M (2001) The cultural formation of teachers' class consciousness: teachers in the inner city, *Journal of Education Policy*, **16** (4), pp 315–31

Marginson, S (2000) Rethinking academic work in the global era, *Journal of Higher Education Policy and Management*, **22** (1), pp 23–35

McInnis, C (2000) Changing academic work roles: the everyday realities challenging quality in teaching, *Quality in Higher Education*, **6** (2), pp 143–52

Morley, L (1999) *Organising Feminisms: The micropolitics of the Academy*, Macmillan, London

Morley, L (2000) The micropolitics of gender in the learning society, *Higher Education in Europe*, **25** (2), pp 229–35

Morrison, K (1998) *Management Theories for Educational Change*, Paul Chapman, London

Ozga, J (1998) The entrepreneurial researcher: reformations of identity in the research market place, *International Studies in the Sociology of Education*, **8** (2), pp 143–53

Shore, C and Selwyn, T (1998) The marketisation of higher education: management, discourse and the politics of performance, in *The New Higher Education*, eds D Jary and M Parker, Staffordshire University Press, Stoke on Trent

Shore, C and Wright, S (2000) Coercive accountability: the rise of the audit culture in higher education, in *Audit Cultures: Anthropological studies in accountability, ethics and the academy*, ed M Strathern, Routledge, London

Trowler, P R (1998) What managerialists forget: higher education credit frameworks and managerialist ideology, *International Studies in the Sociology of Education*, **8** (1), pp 91–109

Wilmott, H (1995) Managing the academics: commodification and control in the development of university education in the UK, *Human Relations*, **48** (9), pp 993–1027

11

Reflections on Widening Access to Medical Schools: The Case of Southampton

Angela Fenwick

Medical schools have been under attack for a number of years for continuing to select their students from particular groups whilst appearing to disadvantage others. McManus' influential report (1997), in which UCAS data released by the Council of Heads of Medical Schools (CHMS) were formally analysed, did not indicate that medical schools were, on the whole, disadvantaging applicants from lower social classes.[1] Male applicants and those from ethnic minorities were more likely to be disadvantaged during the selection process and this was indicated by the difference between the percentage of these groups applying and the percentage being given a place. Following McManus' article, CHMS requested all medical schools to look at equal opportunity issues in their selection process and draw up action plans to cover these. Medical schools are now required to monitor their applications and offers to identify any possible bias in the selection process.

Perhaps the most central issue in terms of access and participation is the over-representation of applicants and entrants who are from social classes I and II: significantly more people apply from these two groups.[2] This is apparent at Southampton School of Medicine where these groups have constituted around 70–80 per cent of entrants for the last four years, although this figure appears to be decreasing. That under-representation of people from social classes III to V might not be considered a 'good thing' in higher education as a whole has been discussed elsewhere in this book. However, in relation to medicine, the issues are brought into sharp focus. It can be argued that the medical profession has a responsibility to train doctors who are representative of the population as a whole in order that the pool of doctors can meet the health needs of society. Indeed this is a principle articulated by the CHMS (1998): 'The social, cultural and ethnic backgrounds of medical graduates should reflect broadly the diversity of those they are called upon to serve.' Hamilton, from Durham University, has also speculated that training people from less advantaged backgrounds may confer two additional benefits. Firstly, graduates may return to practise in areas in which they have grown up and secondly, their presence in medical schools could serve to raise the profile of issues such as inequalities in health for all students (Powis, 2001).

If medical schools are to incorporate the principle set out by the CHMS then they need to introduce schemes that attempt to redress the imbalance in the social class profile of medical students. Different medical schools are currently adopting different strategies to widen access. One approach is to try and encourage high achievers from disadvantaged groups to apply for medicine. Given that we know that pupils make early choices about career preferences, a possible strategy is to target these groups at an early age. For example, Sheffield is attempting to attract people through the compact scheme and an early outreach scheme. The early outreach scheme is trying to identify potential students in secondary schools as early as year 9, and then, from year 11, to provide advice and support for work experience, applications and interview (Angel and Johnson, 2000). Glasgow University is operating a scheme aimed at pupils between ages 10 and 18 in local schools with low progression rates which introduces them to higher education. The medical school participates in sessions on what medicine as a career might be like (Lumsden, 2001).

Whilst such schemes can be viewed positively in that they may help raise pupils' aspirations and encourage more high achievers from disadvantaged groups to see medicine as a possible career option, they may in the end have little impact on percentage figures. As Dearing acknowledged (NCIHE, 1997) and as Clark (2000) reiterates, 'The main factor influencing patterns of participation in higher education is achievement in qualifications required for entry.' This is compounded in medicine as it is a subject that requires applicants to achieve high grades in the traditional qualifications.

The School of Medicine at Southampton operates within the context of a 'research-led' university, competing to be regarded as one of the 'best' universities in the country. In the league tables, which were constructed following the results of the 2001 Research Assessment Exercise, Southampton was either placed 10th or 11th in the country depending on the newspaper reporting the figures. This was hailed as a major success, particularly as research is the primary mission of the institution. Two out of three subject areas submitted from the School of Medicine gained a grade 5 score. The School also achieved a score of 24 in its 1999 Quality Assessment Exercise. However, the University is not performing particularly well in terms of widening participation. An analysis of the HEFCE performance indicators shows the University operating below its benchmark figures in 1999/2000 for all the categories relating to the participation of under-represented groups in higher education (University of Southampton, 2001).

The Widening Access to Medicine Project (WAMP) in the School of Medicine was set up following a working group that looked at strategies for widening participation. It is currently overseen by a core team of six people, of which I am one, with a larger Steering Group that also comprises further education college partners in the project. We are at the early stages of development and in this chapter I outline what we have done to date and explore some of the issues that are arising from my experience of working on the project.

The project team set itself a series of objectives as part of its strategy to widen access and these are outlined in Figure 11.1. We were aware that the high academic entrance requirements were a serious barrier to our target group of people from lower socio-economic backgrounds. We knew we might encourage applications by lowering the academic requirements; however, simply lowering the academic requirements for a particular group was not an option for a number of reasons. First, we would be accused of introducing positive discrimination. Secondly, league tables for universities and medical schools use qualification points or A level scores as an indicator of quality. Any attempt to lower the academic requirement was unlikely to be acceptable especially as, at this time, pressure was being applied to raise the A level requirement from grades ABB to AAB.[3] Thirdly, we were wary of being accused of 'lowering standards': we wanted any initiative to be been seen positively by both students and staff in the School.

- To identify and target currently under-represented groups, particularly pre-18-year-olds from socio-economic groups III, IV and V who have been identified by their schools and colleges to have not yet realized their full potential.

- To collaborate with local and other further education colleges in providing an accessible pathway for the target group into medicine.

- To ensure the pathway provides the support, guidance, skills and knowledge required by individuals to enable successful participation and progression to the School of Medicine.

- To provide a range of exit routes from the pathway that matched individual career choices and potential to succeed.

- To raise aspirations, particularly of those still at school who might otherwise be excluded entry to medicine due to their background or lack of educational opportunity.

Figure 11.1 Objectives of Widening Access to Medicine Project (WAMP)

We chose to try and meet our objectives by adopting a number of strategies. One of these was to develop a pre-degree level O course, starting in 2002/3 at New College, a faculty of the University with a specific remit for widening participation. As we are expecting applicants for this course to study for an additional year, the academic entrance requirements can be lower than for entrance onto the Bachelor of Medicine (BM) course. The aim is for the level O course to help students to achieve the same academic standards and non-academic requirements as those applicants applying directly to the BM course. The entrance requirements for the level O and the BM programme are set out in Figure 11.2.

In order to select students onto the level O course from the target group, the School has introduced a set of screening criteria which candidates must meet before being considered for selection (see Figure 11.3). This was especially important in view of the fact that the inability to target young people from lower socio-economic groups has been identified as one of the problems associated with widening access schemes (CVCP, 1998). Selection for entrance into the School takes place prior to the level O course; once selected, students have automatic entrance to the School as long as the learning outcomes of the level O course at New College are achieved at a satisfactory level. The School has ring-fenced 20 places for students coming through this route, 10 per cent of the total intake. By 2004, when the intake will rise to 240, 30 places will be ring-fenced. This ring-fencing of places in the School was achieved by asking for these additional places

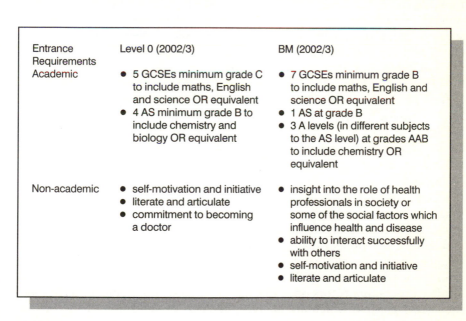

Entrance Requirements Academic	Level 0 (2002/3)	BM (2002/3)
	• 5 GCSEs minimum grade C to include maths, English and science OR equivalent • 4 AS minimum grade B to include chemistry and biology OR equivalent	• 7 GCSEs minimum grade B to include maths, English and science OR equivalent • 1 AS at grade B • 3 A levels (in different subjects to the AS level) at grades AAB to include chemistry OR equivalent
Non-academic	• self-motivation and initiative • literate and articulate • commitment to becoming a doctor	• insight into the role of health professionals in society or some of the social factors which influence health and disease • ability to interact successfully with others • self-motivation and initiative • literate and articulate

Figure 11.2 Academic and non-academic entrance requirements for the level O and the BM programmes

Applicants would normally be expected to meet two of the following:

- Resident in an area with a postcode that entitles institutions to claim the widening participation funding uplift, or a member of a travelling family.
- First generation applicant at HE.
- Parent/s or guardian in receipt of means tested benefit.
- Living alone without independent financial support or in residential care/hostel accommodation.
- Eligible to receive Education Maintenance Award or similar grant.

Figure 11.3 Screening criteria for level O

within recent bids to HEFCE for additional medical student numbers which formed part of the government drive to increase the number of doctors. By doing this we are able to counter any accusations that might be made that we were taking places away from high academic achievers.

The School does not normally interview school-leaver applicants for the BM programme: evidence for achievement of the non-academic and academic criteria is gained from the UCAS form. We are aware that schools and colleges, particularly those with high progression rates to higher education, are likely to coach students on how to fill in application forms. Students might also get advice from family and friends; and furthermore, some students have more access to activities which carry with them more status and cultural capital (Gamarnikow and Green, 1999). In view of this we decided to drop two of the non-academic criteria (insight into the role of health professionals in society and the ability to interact with others) for entrance onto the level O. These criteria now form learning outcomes for the level O course and were replaced by a criterion asking for a commitment to becoming a doctor. We also decided to interview qualified applicants to enable this group to supply evidence of achievement for the non-academic criteria, from both the application form and from an interview.

The level O course itself is structured around two areas: units in Human Structure and Function and units in Professional Practice. The latter are organized around projects on health and illness and involve work placements. Developing appropriate support mechanisms has been a particular concern for the project team. We have designed a support network which includes the following: personal tutors at New College; health professional mentors located in the work placements who we hope might also become students' personal tutors once they enter the BM programme; and student mentoring groups, which are likely to become an extension of the current student-led system of peer support ('student families') in the medical school. Our intention is that this group of students might be at an advantage compared with other students once they enter the BM programme: they will be familiar with both the university environment and different health care environments. The level 0 course will also have prepared them specifically for the BM programme in terms of both content and assessment methods, giving them, we hope, an academic advantage and boosting confidence.

An important plank of our strategy was to work closely with further education colleges. We originally involved three Southampton colleges – Southampton City, Taunton and Itchen – as well as Lewisham from London. We have since involved an additional two partner colleges – Totton and South Downs – and may involve more in the future. The formal link with these colleges has enabled us to gain access to the institutions and to publicize the route into medicine, identify potential students, as well as draw on their expertise in the development of the project. For example, the further education colleges helped to identify equivalent qualifications to the standard entry requirements of GCSEs and AS levels.

In addition, we appointed an outreach worker to work closely with the further education colleges and with local comprehensive schools to help raise aspirations and publicize the pathways through a whole range of activities. These included talks in schools and colleges, a two-day further education student conference, and a summer day-school for year 10 pupils.

The project has thrown up a whole series of problems, tensions and dilemmas at a number of different levels. One of the most pressing, currently, is recruitment of students onto the level 0 course for 2002/3. The School can accept up to 20 students and New College's current minimum requirement for running the course is 10 students. The original deadline for applications was October 2001 and we received only 16. Of these, a number were rejected on the grounds of not being able to meet the academic requirements, not meeting the non-academic requirements at interview, or were classified as being overseas. We may currently be able to give an offer to less than 10 students and there is no guarantee that all these will accept or choose to come in October 2002. We have extended the deadline for applications but the small number of applicants to whom we can make offers seriously jeopardizes the project. We originally focused our attentions on school leavers but are now also trying to encourage older people up to the age of 39 to consider applying through this route if they have met the screening criteria.[4]

There are likely to be a variety of reasons for the low numbers of applications. Medicine as a career does not look particularly attractive given the recent spate of negative publicity the profession has received. Many local schools and pupils are still not aware of this new pathway into medicine. Ball, Maguire and Macrae (2000) indicate that the reasons behind young people's career choices are complex and cover structural, academic and personal factors. Foskett and Hemsley-Brown (2000) in a report on how young people perceive a career in medicine found that it was known as a subject requiring high qualifications. Young people who were not part of families where members pursued a professional occupation lacked confidence in their ability to achieve these, were reluctant to stay in education for long periods of time and were more concerned about the financial consequences of studying in higher education. Addressing these issues is a long-term project and not one that the School can address on its own.

There have been lessons to learn from the selection process. The screening criteria were introduced as a way of trying to ensure that we meet our target group. However, they were difficult to construct both because there was a concern that whatever we did we were unlikely to get it 'right', and because it was an uncomfortable process to engage in – equal opportunity projects are usually about including people rather than explicitly excluding people. Applicants were asked to tick boxes next to each of the screening criteria on the application form and, as we did not want to engage in the process of classifying applicants once we had received their application, we asked the colleges to sign to say that this information was correct. In effect, we have left the screening process to the applicants and to the colleges.

Operating this screening process may be difficult in the future. Currently applications for the level O course are not made through UCAS allowing us, during the pilot, to keep some level of control over how far we extend the scheme. If we go through UCAS it is unlikely that we will be able to operate the screening process as the course would need to be available to everyone in the EU, and would have to be open to anyone who applied. Most of the colleges involved currently had an input into the development of the screening criteria and agreed on the process. The more we open up the project to other colleges – which looks like an essential step in order to encourage more applications – the less likely it is that this process will be able to be sustained. At this stage it is unclear how we will keep the level O as an access route for our target group.

When we were developing the academic requirements for the course we were aware that pupils from lower socio-economic groups were likely to apply with non-traditional qualifications. We were therefore keen to stress that the standard requirements of 5 GCSEs and 4 AS levels were to act as a benchmark. As previously mentioned, the further education colleges advised about possible equivalent qualifications; for example, key skill levels and subjects and AVCEs and National Diplomas. However, perhaps because of our lack of experience in this area, the selectors in the School found it difficult to work out whether applicants were academically qualified.[5] Few presented a neat set of qualifications: some had taken their AS levels on to A2 level, we were presented with access modules that we hadn't anticipated and became aware that some applicants were unable to study certain science modules because the college didn't offer them. Straightforward points equivalents are problematic because of the specific subject requirements and the need to show we are not attempting to lower academic standards. We have responded in a number of ways: looking at each individual student's package of qualifications and asking for further agreement on possible equivalents and concessions from the Selection Sub-committee where it seemed appropriate. We also held a meeting for the panel of selectors to finalize selection decisions. We invited the outreach worker and a Steering Group representative from a further education college with experience of working with a variety of post-16 qualifications; this meeting was invaluable and served as staff development for School of Medicine selectors.

If we were able to offer a very flexible curriculum in the level 0, we might be able to construct more flexible academic entrance requirements; for example, accept an applicant without chemistry and offer this in some way as part of an individual learning plan. However, it may be some time before this approach would be seen as acceptable both in terms of the possible resource implications and because of the context of working within this type of institution.

Working within a 'traditional' university on a project of this kind has been difficult in a number of respects. On one level, the University has been very interested in what we are doing as it is a new initiative and fits in with its Widening Participation Strategy as well as contributing to New College's specific widening participation remit. On the other hand, however, it has been difficult sometimes to get support and guidance from the University, precisely because it is a new initiative for them. As Southampton is essentially a 'selector' institution that has a mission to compete internationally in research, making connections and building relationships at a local level with schools and further education colleges has not been one of the University's priorities in the past. The project's outreach worker has found it difficult to establish relationships with some schools, sometimes because they have not returned calls or answered letters. We are now considering additional ways to build these links; for example, by making contacts with schools through the further education colleges.

A practical consequence of the project being located in a traditional University is that the level 0 does not carry with it any academic award: the University has no provision for level 0. This essentially means that the level 0 has no currency outside of the University: any student who completes the course but who wants to apply to another institution will have no portable qualification, despite having successfully completed a year's course at a university. We are currently waiting to see whether the University finds a solution to this problem. An alternative solution would be to get an outside body such as the Open College Network to validate the course.

Some more minor problems have been more easily resolved. For example, the University guarantees places in halls for first-year students. When we highlighted lack of accommodation as a problem for level 0 students the University extended this entitlement to ensure that they could have a place in halls for their first year and again during their first year of the BM, if they required it.

A major anxiety for the project team has been the lack of government grants for students. If students are unsure about funding themselves through a three-year degree, the five-year BM will look considerably more daunting and, starting with a level 0, this becomes a six-year commitment. We have attempted to find sources of funding for both hardship funds and bursaries for the level 0 students (and this has also highlighted the needs of others on the BM). The University has agreed to extend the opportunity bursaries to a five-year period, raising this bursary to £3,500. The level 0 curriculum has also been organized so that students can work on some days of the week if they wish or need to. Although we may make progress in these different areas there is an urgent need for student finance to be addressed at national level. Whilst this government is now reconsidering its policy on student grants, any positive developments in this area are unlikely to be in place for the start of the level 0 course in 2002/03.

Working within the School and University on a project such as this feels like being at the centre of a number of contradictions. On the one hand, the School positions itself positively in the arena of widening access to medicine, whilst at the same time raising the A level grade requirements. The University is seeking to strengthen its Widening Participation Strategy but the focus for development is on New College, one faculty, rather than working in an integrated fashion across the University. It also required us to ask applicants for a fourth AS level. Engaging in this type of development work, which is incredibly time-consuming, takes time away from undertaking research which, as already outlined, is the primary mission of the University and which carries more prestige and weight in relation to promotion. Southampton's new Vice-Chancellor was reported in *The Times Higher Education Supplement* (28 September 2001) as questioning whether widening participation should be part of the policy of a research university. Given current constraints on higher education institutions it could be argued that this is a valid position for a senior manager of a research university to take. However, if it is not within the remit of institutions such as this, where does the responsibility lie for training doctors for the NHS and society?

The project is still at an early stage in its development and we are yet to see a first cohort of students or see many tangible benefits from the outreach work and partnerships with the further education colleges. In some respects whatever we are able to achieve will be only a small step towards widening access to medicine. However, the 1999/2000 percentage of first-year students from social classes III to V was 26 per cent. If we are able to increase the numbers by 10 per cent with students progressing from the level 0, we might begin to make an impact on the social class profile of medical students at Southampton. On a more pessimistic note, the raised academic requirements from 2002/03 may result in fewer applications to the BM, and therefore fewer offers of places, for students from these groups: what is given on the one hand is taken away by the other. The current government strategy of increasing the number of doctors has led to an increase in the number of places available in the country to study medicine, whilst at the same time the trend for applications appears to be downwards. If this continues it may lead to a decrease in the academic requirements for medicine in the medium to long term as medical schools attempt to draw in a larger pool of applicants. However, I think this is unlikely to happen in the short term. We are operating in uncertain times.

Notes

1. Only two medical schools out of a total of 27 in the data set showed any significant evidence of lower social class being a disadvantage after application; Southampton medical school was not one of these two.
2. I use the Registrar General's social class categorization system here as this is what UCAS uses in equal opportunity monitoring.
3. See for example *The Times* league tables for medicine in May 2001. Average A level scores made up 20 per cent of the total score awarded to each medical school. Southampton, placed 5th, had the lowest A level score in the top 10 medical schools and was likely to have been placed top of the league table if it had had higher A level requirements. After resisting any rise for a number of years, the School of Medicine Selection Sub-Committee approved an increase in the A level grade requirements from ABB to AAB in June 2001 as a large percentage of students with offers were tending to put this Southampton School of Medicine down as their insurance choice, making predictions of student numbers difficult.
4. The age limit for the entry to the School of Medicine is 40.
5. Whilst we accept equivalent qualifications for direct entrance on to the BM, in reality few school leavers apply with post-16 qualification other than GCSE and A levels.

References

Angel, C and Johnson, A (2000) Broadening access to undergraduate medical education, *British Medical Journal*, **321**, pp 1136–38

Ball, S J, Maguire, M and Macrae, S (2000), *Choice, Pathways and Transitions Post-16: New youth, new economies in the global city*, Routledge/Falmer, London

Clark, T (2000) Summary background paper prepared for the Policy Forum on Higher Education, Access and Success in the UK and the USA: Widening access to UK higher education (unpublished)

Council of Heads of Medical Schools (CHMS) (1998) *Medical Education and Research: CHMS Statement of Principles*, CHMS
http://www.chms.ac.uk/key_prin.html

CVCP (1998) *From Elitism to Inclusion: Good practice in widening access to higher education*, Committee of Vice-Chancellors and Principals, London

Foskett, N and Hemsley-Brown, J (2000), *Perceptions of Medicine as a Career Amongst Young People in Schools and Colleges: A pilot study*, Centre for Research in Education Marketing, University of Southampton

Gamarnikow, E and Green, A (1999) Developing social capital: dilemmas, possibilities and limitations in education, in *Tackling Disaffection and Social Exclusion: Education perspectives and policies*, ed A Hayton, Kogan Page, London

Lumsden, M A (2001) Access to undergraduate medical education is being broadened, *British Medical Journal*, **322**, p 494

McManus, I C (1997) Factors affecting the likelihood of applicants being offered a place in medical schools in the United Kingdom in 1996 and 1997: retrospective study, *British Medical Journal*, **317**, pp 1111–16

NCIHE (1997) *Higher Education in the Learning Society*, HMSO, London

Powis, D (2001) Selecting medical students: a discussion paper, (unpublished) Medicine League Tables, quoted in *The Times*, 15 May
http://www.thetimes.co.uk/article/0,,714–125594,00.html

University of Southampton Planning Department (2001), *HEFCE Performance Indicators*, (unpublished)

12

Mentoring: A Black Community Response

Howard Jeffrey

Introduction and background

The idea of mentoring is not new. It has its origins in Greek mythology where the poet Homer describes how Odysseus chose a man called Mentor to be a guardian and tutor for his son when he was away at war. Thus, the term mentor came to mean any trusted counsellor or guide. The mentoring of young people by adults has been used successfully in the United States for generations. This chapter will describe how the North London Mentor Programme (NLMP) helped North London College (now part of City and Islington College) to develop an 'achievement culture' for black students,[1] which helped significantly to increase the number progressing to higher education. It will also try to highlight some of the issues, concerns and good practice generated by the mentor experience.

The College is located in Islington, a multi-ethnic inner city area where extremes of wealth and poverty coexist. In the southern end of the borough, employment opportunities are few and mainly in the service industries. In 1988 Islington was one of the top 10 most deprived boroughs in England and at that time youth employment was generally high but particularly so amongst black young people. North London College (NLC) was a small and neglected college with the lowest funding in ILEA. Its students were recruited from its immediate locality and from neighbouring inner city boroughs with similar profiles. A significant amount of the student cohort was black and there was a higher proportion of females than in other colleges.

The NLMP began in September 1989 and was the first student mentoring programme in Britain. It was initially funded for one year by the Further Education Unit (FEU) of the Department of Education and Science as a demonstration model for dissemination throughout the country. The idea for the Programme emerged as a result of observations I made during a two-week study tour of the United States in 1987 where I looked at a number of initiatives designed specifically to meet the need of unemployed black people in New York and Washington. In 1987 the concept of mentoring was not part of the armoury of support systems used by British educationalists to address the needs of black students. In fact the term mentor was absent from the education vocabulary of the period.

Rationale

The Mentor Programme was established at North London College as a direct and practical response to a number of equal opportunity issues confronting the college in 1988. These issues included poor achievement and retention levels amongst black students; the over-representation of black students on lower-level courses; the need to widen access to higher education for black students; and the lack of opportunities for young black people in skilled and professional employment (Jeffrey, 1988). There was strong correlation between the latter concern and the small number of black students progressing to higher education in the late 1980s.

The black communities' concern about the low achievement levels of black students had been well documented (Yekwai, 1988; Coard, 1977). Research indicated that the nature of disadvantage and the economic and social position occupied by black people had changed little over the years. Career opportunities remained limited and they continued to suffer from higher levels of unemployment than their white counterparts (GLC, 1988). Despite a strong commitment to education by young black people and their parents (staying-on figures for black students in inner London were consistently high) their examination results had been disappointing. The London Strategic Policy survey noted that young blacks were ill equipped with the traditional qualifications needed for a worthwhile career (GLC, 1988). This view was confirmed by an ILEA examination survey, which highlighted the poor exam results achieved by Caribbean and Bengali students (ILEA, 1989). Further reports in 1989 and 1990 (Jeffrey and Jeffrey, 1989; Anderson, 1990; Jeffrey, 1989) commissioned by Islington Council to look at the quality of educational provision for ethnic minority students in the college and in the borough confirmed that levels of achievement were poor. The reports detailed the lack of black role models in positions of authority within the borough. Few of the lecturers at the college were black and none were in recognized mainstream positions, with authority and status.

In 1988 the college's Equal Opportunities (Race) Committee convened a training day to address the issues and concerns detailed above. The event was a great success and helped the Committee to build a platform, supported by a small group of committed enthusiasts who would help to drive the recommendations forward. As the college Multi-Ethnic Education Coordinator I was responsible for implementing the recommendations generated by the training day, one of which was the desire to develop some kind of positive action measure.

With the full support of the college Principal, Diane Brace, I approached the FEU for funding to pilot a mentoring scheme designed to support black students at the college. The FEU offered the college a modest grant to run a one-year pilot scheme involving 15 students. In response to the huge demand from students and the surprisingly large supply of mentors, the scheme was extended to 30 students immediately. The first programme had a surplus of mentors and some remained unmatched throughout the first year. In its second year, the Programme was expanded to include more students, and extended to the Islington Sixth Form Centre and City and East London College. All three institutions subsequently merged to form the current City and Islington College.

From its inception the Mentor Programme was developed as a way of enabling successful members of the black community to share experiences, impart skills and knowledge and to give support and encouragement to less advantaged members of their community. The Programme aimed to raise the expectations, and improve the achievements and life chances of black students studying at North London College who had underachieved in the past. This aim was to be achieved by establishing a programme of academic tutoring; social and vocational guidance together with intensive paired work with role model mentors.

Students

The Programme targeted black students aged 16–25 with priority given to those within 16–19 age range. In order to be selected for the scheme students had to satisfy at least one of the following criteria:

- the intention to attend the college for at least two years;
- an ambition to progress to higher education;
- no parental experience of higher education;
- a history of underachievement;
- membership of a group where English was not the first language.

Students were selected from across the ability range represented at the college. They included students on pre-vocational courses; those with language support needs as well as 'high-flyers'. Many of the students came to the Programme with a history of poor educational achievement and a portfolio of unfinished courses, lower-level qualifications and poor grades. All students who joined were expected to have some ambition and to demonstrate commitment to the Programme's aims and objectives. The majority of students were ambitious; they wanted to succeed though they were often unclear as to what they wanted to do. Some lacked the skills they needed, others were unsure how to proceed or of the qualifications they needed to help them on the road to success. At the start of the first programme very few students indicated a wish to progress to higher education.

Mentors

The mentors were recruited from a range of social, academic and vocational backgrounds. They were all black and included business people, academics, lawyers, media personalities, and people from the public services. Some of them had battled their way to success from disadvantaged backgrounds and often succeeded in spite of prejudice. Many joined the programme because of a strong sense of commitment to the black community and their willingness to inspire and instil confidence in their selected mentee. The exposure they provided was as much cultural as vocational, and many gave their students a tour of the success-orientated ethos that governed their working life. They provided work experience, work shadowing and job opportunities that gave their students an insight into the world of work. By developing close and nurturing relationships the students were able to observe their mentors at work and home and began to realize that surmounting hurdles can lead to desirable rewards in terms of job satisfaction and lifestyles. One mentor, Geri Mcleary of Touche Ross, remarked, 'The Mentor Programme has given me the opportunity to help a young person, and the satisfaction of knowing that I have really made a positive contribution to someone's life.'

What enhanced the process

In formulating its aims and objectives the Programme had relied on a considerable body of research material drawn from the United States, industry and the black community itself. We were adapting a model that was tried and tested and had been successfully operating in the United States for decades.

From the beginning the Programme operated as an independent scheme with the active support of the Principal and the new Steering Group comprising ILEA officers, representatives from the black community, and the corporate and voluntary sectors. It raised its own funds from non-statutory sources and made its own decisions in consultation with its advisory committee. After the one-year FEU funding ceased, links with the corporate and voluntary sector were actively pursued. The Programme needed to acquire a more secure financial basis. At this juncture we approached the London Enterprise Agency (LENTA), which was in the business of developing partnerships between public and private sector organizations. LENTA organized a sponsorship event launched by a government minister to publicize the Programme's mission to its members and other interested organizations. The event was very successful, resulting in positive publicity and immediate offers of sponsorship.

The media interest generated by the event played a crucial part in helping the programme to attract funding from a wide range of corporate, statutory and charitable organizations. Initially, most of the funding for the project was provided by corporate sponsors. This comment from John Rice was typical of the support received, 'Unilever supports the Mentor Programme's aim to provide opportunities for talented young people to share the experiences of work with mature working people. The project enhances the knowledge and training of candidates for future employment'. This pattern of funding changed in line with new corporate sector priorities and the growth of government support for mentoring.

It was opportune that at this moment BP Oil had just launched its extensive *Aiming for a College Education Project*, with the mission 'to work with and support education, to the mutual benefit of the company and the many communities to which BP belongs'. BP Oil became the Programme's first sponsor and its most important and influential one. The methods the Mentor Programme was employing to increase the number of black students accessing higher education conformed well with BP Oil's education mission and was wholeheartedly supported by Judy Porter, Project Manager, BP Oil, who stated:

> The Mentoring Programme enables the practical demonstration and achievement of this mission through active partnership. The encouragement and motivation of young people through caring role models and the opportunity for those established in industry to share their personal experiences and knowledge has been successfully provided by the Mentor Programme.

BP Oil's continued support for the Mentor Programme's activities over many years gave the scheme a robust credibility in the eyes of the funding establishment and enabled it to attract a wide range of funding. As one sponsor noted, 'If it is good enough for BP it's good enough for us.' Although the Programme is indebted to many sponsors over the years, BP Oil always helped us generously when we most needed it.

The Programme's ability to raise funds independently of the education establishment and divorced from its failed strategy for dealing with education underachievement greatly enhanced its development. Later, as funding became scarce after the first three years, the pitfalls of this strategy became clear. However, that rare independence, uncommon in the education sphere, enabled the Programme to develop a unique and black perspective that really made the difference. This method of operating was particularly noticeable in its early stages.

The operation of the Programme itself clearly enhanced the process. It used mentoring as a way of fostering achievement and lifting aspirations.

Central to the success of the Programme was the black community, which provided mentors for each student. These were people who had achieved success and acted as positive role models that provided support and guidance for the students. This was very important because many black young people do not see, let alone meet, successful people from their own community. This comment from Trevor Phillips, a mentor on the second programme really captured the positive mood of the black community:

> In my book role models do count today. Thus wealthy and prominent black people have to be active and provide role models for the young... The government should give support to the sort of Mentor Scheme run by Howard Jeffrey at City and Islington College, giving young people the chance to gain support from successful black adults.

The Programme was aware that structural disadvantage and institutional racism often acted as barriers to achievement and a block on students' ambition. To overcome these barriers the Programme mobilized the self-help tradition of the black community via its mentors and their networks. The Programme also tried to empower its students by providing them with practical solutions and inspirational examples of black achievements, which reinforced the positive. A former mentor, Sharon Annafi, described one such example:

> In February I had the great privilege of receiving the Queen's Anniversary Prize from the Queen at Buckingham Palace. Approaching the time of the ceremony I was nervous but excited... the palace is how I envisaged it to be, plush with a strong sense of tradition. I was very proud of our programme, as Mentor was the only black organization to win one of these prestigious awards. It was an unforgettable day.

Participation by students at these types of events greatly enhanced the credibility of the message.

Kane (1994) pointed out that the approach 'represented a departure from the traditional ways of dealing with poor academic achievements, namely: to tackle structural causes of inequality; or the deficit approach, aiming to compensate for perceived disadvantage'. Though the primary emphasis of the Programme was not remedial, the effect of disrupted or poor education was acknowledged and thus practical help including basic skills support was an integral part of the mentoring provision. For these reasons Kane said:

> ...the emphasis on raising self-esteem though important was secondary to practical steps, which raised achievement... The programme perceived low self esteem as the result rather than the cause of poor achievement; thus the students' improved academic performance would enhance their self-esteem. (Kane, 1994)

The concept appealed to the college and the Steering Group because it was direct and immediate. It simultaneously satisfied a sense of urgency and a desire to cut through 'red tape' in order to offer this unique form of support for the students. The Mentoring approach stood in opposition to some of the established strategies that were being used to address problems of underachievement amongst young black people, with little success. It also provided the College Principal with a fresh and new approach for addressing the issue of underachievement. In times of crisis, such a tried and tested initiative was highly valued. The Programme also provided a vital opportunity for white staff to meet successful black people. For some staff this might have been their first encounter with black people who were not underachievers or in need of their help. At the time, Diane Brace, Principal of North London College, noted, 'The first mentor meeting astonished me, a number of volunteers from the professions, business and entertainment appeared, all enthusiastic to be part of it... It is time, one said, to give something back to members of our community.'

What hindered the process

The abundance of non-statutory funding that characterized the early years became scarce in the mid-1990s. From the start the special funding the Programme received was intended to be a short-term measure. It was envisaged that the Programme would become part of the educational fabric of the institution and its running costs would be built into its budget as they are in the United States. Unfortunately this vision did not materialize. The uncertainty surrounding funding created insecurity that reduced the Programme's ability to deliver its agreed menu of activities. Many of the proposed trips and visits to universities, industry and cultural activities had to be cancelled. The annual residential ceased and trips abroad (to France and Holland) were only partially subsidized. The Programme's precarious funding position undermined its ability to retain staff as we could only offer part-time, temporary contracts. It was not until 1997 that the Programme received its first substantial grant (from the National Lottery), which permitted the employment of a full-time manager and part-time administrative support.

A significant proportion of the funds raised by the Programme had to be spent on staff seconded from the institution. In view of the role the Programme played in improving retention and increasing the progression of black students to higher education it should have been acknowledged as an important part of the mainstream Students Services provision. Integration into the mainstream provision would have ensured its financial security. In hindsight the Programme should have prioritized lobbying college managers and ILEA officially. Had we been able to persuade the ILEA or other government agencies to see the potential of mentoring and offer mainstream funding, many of the difficulties we subsequently encountered would have been reduced.

The Mentor Programme was a 'bolt-on' to the mainstream provision and thus lacked adequate resources, which weakened its infrastructure. While recruitment and selection of mentors and mentees proceeded at full pace, support for the relationship was often neglected due to lack of staff. The programme was often held together by the goodwill of its skeleton staff and help from supportive college tutors and volunteer mentors. Though the absence of adequate resources was important, a more significant factor was missing, namely an appreciation by the college of how hard it was to put such a new and unique initiative into action. All these factors were exacerbated by pressures from both inside and outside the college for the successful programme to expand quickly and produce miraculous outcomes.

Though increased resources would have improved the ability of the Programme to address the needs of the students, we clearly underestimated the extent of these needs and overestimated the ability of mentoring to meet them in isolation. A significant proportion of the students suffered from disrupted or poor education which had severely hindered their basic skills development. This in turn put a temporary block on their ability to progress to higher education. After the Programme's first few years it became clear that there was a gap between the demand for and supply of mentors, particularly in vocational areas like engineering, media, etc. In simple terms there would not be enough mentors for the students who required them.

The Programme suffered from lack of support from main grade tutors and some managers. Diane Brace suggested a few reasons for the difficulty: 'Initially, perhaps suspicious of change, our colleagues also saw problems in the exclusion of white students from the Programme... Controversially, I think that there was also a mood in parts of mid-1980s education that valued sympathy more than success.'

While the Principal was the most significant power-base in the college, cooperation and support for new initiatives is obtained by negotiation and persuasion. This area of development was neglected. More time and effort should have been invested in the process of obtaining support from the college's Academic Board and main grade tutors.

Lessons to learn

At that time it seemed important for the college to go beyond the ILEA's meaningless Equal Opportunities policies and to question our practice, and to reaffirm our obligation to equip each student with skills, useful knowledge and qualifications.

Within the college, there were a number of decisions and difficulties. Which students should join the Programme from those who applied?

Should it be on recommendation from tutors, from interview, from need, from perceived potential, from willingness to work within its rules? Whatever the method used it was open to suggestions of elitism. As the Programme matured, these issues were addressed and good practice began to emerge.

The Programme faced criticism from colleagues, who argued that using a comfortable lifestyle as a lure is somehow incompatible with the equal opportunities background to the project. The project was also accused of elitism and discrimination. These criticisms annoyed one mentor, Sir Herman Ousley, who said:

> I see it totally positively. I am being asked to share my skills to broaden someone's horizons. It's amazing that what the student sees as a negative experience can be seen in a positive light... What is wrong in black people living in comfortable houses, driving good cars and enjoying the opera?... That doesn't preclude having caring values and a sense of responsibility to the community at the same time.

It became clear that the caring, focused mentoring approach to supporting young people created a unique environment that should be extended to the whole college. This led to the college expanding its student service facility and locating it in a common space. The creation of these supportive teams negated the need for charismatic mentors to meet the students' needs through a one-to-one relationship. As a result of the Programme's successful first year the college recognized the need to create a context in which all college students had the opportunity to connect with professional support workers in their time of need. This development pre-empted the whole Connexions movement.

The Programme brought mentors together to share experiences and determine ways of acting in concert around issues of strong mutual concern. In particular, these sessions focused on the often-expressed desire of mentors to be part of a broader support network for the young people. Around this desire, mentors could be encouraged to press for the kinds of changes outlined in the preceeding section.

The experience of the first programme proved that mentoring was not the cheap fix that many commentators had predicted. In fact it was quite expensive to deliver properly. The success of mentoring led logically to a set of reforms that would be extremely expensive. The cost of introducing these reforms to the college was way beyond its funding capacity. The Mentor Programme not only offered direct assistance to the disadvantaged, but served as a catalyst for the more encompassing reforms currently sweeping the country like Excellence in Cities, Connexions, etc.

The success of the Mentor Programme drew the college's attention to two other issues of social policy: first, how to provide black young people with the relationship with successful black adults that they so badly needed, and second, how to get successful black adults to address and inform the debate about black youth underachievement. By raising these issues the Mentor Programme challenged the college to go beyond what voluntary mentoring could realistically achieve as an isolated strategy.

It became clear to the college that trying to solve the complex problem of the low progression of black students to higher education through mentoring alone was not realistic. In fact what mentoring did was to help the college to highlight some of the barriers to higher education that the students were encountering. It also helped the college to identify possible strategies that could be used to address some of the barriers, and highlighted the need for the college to obtain extra resources to address the barriers.

Outcomes and conclusion

For the thousands of participating mentor students, many of whose past record has been one of underachievement, the Programme has played a major role in improving their grades, developing their personal qualities and skill, raising their confidence and enabling a significant number to progress to higher education. Several students reported that they became more aware of the career options available as a result of work experience/ shadowing. Many decided to go to university on the advice of mentors or Programme staff. The value of this support was summed up by Junior Sesay, Project Manager, BT: 'The Mentor Programme has provided me with the chance to realize my career aspiration of becoming a professional engineer. I owe the Mentor Programme a lot, it enabled me to become an achiever rather than a dreamer.'

Since its inception more than 700 mentors and 2000 students have joined the Programme. The Programme has helped students to obtain places at a broader range of universities. To date, over 500 students have progressed to higher education, some of them to the most prestigious universities in the UK. The increased university progression of black students at the college would seem to indicate an improvement in their attainment levels. Most of the other students completed their course and either entered employment or went on to another course within further education. In 1989 only a handful of students progressed to higher education from the college. Today the number has risen to nearer 900 each year and the college takes real pride in the way it has responded to the needs and aspirations of its local community.

For its part in this successful development, the Mentor Programme was awarded the first Queen's Anniversary Prize for Further and Higher Education alongside top universities such as Oxford and UCL in 1995. The citation read, 'This scheme is innovative and imaginative and meets the needs of students. The initiative has played an important part in increasing morale and achievement in the community. It is a model for others.'

The Programme's achievement reflects a shift in attitude as well as in performance, since many students arrived at college with a typical under-achiever's profile of poor attainment and low expectations. The grades of many students on the programme visibly increased. For example, one student, initially thought to be capable of only a low-level course, has progressed through the BTEC route (BTEC First followed by BTEC National) and is now in his final year of dentistry school. Before starting the course, he commented:

> I cannot say enough words to describe how helpful and supportive [my mentor] has been to me throughout my course. As a result of this I am now due to enter dental school to study dentistry. The Mentor Programme can be summed up in two words: absolutely brilliant. (Colin La Fond)

The improved academic performance led to the prestigious Morehouse College, USA (whose alumni include Dr Martin Luther King, Samuel Jackson and Spike Lee) to offer full, four-year scholarships to six mentor students. Tom Jupp, then City and Islington College Principal, said. 'We are immensely proud of our students... and it is a tremendous accolade for the college too... These scholarships are ground-breaking. Our students will now become role models for young black men in the UK.'

Since the mid-1990s former mentor students have been returning to the programme to act as mentors. 'The Mentor programme has given me a chance to get lots of experience and meet new people. I have really enjoyed being part of the Programme, and one day I will be a mentor myself'. (Abolaji Shonubi, Project Manger, Rolls-Royce).

In the long term, the Steering Group hoped the programme would be replicated in other colleges, and eventually be absorbed into mainstream education. As Timothy Cook, City Parochial Foundation, said:

> Turning good ideas into effective practice is never easy. However, the Mentor Programme has achieved just that with its pairing of students and mentors. Some outstanding successes have been achieved and the foundations laid of an important model of educational development.

It is gratifying to know that since 1989 the Mentor Programme has grown in popularity. Many schemes have a wider brief and are not exclusively for ethnic minorities. Mentoring has become accepted as a major mainstream student support activity with more than 1,000 schemes operating in schools, colleges, universities and other institutions.

Note

1. The term 'black' refers to people of African and Caribbean origin and those who originated from the Indian sub-continent, particularly those of Bengali origin.

References

Anderson, B (1990) *Race Equality: Consultation Report*, London Borough of Islington

Coard, B (1977) *How the West Indian Child is Made Educationally Subnormal in the British School System: The scandal of the black child in schools in Britain*, New Beacon, London

GLC (1988) *London Strategic Policy Survey*, Greater London Council Strategic Policy Unit

ILEA (1989), *GCE Examination Survey*, Inner London Education Authority

Jeffrey, H (1988a) *College Annual Review Evaluation: Equal Opportunities*, North London College

Jeffrey, H (1988b) *Annual Report: Multi-ethnic Co-ordinator*, North London College

Jeffrey, H (1989) *North London College Ethnic Monitoring Survey*, North London College

Jeffery, H and Jeffery, L (1989) *Race and Education*, report for London Borough of Islington

Kane, L (1994) *Conference Report: Diversity in Mentoring Conference, Atlanta, 1994*, City and Islington College

Yekwai, D (1988) *British Racism – Miseducation and the Afrikan child*, Karnak House, London

13

Making Links with Schools and Colleges

Harinder Lawley
with Ian Stirling, City and Islington College and
Jan Oztun Ali, Gladesmore School

Context

Looking at the discourse of educational policy over the last 10 years, what is striking is the incrementally increasing emphasis on partnership and collaboration as a means of widening and increasing participation in further and higher education. Despite increasing competition between institutions (as described elsewhere in this book), whether we talk about intra-sector relationships between schools, further and higher education, or cross-sector associations between employers and educators, the message from successive governments is the same – recruit more students but also look for more direct contact, dialogue and a better 'fit'. This is further supported and evidenced in the work and recommendations of national enquiries and commissions such as Kennedy (1997), Fryer (1997) and Dearing (NCIHE, 1997), which in seeking more inclusive and integra-tionist approaches to widening participation in education as a whole, argue that in liberal democratic capitalist societies economic prosperity and social cohesion are inextricably linked.

Having achieved some movement from an elite to a mass system, policy makers now urge the higher education sector to address how to achieve a more representative student profile that reaches out to economically and socially excluded groups (HEFCE, 2001). In introducing alternative models of a new higher education we are asked to recognize and accept the rele-vance of a broader vocational and academic offer as an underpinning objec-tive, developing the notion of an economic ideology of education based on state priorities (Edwards and Miller, 1998). Slipped into the message is the formal introduction of the concept of lifelong learning, the metaphorical 'oil' that eases personal and professional development and acknowledges the value and place of work-based learning as a legitimate and alternative route to the skilled and 'qualified' workforces that underpin economic prosperity.

Introduction to the Scheme

It is against this backdrop of the redefinition of state-funded education that institutions such as the University of North London have endeavoured to work. Supporting the positive value of the equity and inclusion agenda the institution has attempted to engage in the debates and re-conceptualization of the shape, nature and purpose of higher education at the national and strategic level and taken specific actions to change practice on the ground.

This chapter considers one of these actions, the formulation of a school, college and university partnership, commonly known as the Compact Scheme. Initiated in 1994, the Scheme illustrates a partnership initiative that set out to work with targeted students in all three stages of education, compulsory schooling, elective further education and selective higher education.

Working with local further education colleges and secondary schools, the primary purpose and aim of the Scheme was to level the playing field in terms of providing access to higher education for specific groups who were under-represented in the sector. While the Scheme is not in itself unique it has distinctive developmental characteristics that set it apart from other local initiatives.

The most important of these is that the Scheme was designed around the strategic goal of raising aspirations about higher education and providing a means of enabling students to make an informed choice about their choice of progression routes. This emphasis on personal empowerment and choosing the right pathway, highlighting a range of opportunities that included employment, training and education was distinctive. Although the Scheme grew to have a membership of 28 schools and college partners, this chapter will focus on the model developed at one school and a further education college over an initial period of four years.

Following discussion by the university's Access Advisory Committee, a cross-institutional group reporting to an academic board through the deputy Vice Chancellor (academic), the Head of Access Development was asked to investigate, consult and propose an institutional strategy. Agreement secured, the plan was supported by a successful bid to the HEFCE's Non-award Bearing Continuing Education Project. This provided the additional resources and commitment to underpin the initiative for a four-year period and provided a means to develop an integrated embedding strategy as one of the outcomes, a key element and condition of project funding.

Following evaluation of the initial pilot project the Scheme was main-streamed and continues as a long-term activity, forming a central part of the university's widening participation strategy.

Aims of the Scheme

The Scheme took as its starting point a positive identification of potential partners among local North London institutions within a geographical area spanning six boroughs. Partnering institutions were selected on the basis of demonstrating an explicit and visible commitment to the widening participation agenda; a shared ethos in terms of taking positive action; a recognition of the barriers and a vision of an alternative, more inclusive, engaged and empowered student body. These criteria were used to formulate goals and specific actions that set out to raise and facilitate aspirations, motivate progression and foster positive messages about the value of continuing and lifelong education to a wider constituency of contacts that reached beyond pupils to staff, parents, families and others associated with the educational process.

It was the commitment to negotiated agreement between participating partners that underpinned the Scheme and helped to maintain a democratic balance between providers and players. This informed the process at every level from the strategic, evidenced through invitations to head teachers and senior college staff to join the university's Board of Governors and the formulation of 'associate' college/school relationships, to the operational level where practitioners and students were involved in designing and planning the activities together. This model of vertical integration and support provided an unequivocal signal of intent to both internal and external audiences and served as a dual-function lever that both 'pushed' and 'pulled' as needed.

The Compact sought to foster widening and increasing participation in higher education by adopting a holistic approach to working across whole communities. Through dialogue the Scheme nurtured links with local groups that explicitly addressed the identification and development of aspirations before moving on to consider what the progression opportunities were, and how to succeed in getting what one might want from education both through compulsory schooling and subsequently as older learners. Again, this address to learning in the longer term was deliberate and sought to extend and exploit the familiar culture of consumerism towards education with the aspiration of inculcating a culture of lifelong learning. What we hoped for was that further and higher education would become the local 'supermarkets' where one picked up whatever was needed, whenever it was wanted and in the size and format that best suited the purpose.

Of course this was not without its challenges, the biggest being that many of the target groups were anxious to leave school/college and all that was associated with it as quickly as possible in order to start working. This was closely followed by the difficulties of thinking 'outside of the box' for practitioners who, in the main, focused on their particular subject area or element of delivery. Nevertheless, this extension beyond personal areas of expertise to link up thinking across the Compact was and continues to be an area of huge potential and one that might be fruitfully explored further if 50 per cent participation rates are to be achieved.

Targeting

Set in an inner-city urban context, the rolling two-year-long scheme initially focused on targeted minority ethnic and social class IV and V students enrolled on any level 3 programme.

Given the relatively high concentrations of both categories in the local population this effectively meant that the scheme was widely accessible and relevant to students in both the school and college.

The decision to start with 16-plus cohorts for the pilot was taken following consultation and agreement between partners and is a reflection of the issues pertaining to progression at the time we started actual delivery, 1995–96.

The period from 1984 to 1995 saw major changes in the higher education sector. Not only was there a significant expansion with notable growth in applications and progression but there was also increased competition between institutions for those students. While the reforms of 14–16 education and subsequent improvements in attainment rates account for some of the changes, much of this increase was attributable to higher levels of participation in vocational level 3 courses such as BTEC National, Access courses and GNVQs, although this last group was only just emerging as a cohort.

With the loss of access to state benefits at 16, significant numbers of the target groups were opting to stay on at school or transfer to college instead of joining government-training schemes. Many of these students opted for vocational rather than academic qualifications as a training route leading to employment opportunities. However, the potential to use these programmes as an alternative route to higher education offered a different window of opportunity and, given relatively limited local employment opportunities, further study became a more attractive proposition.

Whilst it might be argued that targeting post-16 learners offered a relatively safe, self-selected group, it was not necessarily the case that everyone in the group intended to progress beyond level 3. Indeed students at both the school and college were involved in a range of programmes spanning a mix of level 2 retakes and level 3 options and often with no clear idea of what they might do next.

It is also worth noting that this represented a new departure for the university in that it was venturing into unknown territory, working with new client groups and schools at a time when this kind of work was still considered relatively new and innovative for higher education institutions.

The structure

The Scheme invited students to join up and explore the higher education environment, moving from general information and contact at the outset to more specific subject-based advice and guidance during the course of the two years or the length of their academic programme. Based on a stakeholder model, the key partners were the individual student, the school or college, and the university. Each had a role to fulfil and responsibilities to carry that culminated in the specification of successful completion criteria offering progression to any degree or diploma programme at the University of North London for students wishing to apply.

For students, the Compact offered an interactive programme of activities over the two-year period. Sessions included opportunities to talk to university staff at school or college, parents' evenings, open days and events, places on customized short courses, chances to get involved in curriculum development, mentoring, student and work shadowing opportunities, special 'question and answer' events on issues such as funding, family taster courses and targeted community language seminars. These were in addition to the more usual university talks, tours and UCAS sessions. Importantly, the Scheme provided a vehicle for students to discuss, share and feed back their views on their experiences with a range of different staff and others, including student mentors already in higher education.

Participation was voluntary but students electing to join the scheme were given the terms and conditions of membership before signing an agreement that outlined what was involved, their responsibilities and what they could expect from the school, college and university. The partnership agreed that although the primary purpose was to raise aspirations, students would be asked to name the University of North London as one of their six UCAS choices. This was both to encourage them to make an application and, if they wanted to progress to the university, give them a customized progression route in.

Outcomes

Although the Scheme was initially designed as an enhancement programme the structure was revised at the end of the first year to give an alternative points offer. This was to award recognition for the participation, commitment and motivation of students meeting successful completion criteria.

While students still had to meet the appropriate entry criteria for their chosen pathways, the enhancement award was taken into the calculation and included in the conditional offer. Borderline cases were also given a hotline reference and special consideration if entry criteria were not met, subject to tutors' recommendations.

Staff involvement

The Scheme also recognized the need for staff engagement in changing perceptions and therefore provided a wide range of opportunities for staff at partner institutions. These attempted to cover both personal and professional development needs and ranged from routine and procedural activities such as coordination meetings to more enhancement-related sessions. These included faculty staff development events, access to university facilities and resources such as specialist labs and the learning centre, invitations to lectures and events and a chance to develop new ideas and approaches to curriculum design and pedagogy. In one case it led to joint teaching on undergraduate programmes and there were clearly opportunities to build in more exchanges in the future.

While participation of the university staff was mainly voluntary, an existing institutional framework for access coordination was further developed and enhanced. Ring-fenced project funding was delegated to the Dean of each faculty to support the delivery of activities and ensure 'local' (internal) priorities and interests were integrated into university plans. Annual institutional and funding body monitoring and evaluation requirements ensured rigorous scrutiny, highlighted progress (or lack of it), and provided a lever for action. In practice, annual plans were agreed and taken forward by named academic links coordinators at principal lecturer level and progress was reported through the Academic Links and Continuing Education Advisory Group (the successor to the Access Advisory Group). This group not only ensured that progress against project targets stayed on track but also provided a forum for the discussion of good practice and the sharing and exchange of experience across discipline boundaries. In turn this led to more informed policy formulation and development and revision of strategic documents such as the Access Policy (1995), the (regional) Collaborative Links Strategy (1998), and the university's operational plans for successive years.

Issues

The initial work was set up to trial the transferability of successful approaches used with mature students and colleges. Although working with the target group of 16–19 represented a new area of work for the university, it was taking a deliberate step to address disadvantage earlier so that second chances or remedial steps were not necessary. By doing this it was moving beyond an access policy that recognized alternative routes in post-21 education and was testing the viability of equivalent qualifications at traditional matriculation points.

Making the scheme a pilot study based at the University of North London and supported through time-bound external funding helped in ensuring clear objectives were set and monitored. It also conferred academic status as an action research activity and assisted in getting support from key staff internally.

However, working with younger, potentially 'traditional' students created waves and tension within the institution in terms of the appropriate expertise and location for such work, raising a series of questions. Was it an academic activity or really just another way of marketing to different audiences? Should it be part of the marketing schools and colleges liaison brief? Wasn't a key element of the definition of Access related to maturity (in age) at the point of entry? If the university was going to target younger students shouldn't it focus on high achievers?

The strategic decision to define it as an academic development activity for the university staff was critical in determining how it would be developed and embedding it into the mainstream culture of the institution. The active and visible support of senior management alongside its inclusion as part of the Access Policy served to champion the innovative elements as a legitimate and necessary extension of the university's widening participation agenda and subsequently contributed to a variety of spin-off activities that continue several years later. These include inset work led by the School of Education ITEM team, partnership in research projects, other outreach work such as involvement in National Science Week and CREST awards and curriculum development initiatives.

Setting up and implementing the scheme also proved to be a challenge. While it was relatively easy to set out what the partnership wanted to develop on paper, making it happen proved more difficult. Identifying networks of key contact personnel and negotiating roles and responsibilities across all three kinds of institutions was time consuming and sometimes unsuccessful. The lesson learnt was that collaboration is in itself a resource intensive activity and requires commitment, faith and persistence on all sides, particularly at the early stages when mutual trust is being developed.

There was (and continues to be) a clear lack of articulation between all three sectors nationally and this clearly had an impact on expectations. Different ways of working and timeframes became particularly noticeable and required pragmatic approaches to problem solving, including 'working school dinners' on occasion! The difference in the academic year's peaks and troughs for each of the sectors involved became increasingly visible and therefore understanding and organizing activities to make best use of varying resources became particularly important.

Designing effective administrative systems to monitor involvement and maintain direct contact between staff and students became a major issue. The apparently straightforward task of tracking members' participation took on a new meaning as we struggled to find simple ways of recording relevant data that would map into the university's existing, centralized systems. This turned out to be both time consuming and unproductive as individual institutional requirements were very different and data protection legislation made accessing problematic. The outcome was to rely on manual records and personal contacts, a simple solution that was actually more satisfying and productive in the long run as relationships developed.

Raising expectations of staff and encouraging them to consider accessing specialist technical equipment, lecture theatres, and language and learning centre resources all required sustained effort but were successfully negotiated and contributed to the evolving relationships. It is easy for higher education institutions to forget that these resources are not always available in schools and colleges and access to them is valued and appreciated for shared use at times when the university is less busy but pupils are still at school or college.

Equally, joint staff development sessions were valuable promoting cross-sectoral understanding and awareness. While it is dangerous to generalize, it was not uncommon at the time for many higher education staff to be unfamiliar with changes to post-16 curricular studies just as school and further education staff were equally only partially informed of changes in undergraduate studies. This often explained the behaviour of certain staff who were resistant to the scheme or raised objections about working with different types of qualification routes. This was not unique to the University of North London and its partners and is probably still the case in many institutions.

Regrettably, the widening of routes into higher education study enabled by the Compact was not accompanied by a parallel increase in the dissemination of accessible information on critical differences between new routes for admissions staff, so this presented an issue for immediate action. The Compact provided a vehicle for addressing and easing the progression of students by stimulating detailed discussions of the appropriate entry requirements. Details on all aspects of progression criteria, including those relating to specific combinations of Access course units or GNVQ programmes, were offered by academic staff along with advice on how to secure a guaranteed conditional offer. Tutors at all three stages would then use these when interviewing level 3 students. Discussions were also held on how to develop a curriculum in further education/schools to match that which would be needed for success in higher education. Consideration was given to how higher education programmes might need to change to reflect and build on what was taught in the much wider range of pre-university qualifying routes.

Undertaking curriculum matching and progression sessions was a useful way of building awareness and understanding of the issues, exploring, and sometimes initiating, new (university-based) short course developments such as customized 'brush up your maths' programmes and cluster based taster courses as a result. In preparing for these activities we were mindful of pedagogic issues and attempted to ensure that the programmes and curricula that were developed reflected the learning styles as well as the interests and progression requirements of the learners.

While partnership and collaboration were primarily focused on promoting student centred activities it was also important to recognize and value the role of practitioners in achieving positive outcomes. Exploiting joint research opportunities and developing new models of staff interaction were both important elements of the strategy and provided fertile ground for staff across all three sectors, leading to career development opportunities and CV enhancement across the board. Although the desirability of this may seem obvious now, this was hard-won territory when competing with all the other pressures on time, resources and expectations.

It continues to be a constantly negotiated process but higher education institutions would do well to remember the value of developing new research activity in this area and therefore build it into their programmes of work. Similarly, schools and further education institutions might see it as one way they can demonstrate confidence and enhancement to their staff, offering it as part of the continuing professional development portfolio they make available.

Surprisingly, marketing the Compact scheme to learners was relatively straightforward. Initial information was circulated through teachers and tutors and followed up with open discussion sessions at the university. The target groups quickly identified the enhancement opportunities on offer and joined in significant numbers, year on year. Rising from an initial cohort of 63 students in year 1, this figure rose to over 300 by the fourth year. This created its own problems, as we had not anticipated that it would be so popular and were therefore stretched in terms of staff availability to resource and administer all the activities. It would be fair to say that patterns of student participation reflected the individual efforts of Faculties in engaging in the scheme although national trends in the popularity of subject choices would also have been important factors. Progression to the university rose from 19 in year 1 to over 90 in year 4.

While it was pleasing to see that many of the students elected to progress to the University as a result of their positive interactions over the pre-entry period, our collective performance measures were about progression to higher education more generally. These statistics also showed improvement on a yearly basis but we would be cautious about attributing this change simply to participation in the scheme, as there were significant other internal and external factors that might also have contributed. Data capture on this is less accurate as it depends on painstaking follow-up by individual staff, a problem highlighted earlier, but a point worth noting is the number electing to live at home and stay in the London region to study. We know that the decision-making process in making choices about whether or not to study is a complex one but we hope that the students we have worked with will be better informed about the factors to consider in making the right decision for themselves.

Conclusion

The scheme is considered successful by both the school and the college and has subsequently been revised to work with pupils aged 12 and over. This is in recognition of our own and others' (Woodrow, 1998) research activities that demonstrate the positive effects of building aspirations from a much earlier stage. It is interesting to note that the government also recognizes this and has launched national initiatives such as the Excellence Challenge to support such work.

The ongoing collaboration over the last seven years has benefited from key national initiatives in two ways. First, the university has led the opportunity to make successful joint bids for further related work, and second, it has been able to draw on and learn from the experiences of other similar projects. These include the subsequent development of schools as City Learning Centres offering shared access to resources for community groups and organizations, widening participation action research that has piloted particular models of partnership such as regional HEFCE/FEFC projects and, most recently, Excellence Challenge initiatives that promote working across sector boundaries.

Parallel national policy changes have also led to significant shifts in funding methodologies for both further and higher education and these too have moved the agenda along in terms of actively recognizing and supporting diversity in learner profiles in post-16 provision. This extension and enhancement of partnership working and resources coupled with initiatives to foster parental involvement has provided another direct route into working with new and different (often marginal or excluded) populations of potential learners.

Engaging in this kind of detailed insight to working practices and development of new approaches that set out to offer coherence and a good fit can only be achieved through close communication between the schools, further education, higher education, and local communities. We must understand that changing attitudes and perceptions takes time and will require cultural shifts in behaviours and expectations.

Sharing our collective experience has highlighted many things, including recognition that each sector has different ways of working, understanding, reading expectations, and yet we share common goals. We have realized that there is as much to learn as there is to offer and that negotiated pragmatic solutions are often the best way forward.

While it is usually accepted that it is the responsibility of the education sector to provide the curriculum and teaching we would also argue that it is our duty to work with and support individuals in reaching their personal aspirations.

If we are to widen participation there needs to be a more explicit link between the identification and articulation of these aspirations and the willingness of educational providers to listen, integrate and build these into

210

the design of courses that learners might then progress to and succeed in at university. This provides for a dynamic situation, reclaiming and recognizing the role of the learner as an active rather than passive partner in the process of shaping the educational offer, reflecting the learners' changing needs as society, and opportunities within it, change.

If we are radically to increase participation rates to reach government targets and new students, many of whom may be the first members of their family to progress to higher education, we will have to rise to the challenge of developing new programmes with a wider appeal and relevance. This will necessarily need to be based on more open and democratic relationships between a range of partnering organizations and user group representatives.

The University of North London Compact Scheme offers one example of how to open up debate on widening participation at the local level and demonstrates how small changes in working practices can make major differences to student aspiration and progression.

References

Edwards, T and Miller, H (1998) Change in mass higher education, university, state and economy, in *The New Higher Education: Issues and directions for the post-dearing university*, eds D Jary and M Parker, Staffordshire University Press

Fryer, R (1997) *Learning for the 21st Century*, First Report of the National Advisory Group for Continuing Education and Lifelong Learning, DfEE, London

HEFCE (2001) *Consultation 01/62: Supply and Demand in Higher Education*

Kennedy, H (1997) *Learning Works: Widening participation in further education*, FEFC, Coventry

National Committee into Higher Education (NCIHE) (1997) *Higher Education in the Learning Society*, HMSO, London

Woodrow, M (1998) *From Elitism to Inclusion*, CVCP, London

14

Guidance and Choice in a Changing Context

John Beckett

Introduction

In this chapter I describe some of the trends in student choice that have taken place over the past 10 years while I have been working as a higher education adviser at the City and Islington College 6th Form Centre. The College is located in an inner-London area and attracts a wide range of students. In this chapter I look at how students make choices, explore some of the factors that influence their decision making and then go on to outline the ingredients for a successful higher education advice and guidance programme.

For the past 10 years I have done surveys of where (and how many) students from City and Islington 6th Form Centre have applied to higher education and how successful (or otherwise) they have been. The Centre has around 1,200 students with approximately 900 of these on advanced level courses. It is located in Holloway, Islington in North London and serves the local and adjoining boroughs. The majority of students come from Islington and Hackney and, as a result, have often attended failing schools during their secondary years.

Some of the conclusions and recommendations that I draw from the surveys originate from our efforts to meet the particular needs of this group of students. However, the trends that I have identified and the strategies that we have developed should inform any discussion of widening participation and increasing access.

Increased numbers

Over the last 10 years the major trend has been the increased number of students applying for and gaining entry to higher education. Around 80 per cent of each year 13 group now applies and around 80 per cent of those successfully start courses. The expansion in numbers was particularly noticeable in the early and mid-1990s but then plateaued off and in the last year actually declined. There are complex and varied reasons for this. Two important ones are worth highlighting. The first concerns the social nature of the student body, which has become much more locally based, 'working class' and 'disadvantaged'. Knowledge of and aspiration towards 'university' as an option post sixth form amongst this group is more limited. More crucially, the system of financial support for students changed. The slow-down in the increase and then the actual decline this year can be matched perfectly with decreases in the amount of student support available – grants were gradually phased out as loans were phased in. The 1999 entrants were the first to go without grants but the damage had already been done several years earlier with the introduction of the student loan system. Borrowing money is not something many 'working class' students or their parents will entertain. The student would much rather work increased hours in a part-time job to gain the necessary money or, simply, retreat from the higher education possibility saying it was not affordable. In Chapter 4, Callender shows that my perceptions at local level are confirmed by research at national level.

Place of study

One of the most stunning differences between 1991 and 2001 is where students have started their university life. In 1991 there were still polytechnics and universities with separate applications systems – UCCA for universities and PCAS for polytechnics, which made the process more complex. But at that time my surveys showed that the most popular universities were Sussex, Leeds and Manchester – all 'old' universities and all outside London, two of them over 200 miles away. Sussex set up perhaps one of the first widening access initiatives in its SAIL (Sussex and Inner London) scheme. Nevertheless, the fact that 91 of 210 applicants to university in 1991 included Sussex in their choices is a remarkable one when compared to today's figures.

Some figures from the most recent survey of autumn 2001 higher education starters show that the landscape has completely changed 10 years on:

- 9 out of the most popular 10 universities are in London. Put another way, 57 per cent of our new entrants are attending just 9 universities, all of which are in London.
- 74 per cent of students are studying in London. Last year's figure was 68 per cent, 5 years ago it was 46 per cent.
- 86 per cent are studying within an approximate 50-mile radius of Central London.

- 20 per cent (52 students) of our entrants are at either Westminster or Middlesex (two post-1992 universities) whilst only 14 students are at arguably the most prestigious of the London universities (UCL, LSE, King's and Imperial).

So there has been a dramatic shift towards studying at university whilst continuing to live at home and an equally strong rise in the popularity of 'new' post-1992 universities. The three most popular subject areas are business, computing and media-related, areas perceived by students, rightly or wrongly, as having the best and most desirable career prospects. 'I want to do a degree that will get me a good job' is a plea often heard in the careers room. However, students are not choosing courses that have traditionally secured high-pay, high-status employment. In two of the most competitive vocationally oriented degrees – law and medicine – the figures are not good. There has been a 50 per cent decrease in law (9 entrants compared to 18 last year) and, for the second year running, no entrants to medical schools. This is despite there being seven strong candidates and various schemes to facilitate entry for non-traditional applicants. Lack of financial support is a key factor in these changes.

Of the small number studying over 50 miles from home almost half were from white, professional backgrounds. This is mirrored by the situation with regard to gap years (which usually combine work and travel) with only a small number of students deferring their entry until 2002. Only 6 per cent (just 16 students) of the total entrants are taking this opportunity as compared to the mid- and late 1990s where the proportion reached a peak of around 22 per cent.

Diversity of students

Various factors over the past decade have influenced the changing patterns outlined above. One of the most crucial is the constituency of the student body at this college. From having a significant middle class cohort in the early 1990s there has been a shift to students from the local, much poorer boroughs in each year group. Given the poor state of the secondary sector in Islington and Hackney, parents have 'moved' their children elsewhere – a result of the so-called 'white flight' – and they often do not return for their post-16 education. This actually makes some of the findings even more worrying. Whilst current students are undoubtedly getting into higher education they are not accessing all areas. Despite increasing student numbers overall the 'traditional' universities, with some notable exceptions, have not exactly opened their doors widely as has been shown starkly over the past two years with the slow progress of widening access programmes. Whilst widening participation departments are springing up in some of the elite universities, undergraduate places gained by students under that remit have not yet increased in any significant way. This is clearly shown in the figures above with traditional London universities and most of the provincial Russell Group universities where we have only a handful of entrants this academic year. Clearly the students at the core of these statistics have certain needs, which must be understood and then met as far as is possible, if they are to make a successful transition to appropriate courses, wherever and whatever they are, in higher education.

Student finance

Also, as I outlined above, the introduction of fees and loans has had a significant impact on student applications. The powerful influence of money (or the lack of it) in terms of student support over the past five years cannot be overestimated within this decision-making process. With students from non-traditional/working class backgrounds, no matter what the other influences are, finance underpins everything. When the government abolished grants and introduced tuition fees, payments and loans the policy-makers made two gross errors. First, the new system was not explained well enough to those it was going to affect the most and consequently there was much misinformation and misunderstanding. Also, the extent of debt-aversion amongst these same groups was totally ignored. As the figures in the survey of North London students show this has had a devastating and restricting effect on applications from this group. This is borne out by the recent work done by the National Foundation for Educational Research (NFER, 2001), which estimated that about 20,000 able sixth formers fail to apply to university every year. Callender (2001) notes that:

> The changes in funding policies have led to a steep rise in the financial burden of higher education for the poorest groups. Low-income students now pay relatively more than students from better off families towards the costs of their education. The most disadvantaged students experience the greatest risks, hardship and financial pressures. They also leave university with the highest debt.

One can only conclude that these financial factors are leading to a colossal loss and waste of talent in this country.

Making choices

How is this group of essentially working class students making choices? And how can a guidance system take account of this? Hodkinson (1995) described a complex process of pragmatically rational decision making by young people and contrasted this with the establishment's technically rational view of decision making, largely separate from the context and culture of the individual making the decision. There are many and varied influences on how higher education choices are made. Relatives, friends, work experience can all play a role. Future career plans may be the overriding factor. But Hodkinson found that 'Decisions were based on partial information which was localised, being based on the familiar and the known. The decision-making was context-related, and cannot be separated from family background, culture and life histories.'

A further complicating factor concerns students arriving at choices with often mistaken preconceptions. Hodkinson felt this is why many young people reject careers advice, as it does not fit with their existing schematic view of themselves or their perceptions of appropriate careers opportunities. On this issue, a recent survey (Barkers, 2001) shows that students are still discriminating, sometimes unwittingly, between old and new universities when choosing where to apply. Reputations and the value of degrees at old as opposed to new universities are clearly etched on people's minds whether this information is true or not. There is an important role for the adviser here in countering this when counselling on the appropriateness of a university and a course for an individual. Often the best university for a certain course will be a 'new' university rather than, say, a Russell Group institution. Strong examples here would include media and some business courses. It is also essential that universities and policy-makers do not underestimate the public relations work they have to do to avoid a reinforcement of the traditional binary divide. Government plans to create an elite tier of research universities will not make this any easier. It is clear that advice cannot be dispensed without first getting to know 'where the student is coming from' and taking into account the factors that are likely to influence decisions.

Bloomer and Hodkinson (2000) found that learning careers for young people are seldom linear but often undergo significant transformations. The traditional approach to careers and higher education guidance has assumed that for most young people their future aspirations remain 'locked' once a 'sensible' choice has been made at age 16, 17 or 18. It is almost as though there is only one career path ahead and one higher education route to achieve this. The reality is far more complex. For most students it is fantasy to expect them to make long-term career decisions at 16–19 and any professional giving guidance must bear this in mind. Ideas discussed at an interview in the second term of year 12, only nine months from putting in a university application, can transmogrify into something completely different within a matter of months. Very few 17-year-olds have a clear, definite study and career plan at this point and even fewer are ready to put it into action. It is naive to expect that they will develop their ideas sufficiently to make an informed choice after one short dose of 'guidance'. From this we can surmise that working class young people need guidance and support that is based on an understanding of the diverse influences affecting them and that sees the decision about higher education as the first of many (and one that may quickly change) on a long road. 'Keeping your options open' is a well-worn careers advisers' cliché but it is absolutely the case here. Continual support towards, through and after decision making (and then following up with the monitoring of progress) is essential, a role that can be shared by adviser and tutor (see below).

Individual guidance

Hodkinson noted that the value of professional guidance lies in the quality of the counselling that is given rather than the outcomes and that some people will need more time than others to devise a plan or a series of plans. Also, he concluded that any careers guidance system should be flexible enough to accommodate changes of mind.

It follows from the above that in a truly comprehensive school or college situation students are arriving at the moment for university choice from different backgrounds with a variety of influences and will exhibit a range and a diversity of needs that must be met if they are to make reasonable, informed and sensible decisions about their futures. A strong guidance system should, then, place the focus on the individual student, and adopt a client-centred approach, something that seemed to go 'out of vogue' with careers services throughout the 1980s and 1990s, as rigid action plans became the *modus operandi*. Many 'non-traditional students' will start year 12 knowing that higher education is a possible option for them but often will know very little about it. Being made aware of what is a vast body of knowledge and how to access it is of paramount importance. Assumptions about what they know and do not know are to be avoided. Individual guidance should be readily available on a self-referral basis. Often damage has been done by the outdated, traditional 30-minute careers interview during year 11, which many students do not find useful or memorable and dissuades them from actively seeking advice later. If they are encouraged to access guidance as and when they need it so that their adviser is working with them in a developmental way, particularly during years 11, 12 and 13, then far more positive results, the major ones being the raising of expectations and confidence building, can be seen. This approach demands the existence of a frequently available adviser as discussed below. In the past this was often the case. For example, within the ILEA careers service Advanced Course Specialists filled this role. In more recent years it can be argued that many careers services have in fact de-skilled themselves as far as advanced level guidance is concerned by concentrating on other perceived areas of need. This has undoubtedly left a vacuum in guidance provision that schools and colleges have been slow to fill. Whether or not the new Connexions provision will redress the balance is a moot point although in some areas in the country commitment has been maintained to this level of guidance and support in any case.

The components of a strong guidance programme

If we start with the premise that higher education is a positive option that should be considered seriously by students without a family tradition of higher education then a strong philosophy for progression work needs to embedded in a school or college's mission and structures need to be in place for this to work well. To add more context to this consider these simple facts:

- There are over 300 institutions to choose from and over 40,000 different course combinations (students have up to six choices only).
- The applications system (UCAS) is a complex one with prescribed dates and deadlines.
- Students come to this from a variety of different backgrounds and will need individually tailored advice and guidance.
- Many students, without the parental support or aspiration at home, can be overwhelmed by the process and amount of research necessary.

So what are the components of a strong guidance programme and what will the structured programme include? Given that the UCAS system and its deadlines dictate timing (students can forward their application a year before their start date or even two years before if applying for deferred entry), it is important to cover ground in year 12. Talks (during the spring and summer terms) about all the options post sixth form/college will be followed by more specific talks on the what, why, where and how of higher education.

Higher education adviser

As there is such a large body of knowledge to encompass, it is essential for a school or college to have a dedicated, permanent and institution-based higher education adviser. This is a huge and pivotal role encompassing as it does working closely with students, managing resources and liaising with both school/college and higher education staff. As such it must be given appropriate status. This immediately requires the management of that school or college to have a positive and forward-thinking approach to the issue of progression. At 6th Form Centre, City and Islington College, the management took the view at an early stage that progression issues were of prime importance and appointed a strong careers team to work closely with students and integrated their work within the tutorial/pastoral system. This is certainly not always the case. It is easier for a sixth form college to have progression to higher education uppermost in its mission – after all, students are only 'on board' for a two-year spell. It seems that it is much more difficult for an 11–18 school or even a large further education college to provide ongoing advice as a variety of other issues may take precedence.

However, my contention is that, in an age of mass higher education, it seems bizarre that we have not put in place the structures that will enable students to make the best use of what has been created for them. During the past 20 years much of the responsibility for this work has been placed on careers advisers from external agencies. But with the privatization of the careers service much of the specialist expertise developed there has been lost (although there are murmurings that the new Connexions strategy may reinstate the concept of a specialist adviser in this area of guidance). On a national scale it is only recently that schools and, particularly, colleges have begun to recruit to this role.

What should the higher education advisers' role be? First and foremost, they must be good communicators with excellent interviewing skills and an empathy with students. Building up a 'trust' relationship with pupils in order to help develop their confidence, self-esteem and self-belief is vital. Much of their time will be spent working with students individually and in groups (see below) as well as working with a range of professional colleagues in their own institution and in the higher education sector. They must be experts in the process of application, by which I mean the application system as dictated by UCAS. They must also be aware and keep abreast of the continual changes in both the post-16 curriculum and financial support for students (barely a year has gone by in the last 10 without change).

Next, of course, a large body of knowledge about what the higher education offer comprises is essential (but useless without the previously mentioned communication skills). Finally, and crucially, a positive, proactive and innovative approach to making meaningful links with those in higher education is necessary. Much of the above may seem like routine good practice but in many places these tasks are performed by staff with other responsibilities and with outdated knowledge, often based on their own higher education experience some 15 to 20 years earlier. How can, say, a head of sixth perform managerial and teaching duties and have the time to individually counsel students about their future plans? This can result in incorrect and even dangerous 'advice'.

Resource base

To underpin all of this (and this comes back to management vision and support once more) dedicated administrative support and a well-equipped and up-to-date resource base is needed that is readily accessible at all times for the students. It is amazing how many schools and colleges just do not have this. Either it is a small section of the library/learning centre or else it's tucked mysteriously away along a student services corridor. The era of 'some books on a shelf' has to come to a close. Higher education reference material is out of date within 12 months so there is a money issue here also. This includes provision of personal computers. More than half of

UCAS applicants for 2002 entry will apply electronically so easy and quick access to a PC in a school/college is vitally important, especially when many students will not have computers at home. DfES views of the future school and college may have PCs in every nook and cranny but that certainly is not the reality today.

Tutorial support

A trained tutor team in the context of a structured tutorial programme should support the higher education adviser. A tutor cannot be expected to be an expert but should have a role in getting to know his or her tutees well and keeping them on track and be heavily involved in the compilation and writing of references. A well-thought-out tutorial programme will allow input from the higher education adviser at the appropriate times as well as other relevant pastoral/enrichment input throughout. This can include sessions on interviewing skills, how to use open days, explanations of the financial support available, study skills for degree-level study and budgeting skills for student life. This description may fit more easily into a school culture than a further education college but colleges are slowly moving towards this approach.

Open days and visits

At the same time higher education conventions and university open days will be taking place. Attendance and preparation for these events is essential. Conventions are often seen as 'handing out boxes of prospectuses' exercises but students can gain much from them by researching beforehand and focusing on a handful of institutions. Whilst it is now possible to visit a university's Web site after reading the prospectus, and even go on a virtual open day on the Web, there is no substitute for the real thing. Many students have not seen a university and a one-day visit can transform their outlook. Ball, David and Reay (2001) found that 'visits to universities were used far less often than prospectuses in students' decision making' and that this related to 'time poverty'. Poorer students could rarely find the time to make visits as they juggled academic work and labour market commitments. Often visits were post-application and used as a means of elimination rather than choice. Costs of travel also discouraged such students. Curriculum constraints may mean only a small number of visits are possible but I would advocate that, such are their importance, subsidizing travel is a must.

Events and summer schools

The inclusion of an annual in-house higher education day is a crucial ingredient. Students gain so much more from events such as these if higher education reps agree to talk around issues about applications (and not just talk about their own institution). Sessions led by ex-students talking about their experiences of higher education are perhaps the most popular and well received, highlighting the importance of maintaining links with ex-students once they have left school/college. Some colleges use recent students as mentors to work with current students. A more recent development has been the summer school phenomenon: week-long (sometimes shorter) inductions into the world of higher education run by universities. Many have been funded by the Excellence in Cities strand of Excellence Challenge. Experience over the last year has shown that these summer schools can have a powerful and positive motivational effect on a student's aspirations towards higher education in general (rather than just towards the hosting university). This has been the experience at London School of Economics and University of East Anglia, for example. And this is a two-way process – lecturers can see the strengths of students coming from non-traditional backgrounds who may not otherwise apply to higher education and, in one case I am aware of, have even begun to question their methods of teaching as a result. It is to be hoped that the universities offering summer and winter schools will track participants and this will lead to higher numbers eventually gaining access to undergraduate programmes, not just a process of creaming off or cherry-picking the most able from disadvantaged groups.

Links with universities

An essential aspect of the process is the ability of schools and colleges to develop meaningful links with those in the university sector, something that demands time and a proactive approach from the higher education adviser. Many of these links or compacts have been developed with more local universities In our case, at 6th Form Centre, City and Islington College, these have primarily been with universities close to and popular with our students. Ironically, though, perhaps one of the most effective links was one of the earliest, the SAIL (Sussex and Inner London scheme) dating back to the late 1980s. Whilst such links need to be for the benefit of the students in terms of facilitating their entry into higher education, they must be weightier than some schemes which only involve the lowering of offers or guarantees to interview. What is required now is a far broader package enabling continuous dialogue and commitments between university admissions selectors and school/college staff and students. This may well include agreements surrounding the actual application process (interviews, offers) but also commitments to other things such as universities giving specific subject talks/lectures, attendance at school-based higher education events, providing mentors and student shadowing and the like. Currently Westminster and UCL are offering some of these ingredients to our sixth form. Building up networks in this way is clearly going to help raise both student awareness of future study options and create good lines of communication between staff in both sectors, often where previously there had been none. Formalized collaborative links between schools/ colleges and universities are starting to develop, particularly at a local level. This is likely to be much more difficult to do on a national scale. It will be interesting to see how quickly these translate into increasing access for disadvantaged students.

Applications system

Unfortunately, all of the above cannot be seen in splendid isolation. Good practice in providing guidance for higher education progression is very much dependent on and, to some extent, dictated by other factors. Most higher education advisers agree that the current applications system, UCAS, is now outdated and inappropriate in an age of mass higher education. Students are forced into making decisions, if they can be termed as such, before they are ready and the process is so complex that it takes over as the most important thing in students' minds rather than the issue of well-researched choice. A post-qualifications system would undoubtedly enhance guidance. If the proposed six-term year becomes a reality this is likely to facilitate such an applications system. More time will allow students for whom higher education is not an automatic choice to make well-informed decisions.

Curriculum 2000

Another area of confusion is Curriculum 2000. Whilst most agreed that the broadening of the curriculum post-16 was a positive step, the mish-mash within the higher education admissions process in the current cycle is not helping students. We appear to have a two-tier system where some universities are taking note of Curriculum 2000 changes and incorporating them into their offers via the new UCAS Tariff system (Middlesex, Greenwich, South Bank are three examples in the current cycle). Conversely, others are acting as if nothing has happened and offers are being made based on A level grades alone. Oxbridge, UCL and King's, for example, fall into this category. This, unfortunately, is another strand in reinforcing the traditional 'binary divide'. Some students are already receiving offers that make no sense (exactly what happened with the advent of BTEC and later GNVQ?), which suggests that if there are to be big changes in educational provision then they should be explained properly to all those affected. It is hoped that this will settle down and wider choice post-16 will enhance students' access.

Retention

Transition and retention are related, and vital, issues. For some, entering university is akin to landing in an alien world where the support mechanisms are different from those in school or college, if present at all. Whilst there seems to be disagreement about the size of the problem (figures quoted range between 5 per cent and 17 per cent drop-out depending on whether students who are changing universities are counted), keeping non-traditional students on track is crucial. Academic reasons (often the wrong choice of course) for leaving courses are cited more than financial, suggesting that more collaboration needs to occur between higher education and schools/colleges to ease the academic transition. Financial support for students is about to change although at the time of writing (and maybe not until the end of 2002) what sort of system we are likely to have is not clear. Disappointingly, it is increasingly looking as though the learner (and therefore parents) will still have to bear the bulk of the costs. Simply, better and focused financial support would very quickly open up horizons for non-traditional students. It will then be the responsibility of the old universities to better understand this group of applicants and move away from their historic selectivity and exclusivity. There are some signs that this is beginning to happen, albeit very slowly. More government encouragement (and less contradiction and confusion in their policies) is required.

Conclusion

Quality guidance and counselling is a vital component in the move to widen access in higher education. Students do not make choices in a vacuum. Their differing social, educational and cultural backgrounds need to be recognized and understood to enable individual, tailored and appropriate guidance to be the norm. For the Inner London students discussed here it is more a matter of helping them gain access to the appropriate places currently denied them (whether these be in medicine, law, drama or media, for example), than getting them to apply at all. They know higher education exists and what the glittering prizes are but often feel that they are unattainable. For many of these students higher education is seen as a risk rather than a right. On its own, though, quality guidance is not enough. It is essential that the school, further and higher education sectors come together in order to understand their differing cultures, and there are positive signs that this is starting to happen. This may well be in the form of seminars, events – all parts of progression accords and compacts – but the overriding point is that everyone involved must see themselves as part of the same process. There has to be more joined-up thinking between the sectors. Widening Access posts in universities have to be given high-level status to ensure that all the important parties are 'on board'. If UK plc is not to continue to waste so much talent each year then funding of student support and resourcing in general has to improve. The only westernized country that uses a smaller percentage of its GDP for higher education is Luxembourg (Poland, Turkey and Mexico, for example, are all higher). Margaret Hodge, the current Minister for Lifelong Learning and Higher Education, has said that educating more people to degree level is an economic necessity and that elitism has never made a nation rich. As the current Education Secretary announced in October 2001, a redefinition of what higher education is and who it is for might help us all move on.

References

Ball, S, David, M and Reay D (2001) *An Exploration of the Processes involved in Students' Choice of Higher Education*, ESRC Final Report, King's College London

Barkers (2001) *The Binary Line Revisited*, Barkers, London

Bloomer, M and Hodkinson, P (2000) The complexity and unpredictability of young people's learning careers, *Education and Training*, **42** (2)

Callender, C (2001) Changing student finances in higher education: policy contradictions under New Labour, *Journal of the Institute for Access Studies*, Staffordshire University

Hodkinson, P (1995) How young people make career decisions, *Education and Training*, **37** (8), pp 3–8

National Foundation for Educational Research (NFER) (2001) *Supporting Students Applying to Higher Education?* NAHT/Sutton Trust

15

Access: The Widening Participation Success Story

Norman Carey

Introduction

Perhaps a 'qualified' success would be a better title to this chapter! This is not an indication of any lack of effort or imagination on the part of teachers or validating bodies, but an evaluation of the development of Access programmes within the parameters of educational policy, institutional frameworks and wider social structures. As Ball suggested some years ago, '...more means different...' (Ball, 1990). There has certainly been more in terms of Access courses and an increase in student numbers in higher education (the APR for 18-year-olds reached around 30 per cent by the mid-1990s). Nationally, in the year 1999–2000, there were 1,031 Access to higher education programmes in 457 institutions, mostly in the further education sector, and 37,726 students registered (QAA, 2001). But how different is this provision from other courses that prepare students for higher education – and what signifies 'difference'?

Access courses were developed in the 1970s to encourage greater participation, particularly from women and ethnic minorities, and it is these two groups which have seen the most significant increase in participation. Nationally, 71 per cent of Access students are women. For university entrants from Access courses to full-time degree programmes, 22 per cent of female and 27 per cent of male students are from ethnic minorities, although there is some variation between different ethnic groups. For example, there is still a lack of representation from white, working class and black Caribbean groups. Respective figures for part-time courses are 23 per cent and 36 per cent. This compares with 15 per cent for full-time and 8 per cent for part-time amongst non-Access entrants. Evaluation of social class is difficult, but the proportion of Access undergraduates from socio-economic groups I and II is 26.1 per cent compared with 52.8 per cent for all; and 14.8 per cent from classes

IV and V compared with 9.6 for all entrants. Overall, about 4 per cent of adult undergraduates have Access credits, although many more are on HND/C courses (QAA, 2001).

Access provision has endured and evolved during a period of significant change. A centrally planned system has given way to a more devolved and fragmented market system. The introduction of foundation degree courses, Dip HEs and the continued success of HNDs and HNCs has meant that the distinction between further and higher education is now less clear and students can progress to higher education courses without attending a university. Vocational qualifications have seen a rise in status and, following Curriculum 2000, the distinction between academic and vocational provision is less clear. Moreover, with the development of commercial and industrial sites of learning, the traditional role of universities in defining and valuing knowledge is changing, which is also challenging traditional notions of authority and accountability.

The development of Access provision has also encouraged new approaches to pedagogy, curriculum and assessment. From experience we know that mature students respond to a learner-centred approach which builds on previous knowledge and experience as well as recognizing existing skills and interests. Traditionally there has been a focus on the acquisition of learning or study skills rather than on a large body of knowledge. Assessment tends to be continuous and based on explicit criteria that target broad levels of attainment, without grading. This encourages learner centred teaching and learning environments and the development of learning and pastoral support. Recruitment has been based on the appropriateness of the course and the perceived potential of the student, rather than on previous qualifications. Access, therefore, appeals to students who may have had negative experiences at school and want a second chance, or to adults who wish to make a career change.

Access in practice

The role of Access provision in widening participation and the changing nature of the provision itself can be illustrated by the way Access programmes have evolved at Westminster Kingsway College. A key strategic objective for the college is to widen participation as a response to the individual and community needs of the London population. The college has recently appointed a Director for Neighbourhood Learning and has developed partnerships with community organizations such as the King's Cross SRB Partnership and the Peabody Trust as well as being the Adult Education provider for the boroughs of Camden and Wandsworth.

Access provision began at Kingsway College (pre-merger) in 1979 as an evening course to prepare students for entry to North London Polytechnic (now the University of North London). This proved popular and highly successful and was developed into a modular system also available during the day. The emphasis was largely on humanities and social science, with a particularly popular Access to Law course. These courses, which were typical of Access provision nationally, have experienced a marked decline in demand in recent years. This is due, in part, to alternative courses such as the Access provision at Birkbeck College and, nationally, to universities now accepting students directly who would in previous years have been referred to Access courses in further education. Demand seems to be moving towards more vocational Access programmes in areas such as social work, nursing, media and computing.

A new customer base has emerged with different and more complex needs. Access provision at the college, and more generally, has responded well to the needs of adult students who must balance work or family commitments; and for those whose first language is not English. Access courses have provided avenues of opportunity for refugees and migrants who may have no record of previous education or qualifications.

Access provision has also developed in other, perhaps more surprising, ways to include pre-access courses, 'Pathway' courses for younger students and courses for adult students with significant learning and social difficulties. One such example is the Independent Living Programme at Westminster Kingsway College, which is a community education project in partnership with St Mungo's Trust. This is specifically designed for people with mental health problems living in hostel accommodation. Students range from those who lack basic skills to some who have studied at degree level, but all students are isolated from 'normal' society. The programme acts as a stepping stone back into the community and further education, building self-esteem and identity, and has recently won acknowledgement of its success in this area by gaining a TES/AOC Beacon Award for widening participation.

The programme focuses on developing basic skills and the core provision comprises accredited units at entry and levels 1 and 2 in key skills such as communication, IT and application of number and in interpersonal skills and personal development; citizenship; budgeting; and legal rights and responsibilities. An interesting dimension is the connection with the British Museum, where students can find out how the museum operates, get to know the exhibitions and artefacts and choose to work for a Certificate in Museum Studies. One of the students currently has a work experience placement at the British Museum and is hoping to start a degree next year.

Access outcomes

The experience of developing and running Access programmes since they were first begun in 1979 can be summarized by a number of developments:

- The higher education system is now less selective and more open to mature students – 98 per cent of Access students are aged 21 years or over.
- Access credits (at level 3) are now regarded as having equal value to AS/A level and AVCE qualifications although higher education admissions staff still have difficulty with the ungraded nature of Access provision.
- Early research suggested that students from Access courses had better rates of progress in higher education in terms of retention, employment and promotion (Rosen, 1990; Yates and Davies, 1986). Recent evidence suggests that Access students are at least as likely to be successful in gaining a higher education qualification as other under-graduates. Furthermore, Access entrants are no more likely than other students to leave for reasons of academic failure (QAA, 2001).
- Access provision has developed and adapted to meet more complex needs and a new customer base.
- The boundary between further and higher education is now less clear as is the distinction between academic and vocational provision; and the traditional role of the universities in defining and valuing knowledge has changed. For students lacking traditional academic qualifications the transition from further to higher education is now easier.

Changing attitudes

Alongside the positive outcomes there are a number of issues. Access is not only about providing more entry routes but is also about changing institutional structures and attitudes in both further and higher education to enable progression. Initially, most Access courses were run as partnerships with specific universities and even as 'feeders' for specific courses. This was certainly true in the case of the Kingsway College Evening Degree Access Course and its relationship with North London Polytechnic. The initiative involved teachers and lecturers in further and higher education who recognized the value of opening up opportunities to 'non-standard' entrants. In the early days of Access, universities and polytechnics played a close and active monitoring role in recruitment and progression in the face of criticism about lowering standards. The aim then was to develop Access students to 'fit' structures and practices in higher education. Since then universities have had to respond to changes in educational policy and cultural values and more recently to an unprecedented expansion of student numbers. They too have to cater for different types of learners and modes of learning. It is arguable that experience gained in partnerships and links with Access providers has facilitated change and adaptation in higher education. University staff have learned to appreciate students from Access backgrounds and to trust the judgement of colleagues in further education as reliable providers and 'guardians' of quality. The development of validating agencies for Access legitimated the status and currency of Access qualifications in general and courses began to reach out to a range of institutions rather than being connected to a single university or degree course. Provision has also developed to include a wider range of subjects and combinations.

That said, it is now a good time to stand back and look critically at the Access formula. It is possible that Access itself is now too traditional and a response of a different kind is required. One significant barrier to widening participation remains that of poverty and deprivation and funding further study is problematic for many Access students. The partial reversal of the Government's misguided policy of removing maintenance grants and imposing tuition fees while trying to promote inclusiveness may not, by itself, result in a significant shift in numbers. Another obstacle is the issue of standards, which continues apace and which has tended to mask an entrenched and elitist approach to education (CVCP, 2000). Access teachers in further education have long been aware that quality has not been traded for widening participation. Indeed, quality has been enhanced but this still needs to be recognized more widely in higher education. Increased levels of attainment are not necessarily a sign of lower standards but are an indication that different types of students are achieving successful outcomes through the provision of different kinds of learning experiences and assessment methods. Some in higher education already recognize this but a significant attitudinal change is required as well as more institutional commitment to inclusiveness.

Widening participation

Widening participation is a term open to different definitions but it is usually agreed that it must involve activities to target under-represented groups. A number of developments in Access provision set out to cater for groups not widely represented in higher education. These include:

Curriculum design

There has been a tendency to base Access course content on parts of existing or traditional programmes or to offer a series of 'tasters' to students, intended to provide subject knowledge in the area to which they wish to progress. This may be well-intentioned but has a certain lack of coherence and does not explicitly address the needs of an increasingly varied student base. Access courses require properly designed curricula which reflect a variety of backgrounds and interests, allow for varied speeds of learning through differentiated materials and assessment, and build in specific learning and pastoral support such as key skills and counselling.

Flexible provision

Many adult students do not want, or perhaps more accurately, cannot finance full-time courses. They need to balance other priorities such as paid employment and childcare. More imaginative and flexible ways of providing learning and support through, for example, part-time courses, working off-site or in other situations, computer-based and distance learning, and electronic communication need to be considered. More widespread use and development of pre-Access type courses is required to facilitate social inclusion and progression.

Vocationally related Access provision

Vocationally related qualifications such as BTEC Diplomas and certificates, AVCEs and franchised degrees have widened opportunities and participation. Initially, Access provision tended to emphasize humanities and social science perspectives and these two areas still account for the greatest number of programmes. More vocationally related courses have emerged in areas such as business, nursing, social work, law, computing, architecture, hotel and catering and engineering. However, these still account for a small proportion of courses. Recent research suggests that vocational Access courses are now recruiting better, especially when part-time (Field, 1999). This aspect requires further development to encourage wider participation in areas that have traditionally been highly selective, such as law.

A robust credit framework

In 1999–2000, 17,706 full Access certificates were recorded, which represents an achievement rate of 53 per cent. However, the inclusion of partial completion increases the rate to around 85 per cent (QAA, 2001). This raises the issue of a comprehensive credit accumulation and transfer system to reflect and record achievement in a more flexible way. Moreover, APEL (Accreditation of Prior and Experiential Learning) should be part of a strategy for making the qualifications system more inclusive and to facilitate lifelong learning. Development of a proper CATS scheme will require greater institutional cooperation and much work has already been done. However, the policy of the Further Education Funding Council (FEFC) to fund mainly whole qualifications has prevented its introduction. Early indications suggest that the Learning and Skills Council may take a more flexible approach when the funding methodology is revised.

Learner-centred system

A learner-centred, achievement-led system with alternative approaches to teaching, learning and assessment is urgently needed. A great deal of development has taken place in this area, particularly in the further education sector. The government initiative to improve quality has renewed the focus on teaching and learning through more regular training and classroom observation and such practices are now developing in the university sector. But further developments in pedagogy and assessment are still required to ensure that specific groups are not disadvantaged by outdated approaches and practices. Good practice in monitoring student progress and giving feedback, and the use of individualized action plans and learning programmes to promote diversity and inclusion, need to be developed.

Quality and standards

Alternative ways of defining quality and standards are needed – not least because the diversity of students and new approaches to promoting learning are still targets for accusations of lowering standards. The idea of quality can no longer be based on vague academic notions, or proxies such as student background, or on narrow definitions of success such as those provided by the A level 'gold standard'. Other more accountable definitions of quality need to be developed such as quality in teaching; quality in learning experiences; and quality of outcomes.

Promotion of lifelong learning

New ways of encouraging a wider group of students to participate in learning need to be developed through, for example, improved advice and guidance systems; more support with applications; more explicit admission criteria and progression routes; and enhanced induction and on-course learning. In addition, there should be a renewed emphasis on the benefits of education – not only in terms of career development but also with regard to citizenship and even pleasure. Aspirations must be raised in society generally and the importance of education on both social and economic grounds given greater emphasis.

Financial support

The CVCP (2000) labelled the project of increasing participation among young people from lower socio-economic groups as the 'last frontier'. The Committee members suggest the roots of the problem lie in poverty and deprivation. This is obviously a wide social problem but is one that could be addressed, at least to some extent, by more targeted financial support for certain groups. A recent study of school-leavers in Scotland argues that despite the broadening of higher education in general, the gap between affluent and disadvantaged young people, and between different social groups, continues (Forsyth and Furlong, 2000). In particular, there is evidence to suggest that the barriers related to finance and social class contribute to many students dropping out, which undermines efforts to widen participation.

Adjusting to wider access

Many questions remain unresolved when evaluating progress in widening participation. Does the unease and insecurity of contemporary society facilitate or hinder change? Does the fragmentation of practice provide 'space' for a more sophisticated approach to develop, one that involves greater inclusiveness? Is the marketization process likely to result in increased inequalities rather than more opportunities? Will increased centralized control of curriculum and finance lead to a more uniform and pragmatic provision? How successful have we been in developing a more coherent, multi-cultural curriculum to foster more communal values? Further consideration of these questions remains essential in order to evaluate the success of Access and ensure its continuing relevance. The future success of Access provision will rest on whether it can be developed to cater for current needs and also whether the wider implications of the Access approach can be embedded into institutional provision as a whole.

Institutional change is always problematic whatever the motivation of teachers and managers. Personal, organizational and financial objectives may differ and conflict. Inclusiveness may be a moral objective for some or a financial imperative for others – and often highlights the tension between 'service and survival' referred to by Blythman and Orr in Chapter 10.

Access provision developed during a period of social, economic and cultural change. But, at the same time, conservative attitudes entrenched in established practices remained an enduring force. Post-modern ideas have challenged established values. From the right, there has been hostility to notions of universal education with progressive social ends and an embracing of market principles. From the left, successive governments and institutions have been criticized for setting up bureaucratic obstacles to social change and are also seen as responsible for the imposition of a uniform culture on diverse populations. Bernstein (1983) is critical of modernist extremes of position, which have failed to generate a morality without partial, political interests. Foucault (1984), in an allusion to deficit models, argues that progressive educational discourse 'constructs' the person as a particular type of learner with specific needs, as a means of regulating behaviour. Difference, suggest Usher and Edwards (1994), can be seen in 'reality' and, therefore, changing our social practices, including those in education, can bring about wider change. Developments in Access provision have certainly contributed to changing practices in education.

Learner-centred approaches may appear to recognize diversity and difference but can easily be transformed into a kind of instrumentalism that merely maintains prevailing cultural values and practices. The content of education is not widely agreed. Some emphasize 'core learning' such as communication, problem solving and personal development; others stress collaborative learning, teamwork and professional development. Pedagogy now involves the 'delivery' of active learning experiences, the enhancement of skills and the principles of high performance. The main thrust, contends Wexler (1992), is the translation of work skills into the academic curriculum that is taught in the context of 'real life' situations. This, however, is not a simple correspondence but a complex process of design, which involves a very different definition of knowledge and wider implications for social interaction.

The government has proposed the development of a 'learning society' as one that systematically increases the skills and knowledge of its members. The emphasis is on a more flexible and better-trained workforce and also on career mobility and needs satisfaction for individuals through 'lifelong learning'. This has been linked to social class, collective responsibility and inclusion. However, in a quasi-market system, quality control is often substituted for accountability, and consumer choice confused with democratic determination. This may only serve to increase fragmentation and heighten cultural differences, and there is a danger that those in authority may lose sight of the wider social purpose. Brown and Lauder (1991) stress the importance of developing a 'common education culture' to help break down class, gender and racial barriers, and recognize that everyone is capable of practical and academic achievement.

The term 'access' certainly implies openness and the possibility of greater inclusiveness. But can the early successes be maintained? Socio-economic changes such as an ageing population, industrial restructuring with new employment and skills needs, and a significant shift in cultural values have provoked a more recent debate on education and training provision, the nature of knowledge and skills, and the nature of learners and learning. It may be worth revisiting a basic question: can Access provide for increasing diversity?

References

Ball, C (1990) *More Means Different: Widening access to higher education*, RSA, London

Bernstein, R (1983) *Beyond Objectivism and Relativism: Science, hermeneutics and praxis*, Blackwell Publishers, Oxford

Brown, P and Lauder, H (eds) (1991) *Education for Economic Survival: From Fordism to post-Fordism*, Routledge, London

CVCP (2000) *From Elitism to Inclusion*, Committee of Vice-Chancellors and Principals, London

Field, J (ed) (1999) *Lifelong Learning: Promoting European dimensions*, NIACE, Leicester

Forsyth, A and Furlong, A (2000) *Socio-economic Disadvantage*, Rowntree Foundation, Bristol

Foucault, M (1984) What is Enlightenment? in *Foucault Reader*, ed P Rainbow, Penguin, London

QAA (2001) *Access to Higher Education: Key statistics*, Quality Assurance Agency, Gloucester

Rosen,V (1990) *Beyond Higher Education*, ALFA (Access to Learning For Adults), London

Usher, R and Edwards, R (1994) *Postmodernism and Education*, Routledge, London

Wexler, P (1992) Corporatism, identity and after postmodernism in education, paper to American Sociological Association

Yates, J and Davies, P (1986) *The Progress and Performance of Former Access Students in Higher Education 1984–86*, Centre for Access Studies, Roehampton Institute, London

16

Student Voice: Working to Ensure Successful Transition to Higher Education

Julia Dinsdale

Introduction

'Bombarded' was the reply I received from a group of mature students when I asked them how they felt after three weeks in higher education. The majority had come from Access or foundation courses where they had believed they were being prepared for higher education. Some felt let down by their feeder institutions, others felt their discomfort was their fault or related to their age and one person added, 'another couple of weeks of this and I'm out of here'. There was general nodding in the room.

That scene is not unusual and is not confined to mature students. The comments are from a piece of social action research carried out over a period of three years, which is still in progress. *Student Voice* is a publication that presents views that students express in focus group discussions. The first two editions were produced in London as part of the Collaborative Widening Participation Project in North and North-East London. The third edition of *Student Voice (Access)* along with continuing research is part of another HEFCE-funded project in the West Midlands.

This chapter describes the research and its general findings. I explore the two issues that run consistently through the research: communication and impartial advice and guidance. Where possible, examples are given of how new approaches are beginning to address these issues and how the mechanisms for institutional change are examined. The work described is the response of one HEFCE-funded widening participation project to listening to the student voice.

The research

The research was motivated by a personal concern that students' voices are not part of the widening participation debate in higher education. I come from a community education background where a continual dialogue with students informs curriculum development and delivery. In the Access movement mature students' views are considered and respected. In higher education, however, students' voices are largely unheard and the offer to students is not negotiable.

In first considering widening participation policy it seemed odd to be asked to put in place activities designed to widen participation which were often 'borrowed' from other projects or considered appropriate by people long divorced from the student experience. I was keen to redress the balance and inform the work I was doing with the views of the students themselves.

The research I have been involved in has taken the form of listening to focus groups, usually 'one-off' groups drawn from students who are following non-traditional routes to higher education. The groups are drawn together by contacts in further education. The students are also contacted once they are in higher education to follow up on their experiences and, in some cases, to engage them as researchers to take the work forward.

Each group is given the opportunity to discuss the journey to higher education positively and to describe their concerns. The outcomes are recorded and the notes returned to the students for amendments and approval before they are used anonymously in publication. The publications are used to inform staff development events, both internal and external to higher education, and to inform the activities undertaken by the project: they are part of our research base. *Student Voice* is now used nationally and has attracted interest from a variety of groups including National Institute for Adult and Continuing Education (NIACE), UCAS and HEFCE.

The attraction for me of using focus groups is that the results are unpredictable. I do not use a series of pre-determined questions, but rather have an idea of the areas I want to cover. Through the process I try to empower people to look at their own role in the education system and what they can do. For example, in the scene described at the beginning of this chapter, the discussion led to the possibility of self-help groups for students to support one another. Just the chance to show how they were feeling enabled some people to think more positively about their concerns. In other situations specific problems have been raised and answered via the focus groups. Solutions have been provided through discussion and have been put into practice with little effort and few resource implications. These 'off-shoots' would not necessarily occur so immediately through questionnaires or one-to-one interviews.

Research findings

The areas covered by the research included the decision-making process about higher education. For some students, this comes early in their experience of returning to learning and clearly leads to a great deal of stress and confusion. Comments included: 'I came on the Access course to open up my choices, now they are being closed down again. There's no chance to learn about the subjects in order to make a decision.' Some students felt unable to make a choice and some did not apply.

This raised the issue of the lack of good impartial guidance to support decision making about higher education. Many people described receiving conflicting advice and guidance. The process was described as a 'matter of luck' or 'a bit hit and miss'. The main ways higher education institutions provide information and advice is through prospectuses, open days or higher education fairs, all of which are partial and competitive. It was generally felt that it is difficult to ask for advice and guidance at such events or that individuals feel too frightened to ask 'stupid questions'. One student said, 'I went in full of enthusiasm and came away deflated, clutching yet another piece of paper'.

The point was also made that open days and higher education fairs are often difficult to get to and the cost of travel is often not justified. Many are held at a time when students are busy with their course and have to make a choice between finishing assignments or attending another open day.

The UCAS process was constantly described either as 'a nightmare' or 'tedious' and without the support of tutors many felt that they might not have completed the process. Completing the personal statement section of the UCAS form caused the most concern for mature students. There is a lack of understanding by both tutors and mature students as to how higher education will 'read' this part of the form.

In many cases the period following application causes anxiety, particularly when students don't hear anything after they have sent off their forms. Some higher education institutions have good acknowledgement systems, which clearly state what will happen, with timescales, but many don't. Some people described being rejected without the reasons being given and wanted some constructive feedback with ideas for what they should do next.

Being interviewed was again seen as a 'hit and miss' process. Although students didn't like being interviewed they felt it was a way of getting more information about institutions and courses and meeting people who would be teaching them. Those who had been interviewed commented on lack of training of interviewers and raised concerns about equal opportunities in the procedure.

The lack of communication that followed acceptance was a concern. Students felt unconnected to their future place of study and the failure to communicate with them directly was generally seen as a loss of opportunity to invest in future student success. Practical matters like wanting timetables in good time to organize childcare and jobs were raised in most of the groups. The fact that these were not available in advance caused a great deal of frustration and added to the whole feeling that higher education was going to be 'remote and uncaring' – a common perception of what 'independent learning' means in practice.

When describing their arrival at higher education institutions students generally reported confusion and dismay. Induction is described as 'too much too soon' and leaves people disenchanted: 'I felt let down by the college'. People leave inductions with large bags of written information to be dumped on shelves and they are still confused about timetables, rooms, how to use IT systems and the library. Yet induction is an essential part of successful completion. Work carried out by institutions with poor retention rates indicates the need for a longer, slower induction period, stretching back to acceptance and forward well into the first semester, with a variety of activities designed to serve a diverse student body.

Often, structural problems experienced by students could be addressed easily: provision of crèche facilities at open days, for example, better signs around campus, a chance to meet with other mature students, a mature-student UCAS form and provision of timetables at an earlier stage. Attitudinal problems, which involve changing institutional perceptions of certain students and other organizations, are more difficult to solve, but if they are solved, in the long term this will make the difference and ensure a successful transition to higher education and in turn successful completion for students.

The overriding message that comes through the research is lack of communication. This includes lack of effective communication between higher education institutions and students and, perhaps more surprisingly, a lack of communication between higher education staff and staff from feeder institutions. There still seems to be a non-recognition on the part of some higher education institutions that the services they have traditionally offered are not designed to cater for a growing diversity of students.

In the case of advice and guidance, higher education institutions have been slow to recognize the benefits that could flow from establishing good guidance services. Research carried out by CVCP (Connor *et al*, 1999) showed clearly that unless good guidance is available to students during the pre-entry stage many students make ill-informed choices and end up leaving their course. The students in *Student Voice* identified the lack of good impartial guidance as a concern. There is plenty of information available both in hard copy and on Web sites, too much in fact. But if you want to talk to someone about making an informed decision about higher education you have to hope you will 'get lucky'. The majority of students would not consider ringing higher education institutions or 'dropping in' and they know they will not generally get a chance to talk to someone about a specific course or explore all the opportunities open to them in higher education. Traditionally, higher education institutions have relied on schools to give guidance to prospective students and have seen their role as purely one of marketing. The marketing element is still strong and influences how open days, visits and higher education fairs are run, and can be a major barrier to widening participation, as any hint of impartiality or collaboration is seen as weakening the institution's place in the competitive market.

A lunchtime conversation at a higher education fair clearly illustrates the need for good higher education guidance.

> I've picked up all the prospectuses, but I still don't know what I want to do and I don't know the right questions to ask...
>
> I'm interested in teaching or social work, but have the daily care of my twin daughters, while my wife works. Would it be better for me to wait until they're older, can I get childcare? I think I need experience to get on to social work.

These disparate questions and comments need time and skill to answer. They cannot be answered by a one-off discussion over a stall piled high with prospectuses.

Some of the post-1992 universities have established one-stop-shop facilities, which provide information, advice and guidance in easily accessible venues. Much of the work is carried out in an impartial way – general advice is given and guidance interviews provided. The people working in the 'shops', however, are usually employees of a university so that there is pressure to sell their own courses. For example, they may help students with UCAS forms only if they are coming to their particular institution.

A recent discussion document HEFCE (2001) again identified that future higher education students will need to come from those students in the lower socio-economic groups with little tradition of higher education. It is these groups that need the most information, advice and guidance and that struggle to get it. Marketing departments will ignore this group at their cost. A new perspective that sees giving impartial information, advice and guidance as a way of expanding the market is needed. A potential student who has been given good guidance will value that service and even if he or she decides not to attend that institution, will often recommend it to others. Access to a range of information is most effectively achieved through collaboration.

What is needed is a recognition that potential students are entitled to good guidance and will often make decisions about where they go for reasons not directly connected with the courses themselves. For example, how close is the course to a child's school so that childcare arrangements can be made. What will the timetable be? Can it fit around the rest of the student's life? What are the transport links like and how expensive will travel be? These are all important questions that need serious consideration and are usually not answered in general publicity materials. One student suggested, 'we need the "Ask Jeeves" facility'. Some widening participation projects, for example the Web site at (Liverpool) uni4me.com, have tried to provide this, but *Student Voice* research still identifies the overriding need for a person to speak to.

The second area of non-communication, the lack of communication between staff in different sectors, occurs in a variety of ways and again seems to flow from various misconceptions on the part of staff in all sectors which is exacerbated by feelings of competition and superiority. This is most strongly highlighted when students are on linked courses such as HND or foundation courses. Many students spoke of being given one set of information by tutors in further education only to have it contradicted by the tutor from higher education. Other students felt that information given to them by their feeder course was wrong or out of date. Tutors in further education also complain that getting information from higher education is difficult unless informal channels exist.

The project response

The three-year widening participation project between Coventry University, the University of Warwick and University College Worcester was funded from the HEFCE Special Initiative Fund. The project has four workers: three project workers, one based in each of the institutions, and a line manager based at Coventry University. I am the worker based at University College Worcester, so many of the activities discussed in this chapter relate to work there; other responses have been developed at the other two institutions and the work at each institution is disseminated across the project regularly.

The full project team felt that in order to encourage institutional change and embed developments suggested in *Student Voice*, it was necessary to work through existing networks to identify key players who were willing to support work within institutions. Time-limited projects like this one are usually positioned on the periphery of an institution and therefore 'powerless' to bring about institutional change. The project group felt it was important to act as a broker connecting *Student Voice* to those who can influence policy and change. This work was helped by funds to support developments in their initial stages with careful consideration given to how they would be embedded in the institution or funded from elsewhere as appropriate.

The beginning of this work in the West Midlands was the bringing together of interested parties including colleagues from further and higher education and schools in a 'transition event' where the *Student Voice* research was used to start discussion and networking around the issues raised. Subsequent work has flowed from this event and has slowly expanded to include more key players. This organic approach has proved useful in building real rather than formal partnerships on which the work is based, and to some extent has addressed the issue of communication so clearly identified as a problem by the students in the research.

Work to meet the need for good advice and guidance developed following discussion at the transition event. More groups to take part in the research were identified and work began on the development of an impartial Access Pack, which offers information and advice in a variety of ways, including face-to-face workshops on finance and preparation. The project then began to identify the key players involved in pre-entry advice and guidance.

I was offered an opportunity to join the Admissions Committee at University College Worcester. This has led to a chance to be actively involved in recommending changes in policy for the institution on such things as open days, credit for prior learning and written communications with students.

Closer work with student support services at University College Worcester, which provide advice and guidance to current students, led to an interest in extending the advice service to pre-entry. Careful work on this has resulted in a successful joint bid to our widening participation project and the local Learning and Skills Council for an impartial pre-entry guidance worker to establish a model of impartial guidance for higher education. The worker will be based at and supported by University College Worcester, but will work mainly in the community. It is envisaged that after the initial stage the model will be disseminated across all the institutions involved in the project and once it is evaluated will be embedded within university systems.

Alongside institutional work the project has engaged a local DfES-funded information, advice and guidance project to ensure that a higher education perspective is included in the work of this project. This has resulted in two-way working with workers in Admissions at University College Worcester taking the Guidance Council Standard awards and being able to offer up-to-date information on higher education to colleagues.

In order to tackle the issue of non-communication between staff, both between different sectors and between departments in the same institution, the transition event was followed by a series of more local meetings, bringing together interested parties to suggest practical work that might be possible. These meetings expanded the number of people involved and came up with a variety of solutions, some of which have been followed through. The important principle behind this approach has been that it has come from the practitioners and was informed by *Student Voice,* not imposed by the project. Work has been at their pace and to fit their own systems.

In some cases whole departments within University College Worcester have decided to meet with colleagues to discuss complementary curricula to allow for easier transition. Other departments have met over lunch to discuss how best to encourage more communication.

The yearly Access to Higher Education Fair at University College Worcester was revamped to include workshops on preparation for higher education and finance and a chance to attend a lecture as well as providing the traditional marketplace for local institutions. Feedback on this event shows that the additional activities, particularly the pre-entry advice, made it an extremely successful event. The number of students participating was twice that of the previous year.

The yearly summer school for mature students at University College Worcester is to be restructured to take account of issues raised in the research. Instead of a two-day event there will be a series of events over the summer period, both social and academic, which will be extended into the first semester to support the normal induction period to try to make it less chaotic and confusing.

Several staff in further education have taken up opportunities to engage in job-shadowing colleagues in higher education. This initiative began at University College Worcester, but will be offered at all three institutions involved in the project. The job-shadowing has been organized by the individuals themselves through the project.

The above developments have been, on the whole, low cost and are in the majority easily sustainable. Two larger-scale bids were received by the project as a result of the transition event. One came from an academic and the other from a student union. The two projects were amalgamated, which has led to closer working between two areas. An offshoot of this has been that the project is now working with departments on a variety of widening participation issues. This has led to interest from other academic departments, not previously involved, which are beginning to identify 'widening participation champions' who will be key players in embedding practice in the institution and effecting institutional change.

One of the bids received by the project was to develop materials for students preparing for higher education and to deliver them in a variety of ways either in the feeder institution, in higher education, via Web site or hard copy. Linked to this was a 'buddying' scheme to be developed with students who used the materials and were supported into the institution and through the first semester by other students and staff. Another bid was to provide childcare-supported time for students to engage in private study, use the student union, or sports facilities.

Both these bids came from ex-mature students, with children, who had struggled to get their own education. Both recognized the need for support for mature students, and the need for institutional change.

The buddying group is in its initial stages and is beginning to identify issues and provide support. The childcare sessions are in place and growing in use.

The preparation and development of materials for a Moving On pack is now in pilot form and has been well received by students and colleagues. The opportunity to deliver material face to face in the provider institutions has been eagerly taken up. There are plenty of study skills materials available, but not many are written by higher education and addressed to potential students with the offer of face-to-face delivery. This is where the *Student Voice* research has been able to inform practice that so far has proved to be successful.

A year after the first transition event the project is planning a seminar for staff from across the sectors on preparation for higher education. This will not only launch the Moving On pack, but is intended to open up further discussion on the need for communication between sectors as well as suggest further action points.

The research is continuing and has now spread across the project to include all three institutions and includes a larger sample of students. Last year's *Student Voice* involved approximately 100 students; we hope this year's will reach over 300. Interestingly, the idea of listening to students' voices has become embedded in a variety of activities, including the development of a mature students' union and a larger-scale piece of work entitled *Community Voice*.

Conclusion

The *Student Voice* research is a piece of pragmatic, small-scale, action research, which does not claim to represent all widening participation students' views. It does, however, give some ideas about how some students experience the transition to higher education, a voice that has been missing until recently.

Key to the research has been how the work is disseminated and taken seriously, not only by the project but by the institutions we are working with and has, therefore, directed our approach to the overall work of widening participation. We have tried to undertake work on transition to higher education through established networks of staff, encouraging them to consider the *Student Voice* material and collectively seek solutions to ensure successful transitions. The work moves forward at a pace that is appropriate, and solutions are not predetermined by the project. We are fortunate enough to have money to 'kick start' some of the ideas, but are careful to discuss ideas of sustainability at the time of development.

This approach has enabled us to gain the support of staff interested in widening participation and who, in turn, act as widening participation champions within all three institutions. It has also allowed us to empower the students in the research to seek some of their own solutions to the difficulties they have experienced and to engage more successfully in their own transition to higher education.

References

Connor, H *et al* (1999) *Making the Right Choice: How students choose universities and colleges*, Institute of Employment Studies and CVCP, London

HEFCE (2001) *Supply and Demand in Higher Education*, consultation paper 01/62

17

The Sussex Coastal Highway

Jacky Harding

Introduction

The Sussex Coastal Highway is an HEFCE-funded collaborative project involving universities, colleges and secondary schools in Sussex aimed at widening participation. It aims to work with school pupils without a higher education inheritance in order to raise their educational aspirations and encourage them to stay on at 16 and progress to university. The project also works with 19–21-year-olds with partial level 3 qualifications in order to design a specific pathway to higher education for them.

Background

In April 1999 HEFCE allocated funding for widening participation to regional partnerships between higher education institutions and other organizations. Sussex Liaison and Progression Accord supported a successful bid to HEFCE for widening participation across Sussex.

The Sussex Liaison and Progression Accord (SLPA) is an agreement between the three higher education institutions (HEIs) in Sussex and a number of local state schools and colleges in the region. It aims to improve links between the various institutions and provides students in the partner schools and colleges with advice about higher education. As part of the Accord, the three HEIs make certain guarantees about offers or interviews for applicants from SLPA institutions applying to specific subjects.

The funding from HEFCE was for three years and involved working with successive cohorts of young people from year 10 upwards in eight schools and eight colleges in Hastings, Newhaven, Brighton, Worthing and Chichester.[1]

The University of Brighton was the lead HEI, and the other HEI partners involved were the University of Sussex and University College Chichester. The project had two separate strands with different target groups. The aim of the first strand was to identify and tackle the reasons for non-participation through early identification of pupils who have the potential to benefit from higher education but came from 'non-traditional' backgrounds – that is, pupils who had no history of higher education participation within their family. The project aimed to provide sustained intervention in order to encourage these students into higher education.

The second strand involved working with 19–21-year-olds with incomplete qualifications for entry into higher education. The aim was to map the needs and aspirations of these potential students, and to identify ways of meeting those needs in terms of future provision by the further education colleges, in negotiation with the HEIs. This strand was funded over one year.

Rationale

The rationale for the project was established against a complex background. Overall the Sussex economy has been buoyant. Average rates of participation and coverage of level 4 qualifications are high, largely due to the presence of the three HEIs. However, beneath this lies a more complicated pattern of localized economic and social deprivation. Many households depend on seasonal tourist-based employment, which is usually low paid. Achievement by pupils in the coastal areas identified for the Sussex Coastal Highway project is lower than national targets.

The Institute for Employment Studies has concluded:

> ...the region includes local areas with some of the lowest per capita GDP in England, and the uneven spread of development has led to pockets of deprivation. There is a growing gap between the advantaged and the disadvantaged, the rich and the poor, and it has been argued that this gap may be greater than that found in most other regions... the growing divergence between affluent areas and areas of deprivation leads to a segregation within the region – the 'south–south' divide which could create long-term problems for economic performance and with it social cohesion. (Institute for Employment Studies, 1998)

Much of the good practice that has been developed in terms of recruiting and retaining widening participation target groups is also good practice in terms of support and retention for all categories of university student. The Sussex Coastal Highway project has sought to address the problem of low participation from both ends of the spectrum. It attempts to deal with issues of family background and cultural capital as well as issues of access, recruitment and support within further education colleges and within the universities.

Working with the schools

This section describes the way in which work with the schools has progressed within the first strand of the project.

The pupils were identified using defined criteria for selection: CATS and/or SATS scores (mid-range and above), Records of Achievement, school knowledge of individual students and their family background, current aspirations and likelihood to benefit from the project. Questionnaires were used to gain more information about family background. Each of the eight schools selected between 12 and 40 pupils, depending on the size of the school and the project's criteria.

This strand focused on a number of activities. Cluster groups of stakeholders from the schools, further education colleges and HEIs were formed in each of the five towns – Hastings, Newhaven/Lewes, Brighton, Worthing and Chichester/Bognor. Typically these cluster groups involved four or five people from the schools, colleges and universities involved in the project in each town. Each cluster group met regularly to plan the activities for pupils within that town. For example, in Hastings a local launch involving pupils and parents and carers of participating young people took place as an introduction to the project. Invited guests included local dignitaries as well as representatives of the Universities of Brighton and Sussex. Day visits to all three universities took place on a regular basis. At the end of the first year most pupils had visited at least two of the three HEIs. Activities on these day visits included tours of the libraries; visits to the Gardner Arts Centre; talks by the President of the Students' Union; visits to halls of residence and student flats on campus; tours of the sports facilities; IT workshops and psychology demonstrations; a geography group work taster session; treasure trail and map reading; experiencing a lecture in a traditional lecture theatre; tour of the sports facilities and a chance to shoot a few baskets; lunch in universities' refectories joined by current undergraduates; a book search in the library; creative writing and adventure education taster sessions; as well as question and answer sessions on student finance issues. In Brighton, a team of year 11 pupils from one participating school have made a video of student life at Sussex University in order to take it back to school and show it to year 10 pupils. Mentoring is also a major feature of the project, and all three HEIs have identified and trained current students as mentors for the young people in colleges and schools. Mentoring is offered to all year 11 school pupils involved in Sussex Coastal Highway.

An independent evaluation of the project is being carried out over three years. The evaluation is carried out by the Health and Social Policy Research Centre at the University of Brighton. The first year of the project was evaluated in summer 2001. The evaluation made recommendations for the project's work in 2001/02. The main data collection method used was qualitative interviews with participants in the project – pupils, their parents and carers, teachers, further education and higher education staff and project workers. Thirty-four interviews were carried out and short questionnaires were also distributed to a larger sample of participating pupils. The evaluation assessed a number of key questions:

Is strand one successfully targeting the specified population?

The target population for strand one was year 10 pupils who had demonstrated through their SATS and CATS scores that they had the aptitude to progress to higher education, but who had no history of participation in higher education in their family. The evaluation found that most of the schools selected pupils who met the project's criteria for participation.

> We looked at their results, CAT and SATS scores, so then we had a list of 90 pupils... we decided to give all 90 of them a questionnaire. It included things like 'Do you think you might want to go to sixth form college?'. 'Do you think you might go to university?'. 'Have any of your brothers/sisters/parents ever been to university?'. From that we targeted kids that may not think about going to university. (Teacher)

However, in one of the project's three geographical areas and in one other school, cohorts other than year 10 were selected: '[One school] had decided they wanted to work with year 11 and 12... quite a number of them had already got careers in mind, some of them were already definitely going to university and had parents who had been to university' (Project Officer).

Are strand one activities appropriate to fulfilling the aims of the project?

This strand of Sussex Coastal Highway aims to work with school pupils with no higher educational inheritance in order to raise their educational aspirations and to encourage them to stay on at 16 and progress to university.

Strand one had provided a range of activities including taster sessions at HEIs, careers talks, cultural visits and parents' evenings. Nearly all pupils enjoyed the activities in which they took part but there was evidence that some higher education staff had difficulty in designing activities for year 10 pupils and would welcome more advice about this.

> A guy came in and actually showed the group a series of different robots and showed a video of how they were developed... They did enjoy that. (Project Officer)

> We used the big microscopes, which was good, looking at blood and things. (Pupil)

Because I teach the degree course it is hard to find some of the language they can understand. It would be really useful to have a guide revealing what subjects the pupils are doing, the level that they are at. (Higher education tutor)

Most of the activities on the strand one 'menu' were delivered by at least two of the three Project Officers. In one of the project areas a more limited range of activities was provided, so that not all participants in the project were offered the same opportunities.

Wherever you live in the project you are supposed to get some kind of mix of stuff delivered to you ... I think it is quite important, for example, if you want to do psychology, Brighton doesn't offer this degree, if you're interested in a sports science degree, Sussex doesn't offer that. (Steering Group Member)

It would be nice to have a little more uniformity in the project, working together. (Project Officer)

What has been the impact of strand one on the pupils involved?

The evaluation reported that there was much evidence that strand one had increased pupils' understanding of higher education and had a positive effect on their attitudes to it.

I thought about going to university but now I have seen it I thought, yes, I would do it rather than just go out and get a job. (Pupil)

I wasn't sure if I had the abilities to go to university, like was I good enough? But I think seeing some of the people has changed this. (Pupil)

He said to me tonight that it is a completely different way of looking at teaching and it is up to you to do the work and not up to them to teach you. He has learnt that that is the difference in just three days. (Parent)

The pupil questionnaire indicated that before participating in the project 41 per cent of the pupils wanted to go to university and by the end of the year this had increased to 71 per cent.

The evaluation also found that despite its positive impact, little dissemination of strand one had taken place during the first year.

I think [dissemination] could be improved. (Project Manager)

I have contacted every Sub Dean in the university but I don't think it gets past the person I speak to. It's like a brick wall. (Project Officer)

Working with the colleges

This section describes the way in which work with the colleges has progressed within the second research strand of the project. The colleges involved were Hastings College of Arts, Science and Technology, City College Brighton, South Downs College, Worthing College, and Chichester College of Arts, Science and Technology. The South of England Open College Network was also involved in this strand. Members of the research team were seconded on a part-time basis from further and higher education institutions involved: the South of England Open College Network, the University of Sussex, Worthing College and South Downs College.

The main aims of the strand two research were:

- To identify gaps in the coverage of qualifications for the cohort of 19–21-year-olds in the five local project areas, who have the interest and ability to progress to HE but currently lack the required entry qualifications.
- To offer a basis for filling gaps in the qualifications of individuals in the cohort.
- To establish agreement across the SLPA on responses to this cohort including HEI admissions policies.

The main methods of gathering research were as follows:

- A mapping exercise to obtain quantitative information about patterns of non-achievement and non-retention across the project's target area.
- Surveys of young people from the specified target groups in order to identify information of a more qualitative nature eg about their aims and aspirations, their perceptions of higher education and their views on how an alternative pathway to higher education could be offered.
- Interviews with further and higher education partners within the Accord to obtain their perceptions of the proposed new qualification.

The Responsive College Unit (RCU) was also commissioned to examine retention and achievement data for all 16 further education colleges in Sussex. The data produced generated an analysis of drop out and failure to achieve qualifications at level 3. The RCU also produced a postcode analysis of this data in order to ascertain potential demand for college-based provision within the five areas of Hastings, Newhaven/Lewes, Brighton, Worthing and Chichester.

The evidence gathered from the young people themselves involved questionnaires, focus groups and telephone interviews. The evidence indicated an overwhelmingly positive response to the notion of future higher education study in general. However, this attitude was somewhat mitigated by a fair degree of uncertainty and confusion from respondents about the role of higher education in relation to more specific vocational goals.

The research also found that:

- Most of these young people are working full-time but would be prepared to undertake a college course provided that they could still earn money.

- Some of these young people have acquired qualifications in the workplace or through part-time study since they left college.
- The most popular career interests are business and public service related areas (perhaps reflecting the local employment scene in the areas from which students came).
- There is enthusiasm for undertaking further and higher education (despite their previous unsuccessful experiences).
- The majority would attend a local college.
- Daytime and evening study were both popular, as were 2–4 contact points a week for the course.
- A one-year commitment was preferred.
- Respondents see the value of acquiring a range of supporting skills within the programme of study.
- The biggest single obstacle to young people returning to education is loss of income. This obstacle would be exacerbated by having to pay college tuition fees.

A number of community and voluntary organizations were contacted and focus groups were set up in Brighton, Worthing, Eastbourne and Hastings. For this part of the research, 30 in-depth interviews with young people were also carried out. The community organizations involved were Generation Arts Project in Eastbourne, Worthing Foyer, Brighton Foyer, the Prince's Trust in Eastbourne, Brighton Babes (young mothers) and Coalition for Youth in Brighton.

The results obtained from the community-based young people indicated deep fears about their ability to cope with the financial difficulties and workload, little confidence in themselves or the system and a clear lack of knowledge about higher education. Additionally, although many were positive about the idea of going into higher education, it was regarded as an impossible dream.

The independent evaluation of strand two of Sussex Coastal Highway highlighted a number of issues:

What has been the impact of strand two?

The evaluation reported that the research conducted by strand two had produced much valuable information:

> It has established that there is a group of young people who haven't had very successful experiences while they were at college but who say they are keen to return. (Project Officer)

> We managed to find a group of people on the fringes, the marginalized young people. Quite a lot of them would love to go [to university] but they see whole mountains of barriers. (Project Officer)

251

The main objective of strand two, development of a proposal for a new qualification based on the identified needs of the target group, has been achieved. The qualification will now be developed and piloted. 'We have got to the point where we can say, "this is what it should look like"... we have got the institutions that want to be involved and we have got the pilot' (Strand two coordinator).

The evaluation reported that there had been some difficulties in the organization and management of strand two, including the number of project officers from the different SLPA organizations employed on the project on fractional contracts, and a lack of clarity about strand two in the original project bid. Participants in the project indicated that some of these issues stemmed from the different perspectives of the individuals and institutions involved. However, some interviewees argued that this range of views and commitments had contributed significantly to the positive outcome of strand two.

> Within the staff team we appointed there clearly were differences about the process we needed to go through... I think there were also differences amongst the parent organizations of the project workers. (Steering Group Member)

> I think they employed everybody they interviewed because they didn't want to upset any of the institutions. (Project Manager)

> The real problem is that it was a committee that was putting things together, the committee itself wasn't very clear... we weren't absolutely sure what we wanted out of it. (Steering Group Member)

> I think if we said we only wanted one [project officer], that person would have gone and delivered what they thought the model was. Presumably, now that they are reporting, the others would have come in and said, 'That's a terrible idea'... Or we might have had a report in which several organizations might have said that they can't make it work and it doesn't make sense to them. (Steering Group Member)

Discussion

A key issue within the widening participation debate concerns funding, and this is certainly very relevant in relation to Sussex Coastal Highway. Funding for widening participation initiatives has usually been on a relatively short-term, project-focused basis as in the case of Sussex Coastal Highway. In the face of this pattern of funding, the issue of embedding the good practice developed within such widening participation projects has been challenging and frustrating. I would argue that it would be very difficult to embed the lessons learned from Sussex Coastal Highway without continued funding.

Staff who work on widening participation initiatives often see one initiative come to an end to be replaced by a very similar initiative a couple of years later. Additionally, the infrastructure built up around such projects such as close and effective relationships between institutions and administrative procedures have to be re-invented and re-formed. This can be both time consuming and energy sapping. Furthermore, it may not be possible to fully evaluate the effects of such initiatives on actual participation of pupils and students involved – for example, in strand one of Sussex Coastal Highway the first cohort of pupils were in year 10. The project is funded for three years, so the cohort will be in year 12 at the end of the project. Traditionally, students progress to higher education at the end of year 13. How does one truly evaluate success if we never get to find out what percentage of the cohort involved actually progresses to higher education? For strand two of the project the issues are slightly different, but no less frustrating. We've found out what young people would like and would need to get them back into higher education, but there may not be the future funding in order to deliver it.

Widening participation in higher education is, by its very nature, a long-term venture and yet it has traditionally been funded on a short-term project basis. On the other hand, funders continually ask institutions involved in such projects to produce evidence of embedding good practice developed by projects within the institution post-funding!

Funding for widening participation initiatives allows institutions in all three phases of education involved in these activities to buy time and other resources to plan and deliver the activities described in this paper. Hard-pressed staff within these institutions would find it very difficult to continue to support these activities without the additional resourcing.

Conclusion

The independent evaluation reported that both strands of the Sussex Coastal Highway have been successful in achieving their objectives. Both the initiatives with school pupils in strand one and the work with 19–21-year-olds had positive effects.

The evaluation also identified a number of ways in which the project might be enhanced and developed, these included:

- Ensuring that for strand one in all participating schools, future cohorts targeted meet the project's criteria.
- Providing higher education staff who contribute to taster sessions with information about appropriate activities for year 10 pupils.
- Providing all participating pupils with an entitlement to a number of agreed core activities.
- Implementing a dissemination strategy for the whole project.

While a dissemination strategy has been developed for the life of the project, the issue of embedding the work of the project into institutional practice after the life of the project remains problematic.

Note

1. The schools and colleges involved are: William Parker and Hillcrest schools and Hastings College of Arts and Technology in Hastings; Tideway School and South Downs College in Newhaven/Lewes; Longhill School and Patcham High School and City College, Varndean College and Brighton, Hove and Sussex Sixth Form College in Brighton; Durrington High School and Worthing College in Worthing; and Bognor Regis and Westergate Community Schools and Chichester College of Arts, Science and Technology in Bognor/Chichester.

Further reading

Bellis, A *et al* (2001) *Sussex Coastal Highway Strand D Research Report*, University of Brighton

IES (1998) *South East Regional Assessment*, Institute for Employment Studies, Brighton

Shorley, F and Winn, S (2001) *Evaluation of the Sussex Coastal Highway Project*, University of Brighton Health and Social Policy Research Centre

University of Brighton (1999) *Proposal for Funding for Widening Participation 1999/2000 to 2001/2002*, University of Brighton

Conclusion: Is Higher Education Gladdening our Existence?

Annette Hayton and Anna Paczuska

> possessors of wealth ... still consider education as their own prerogative, or a boon to be sparingly conferred upon the multitude instead of a universal instrument for advancing the dignity of man and for gladdening his existence.
>
> (William Lovett, 1837)

As we saw in the Introduction, education systems are the products of particular cultures at certain times and they evolve and develop along with wider social, economic and cultural changes in society. At the same time it is important to remember that as well as being shaped by society, education also plays a part in shaping society. That is why various governments and political systems have attached such particular significance to education. There are many historical instances where the struggle for education by oppressed and underprivileged groups has been part of a wider struggle for freedom, self-identity and self-worth. In the past year we have seen Kurdish students in Turkey facing the death sentence for arguing for university courses to be conducted in their own language and girls under the Taliban regime taking extreme risks to pursue their education in secret.

That said, it is certainly the case that society itself is shaped by forces that are stronger and more enduring than education systems. The extent to which education can overcome social disadvantage and play a part in creating a more equitable society has been the subject of much debate by policy makers, politicians and academics and continues to present us with both theoretical and practical challenges. Nearly 30 years ago Bernstein stated that 'education cannot compensate for society' and today the debate continues about how far education can contribute to social change and tackle social disadvantage. So, in order to understand what influences progression and participation in higher education we must explore the complex relationship between education and society.

Much government policy in the UK, from the 1944 Education Act onwards, has sought to address issues of educational disadvantage.

Various strategies were employed by succeeding governments in the attempts to create greater equality in education (Hodgson, 1999). This discourse of increasing equality in education and society was interrupted in 1979 by the election of the Thatcher Government, the approach of which to social policy is epitomized by Margaret Thatcher's famous comment 'there is no such thing as society, only individuals' (*Woman's Own*, 31 October 1987). That deeply political statement set the tone for the growth of an individualism that is evident in many aspects of society today.

Ironically, though, the biggest rise in participation in higher education of previously excluded groups was under the Conservative Governments of 1979–97. Watson and Bowden (1999) argue that this was the beginning of a process that began to overturn 'nearly all of the organizing principles bequeathed by Robbins' in the 1960s that had set the tone for a more equitable system. Nevertheless, the demand for higher education was strong and the drive to create a skilled workforce was a constant feature of the government policy that maintained their support for expansion. Between 1979 and 1996 student numbers went up from 777,800 to 1,659,400, which included a rapid growth among postgraduate students. The Age Participation Index (API) for 18–19-year-olds rose from 12.4 per cent to 32 per cent and the number of women, mature students and ethnic minorities increased significantly. There was also a first-time increase in the proportion of students from working class backgrounds – from 6 per cent in 1990/01 to 12 per cent in 1995/96 (Watson and Bowden, 1999).

However, the expansion of higher education during this period took place against a backdrop of increased individualism and competitiveness. As a result, many young people do not see a link between their capacity to access higher education and their position in society. Ball *et al* (2000) found that they regard success or failure in education or work as an individual issue unrelated to social background. At the same time, research (Ball *et al*, 2000; NCEHE, 1997; Woodrow, 2001) shows clearly that social background is a key factor in determining the likelihood of participation in higher education and that young people from lower socio-economic groups are much less likely to go to higher education.

The relationship between social background and participation in higher education is complex and the decision to progress to university is based on a range of economic, social and cultural factors that influence an individual's decision. This complexity is not only evident in the way that students without a family tradition of higher education now see themselves and their prospects but also evident in the paths that they take through education, with many of them being quite protracted or discontinuous. Their entry patterns are often in marked contrast to the traditional 'linear route' that involves progression to three years of full-time degree study on leaving school at age 18 (Ball, Maguire and Macrae, 2000). Non-standard routes to higher education themselves are not new. The Access movement of the 1980s and 1990s movement did much to establish and validate complementary routes to higher education for older, mature students, and mature students were the main focus of early efforts at widening participation. But since then the focus of government policy has switched to younger students, those in the 18–30 age group. This focus is partly dictated by existing target figures: 'increases in the numbers of people aged 18 to 21 will drive most of the expansion as the proportions entering when they are older are too small to make much difference by 2010 (THES, 20 February 2002). It is clear that if the enduring link between social background and educational underachievement is to be broken then we must challenge the predispositions of young people as early as possible, before they embark on paths that lead them away from education, as well as maintaining and developing access routes for older students.

In the Introduction we posed three questions that need to be addressed if we are to account for the continuing differences in the participation rates in higher education and so begin to understand why widening participation targets have not been met:

1. Are government policies responsive enough and do they encourage and support student progression and participation?
2. Are potential students rejecting higher education because they doubt that it will result in the social and economic benefits traditionally associated with a degree?
3. Is the university agenda itself failing to meet the needs of students and society in the 21st century?

Government policy

Unlike the Thatcher Government, New Labour agrees with the notion of 'society', and the 'Third Way' ideas that form the basis of New Labour's policies include a commitment to a more equal and inclusive society (Giddens, 1998). In many ways the change in Labour politics has been positive. At a strategic level it cannot be denied that 'old' Labour politics failed to secure election success for Labour and so contributed to the maintenance of Conservative governments and Thatcherite ideals for nearly two decades. Also, New Labour's aspirations for increased social justice and the Government's concern about social exclusion represent a genuine change of policy. In addition, there has been a cultural shift, which can be found even within some of the more controversial initiatives such as 'welfare to work', which recognizes that individual potential can be constrained by lack of opportunity. The belief in the capacity of individuals to change, develop and succeed is one of the key messages that come across from the Widening Participation agenda. In this way New Labour's approach differs from that of 'old' Labour – which focused on economic issues and underplayed cultural obstacles. Within the Third Way, however, there are contradictions and discontinuities that have adversely affected policy.

Merit and reward

The Third Way includes a strong belief in a society based on meritocracy. This was originally conceived as an antidote to the welfare dependency regarded as so damaging by the New Labour project, and Giddens (2002), one of the leading exponents of Third Way politics, continues to maintain its importance. Certainly the potential of individuals should be recognized and excluded groups need to develop a sense of agency and empowerment. However, meritocracy, by definition, is based on competition. We have seen the damaging consequences of competition between universities and the chimera of 'choice' that is the result.

Economic imperatives

New Labour is clearly committed to educating more people to degree level. One reason is economic. As Margaret Hodge has explained, the purpose is 'to tackle our productivity agenda and work to maintain our competitiveness'. She goes on to point out that:

> Research suggests that a 10 per cent increase in the proportion of workers with a degree level qualification would boost our gross domestic product by 3.5 per cent. Our competitors recognize the value of a highly skilled labour force. The US, Canada and Japan already have more people qualified to degree level than the UK. If we want to close the productivity gap we must close the skills gap, and that in part is about higher education. In the US, the proportion of the labour force with a degree is nearly 40 per cent higher than in the UK. (Hodge, 2001)

Linked to this, within Third Way politics there is a strong commitment to promoting paid employment. Giddens states, 'The best protection against poverty is holding good job...' (2002: 17). This principle assigns a value to paid work that places it over and above other relations and activities. Within this discourse education becomes entirely instrumental and higher education as a passport to a good job becomes the most commonly cited reason for study. While we would not wish to reject the importance of paid work, to individuals and to society, it is only one aspect of life and one part of our culture. As we have seen, within a 'mass' higher education system a degree is no longer a guarantee of well-paid employment.

Poverty

Reporting to the newly elected Labour Government in 1998 Sir Donald Acheson stated that the gap between rich and poor had increased significantly under the Conservative Government and that the main cause of inequality is poverty. While New Labour recognizes this in some ways, its policy on higher education has failed to take into account the economic realities that are direct barriers to participation in higher education for those from poorer backgrounds. The emphasis has been on initiatives designed to break down education barriers and make higher education more accessible to new groups of students. At the same time the Government increased the financial obstacles for students from poor backgrounds, a point made in a recent report:

> The funding support for students is complex and 'user unfriendly'. The changes adopted following the Labour Government's election in 1997 are widely held to be regressive and a disincentive to participation. (Universities UK, 2002)

It seems that one reason for this type of contradiction in government policy has been the realization that poverty is not the only cause of social exclusion and, subsequently, the rejection of economic redistribution as the major solution is the result. Young (1999) agrees that building social capital is indeed an essential part of addressing social exclusion and also emphasizes the importance of Giddens' recognition that social exclusion can be a dual process, with those at the 'top' excluded from mainstream society as well as those at the 'bottom'. However, Young reminds us that the economic 'exclusion' of the rich and the poor is not a given situation but rather a manufactured risk of modern societies and a feature of the relationship between wealth and poverty. Within this relationship the wealthy may *choose* to exclude themselves – by purchasing private education, for example – whereas the poor do not have the economic resources to make that choice.

Social capital

Giddens rightly maintains that social exclusion is not merely about poverty and the redistribution of economic capital but also about 'developing people's capacities to pursue their well-being' (2002: 39), by which he means the development of 'social capability' or social capital. As Gamarnikow and Green (1999) explain, there are different interpretations of social capital. The more radical explanation offered by Bourdieu (1978) relates educational achievement not just to economic issues or to cultural issues but to the interplay between an individual's economic, cultural and social capitals.

New Labour policies appear to be based on a 'deficit' model where initiatives are designed to address the perceived inadequacies of excluded groups. In her aptly titled paper *Cloning the Blairs*, Gewirtz (2001) explains what this means in cultural terms. She argues that New Labour's strategy to achieve excellence in education at school level by engaging parents in a 'culture of achievement' and changing their attitudes towards education is in fact an attempt to 'make all families like middle class families' and to 'make all parents into clones of Tony and Cherie Blair'. She further argues that there is no doubt that many middle class parents possess or have access to the cultural and social capitals that enable them to exploit the education system to their children's advantage. From this the policy makers have concluded that the way to improve opportunities for working class children is to 'universalize the values and modes of engagement of a particular kind of middle class parent'. In her criticism of New Labour policy Gewirtz makes three points:

1. We should challenge 'the competitive, instrumentalist and "pushy" orientations of many middle class parents' and instead 'expose the damaging effects of these modes of engagement both for children and for society as a whole'.
2. The growing gap between rich and poor is the basis for social structures which underpin the differences in educational achievement between middle class and working class children and it is these social hierarchies we have to dismantle if we are to ensure success for working class children at school.
3. We need new curricula developed in collaboration with a range of interested parties 'which engage and give voice to the diverse experiences and perspectives of working-class children and their parents as well as their middle-class counterparts'.

Gewirtz is talking specifically about schools, but a similar argument could be made about higher education. In government policies on higher education there is the same emphasis on 'choice' and the same attempts to inculcate middle class values (and promote self-confidence and social networks) in working class students. There is also the same stress on 'excellence' and on accessing the best although, as Gewirtz rightly points out, 'there is no room for everyone to be a winner' just as there are only a limited amount of higher education institutions which are deemed to be 'excellent'.

And the same criticism can be applied to the strategy of promoting the idea of higher education to more young people – so long as social inequalities exist, middle class people will get the best out of the system. The higher education system is structured to ensure that the cultural capital of middle class applicants is more valuable to them in the higher education 'game' than that of working class applicants. Their predispositions are more likely to enable them to progress and they have the economic capital to support them. Higher education awareness-raising events, summer schools, master classes and mentoring schemes can help to motivate young people in school about higher education but these initiatives cannot redress the fundamental inequalities that make going to university more likely for middle-class students.

More importantly, perhaps, by stressing 'excellence', 'choice' and the value of 'elite' institutions accessed through linear routes, policy is simultaneously implicitly devaluing the achievements of those who progress to local institutions through non-linear routes. These are the very students who are likely to be 'new' to higher education and from family backgrounds with no history of higher education. Rather than underplaying their achievements we should be promoting the diversity of 'excellence' available at a variety of institutions.

Widening participation policies

In terms of widening participation, policies are often at odds with the needs of students from lower socio-economic groups. In particular their policies:

- underestimate the effects of lack of economic capital for 'non-traditional' students;
- presume that middle class values (such as attitudes towards educational achievement, the preoccupation with educational 'choice' and competitiveness about schooling) are an appropriate (and equitable) basis for developing policies for encouraging non-traditional students: 'not only do they run the system, the system itself is one which valorizes middle- rather than working-class cultural capital' (Reay, 2001);
- fail to take into account the potential risks for students who lack the social, economic and cultural capital necessary to be successful in the current system of progression to higher education.

As a result there are a number of practical outcomes of government policy that inhibit progression from certain social groups, which we outline below.

Selectivity, competition and elitism

As we have seen, selectivity, competition and elitism are enduring features of our education system for which New Labour cannot be held responsible. However, the policy focus on league tables and the concentration on progression to 'elite' institutions underplays the considerable achievements of the students who progress to and succeed in their local institutions and also the expertise of the institutions themselves, which have traditionally catered for students from lower socio-economic groups. League tables and the competition between institutions invoked by them also have implications for student choice – are institutions 'recruiting' students on to courses or genuinely advising them about the best course available for them? More dramatically, as is argued by Ainley *et al* in Chapter 5, lifting the MASN provision means the overall selectivity of higher education will remain unchallenged. The MASN is the maximum number of students set by the Council for each university and higher education college it funds – removing the MASN means that elite institutions will no longer be penalized for over-recruitment. Competition

261

between institutions will be heightened and prestigious institutions will recruit non-traditional students in addition to their usual cohorts and collect their cash premiums for so doing.

Meanwhile the league tables and the criteria used to construct them are creating the equivalent of 'failing schools' in higher education, with institutions experiencing demoralization, and energy-draining inspection and action planning regimes similar to those of schools deemed to be failing by OFSTED. How can disadvantaging institutions that have traditionally provided progression routes for working class students in this way lead to widening access? It is particularly unjust when we look more closely at the way league tables are compiled using criteria relevant only to 'traditional' provision to judge the achievements of the whole sector, as argued in Chapter 9 by Farwell.

Advice and guidance

The applications process is not culturally neutral and, in a climate of competition between institutions, the quality of advice cannot be assured. Students need more personal and individual advice, and support for the applications process needs clear objectives as well as developing self-awareness to enable pupils to be self-confident and analytical about the choices. At present the higher education admissions system is like a lottery. Local links and closer liaison between school, college and university staff can ensure that potential students gain the advice and information that can help them to be clear about the choices they make.

Recent changes in national policy for advice and guidance have been designed to provide individual advice for 13–18-year-olds through the Connexions scheme. This could potentially provide the ongoing independent support that students need and provide some coherence across sectors. But there are concerns that the service might lapse into a deficit model that provides support only for those at greatest risk of dropping out. If this is the case then those considering the option of higher education would not be a priority.

At the same time the Government has introduced the Excellence Challenge and the Gifted and Talented Pupil initiative, which targets those secondary school students deemed most likely to succeed in progressing to higher education. Selection can happen from year 7 upwards and, while giving positive support to a few, will give the rest the message that they are not 'gifted and talented'. Excellence Challenge work is useful but it should be extended to whole school or whole year group initiatives to ensure that potential higher education students are not discouraged at an early age. Rather than piecemeal initiatives, prospective students need comprehensive provision that includes access to independent, student-focused advice, guidance and awareness raising for all.

Qualifications and standards

A levels have been the traditional entry qualification for higher education and the reluctance of governments to relinquish this 'gold standard' has proved a barrier to achieving parity of esteem between academic and vocational areas and therefore a barrier to curriculum innovation. The fear is that if A levels are abolished, then standards will drop. As Stuart (2002) has pointed out, the introduction of 'new' qualifications generally leads to talk of 'standards' and these are then discussed in terms that imply there is universal agreement about what those 'standards' might be, but as Stuart argues:

> The language of standards is not neutral. Currently the idea is connected with ideas of quality, effectiveness and measurement. Measurement that is rooted in league tables, GCSE and A level scores that produce soundbite results that can be judged as 'effective' or 'failing'. The framework for this measurement is rooted in a set of class and cultural principles that include grade success but also, I would suggest, *the appropriate behaviour of those being measured*. (Stuart, 2002: 183) (our italics)

Her point is not just that higher education continues to be biased towards middle class culture, or even that the 'new' Curriculum 2000 has the 'old' gold standard of A level enshrined within it. An additional problem is that most strategies for widening participation, including 'aspiration-raising' activities and 'preparing for higher education' activities, are essentially about ensuring that young people learn 'to fit in'. Certainly, it is one approach to inclusion and participation but it is questionable whether it is one that can challenge the class bias of the higher education sector. Stuart argues that it might be more fruitful to look at the lessons learnt from the Access debate on adult learning and how people are excluded from educational opportunities by the largely unchallenged (middle class) assumptions about the desirability of 'standards' and 'achievement'.

To achieve a different profile of students in higher education we need to consider alternative qualifications and crediting a broader range of achievement rather than trying to squeeze all students into qualifications based on middle class values. This is especially the case now that widening participation policy is focusing on younger students. Widening access is about progression overall and the need to create a multiplicity of complementary routes, which may include different modes of attendance, work in different institutions and part-time or even interrupted study which can be credited through a single qualifications framework.

In Chapter 3 Hodgson and Spours have argued that the mainstream qualifications must change if the number of students qualified for higher education is to increase. They call for a straight-through 14–19 national qualifications system that values both academic and vocational skills, is flexible enough to meet the diverse needs of students, offers clear pathways into work and higher education, and provides a clear benchmark at level 3.

Funding of schools, colleges and universities

Differential funding between schools and colleges means that post-16 work among middle class pupils is better funded than work in colleges (where the bulk of students in poor boroughs go). Proposals for specialization in post-16 will discriminate against institutions that currently cater for a variety of post-16 activities and promote progression for non-traditional entrants to higher education (the government needs to do some joined-up thinking here).

To genuinely support a diversity of higher education provision, institution funding across the whole sector should be rationalized. A submission to the government select committee of enquiry on retention in higher education from the lecturers' union NATFHE (January 2000) pointed out that, while the specific monetary incentives to encourage access to higher education for non-traditional students are useful, the £30 million allocated to this is but a very small proportion of the total £3 billion teaching grant. NATFHE argues that to achieve the 50 per cent participation required by government, 'much greater incentives to recognize the true costs of teaching disadvantaged students will be needed' and estimates that an extra £88 million annual increase in the teaching grant is required. At the same time, its submission focuses on the teaching income for individual institutions and points out that it is the institutions with the lowest teaching income per student (also the institutions with the highest proportions of non-traditional students) which have the highest drop out rates.

The NATFHE document points out that the retention rates for the higher education institutions illustrated in Table 18.1 are close to benchmark predictions, so each institution was 'doing pretty much as expected'. But the table illustrates the stark differences in funding for students between different institutions with very different needs.

In addition, institutional funding should be available to support students through flexible and changing routes. At present if a student completes even three-quarters of a year-long programme his or her institution is

Table 18.1 Drop-out rate and teaching income per student (top 5 and bottom 4 institutions)

	Drop-out rate	Income per student
University of Cambridge	1%	£9,019
University of Durham	2%	£6,785
LSE	2%	£7,311
University of Bristol	2%	£8,497
South Bank University	15%	£4,683
University of North London	15%	£4,326
University of East London	15%	£5,212
Bolton Institute	14%	£4,890

Source: NATFHE (2000) *Dismantling the Ivory Tower*: appendix to submission to Higher Education: Student Retention, Education and Employment Select Committee Enquiry

penalized because the student has not completed the full programme he or she enrolled for. Even if the student's achievement is acknowledged in terms of academic credit, the institution itself is still penalized. This currently applies to both further and higher education.

Student finance

A number of studies have shown the detrimental effects of current government policy on student funding and:

> There is a broad swathe of opinion that changes in the system of student support have been regressive and a disincentive to participation... the sources of support for students, including student loans, present a confusing picture to potential students. The interconnections are not readily appreciated, some sources cannot be tapped until a student has enrolled, and some – like hardship funding – can only be tapped if a student loan has first been taken out... for some groups loans are culturally unacceptable. This means the loan system discriminates against them. (Universities UK, 2002: 167)

Student finance, levels of debt and the need for poor students to work whilst studying full-time are key factors in how students see the potential benefits of higher education. The Government's decision to opt for a system of fees and loans has proved a major disincentive to the very students policy is trying to attract to higher education, as Callender has argued both in Chapter 4 in this book and in her research for the DfEE. One reason is the marked difference in attitudes towards student debt depending on social class:

> Middle class students construe debt in terms of investment and working class students construe it in terms of debt collection. For the student in relatively well-off circumstances, the investment of the student loan (whilst he or she is in receipt of familial support) can actually generate personal profit. (Universities UK, 2002)

From the financial point of view it is now more difficult for students from poor backgrounds to participate in higher education. We need a student support system that is positively weighted to support students from poorer backgrounds.

Transition and sectoral boundaries

As we discussed in the Introduction, entry to higher education represents a transition that entails crossing sectoral boundaries between schools, colleges and higher education. The different educational sectors are all funded differently, have different teaching and learning cultures and in the past have operated largely independently of each other. Progression means negotiating a path through each sector as well as moving between sectors effectively. In recent years the boundaries between further and higher education have become less distinct yet the movement from one sector to another still requires considerable readjustment for the learner (Paczuska, 2000). For this reason government policy initiatives to promote greater collaboration across boundaries and more partnerships between institutions to support transition are to be applauded. But the work must also be adequately resourced and funded. Partnerships for Progression are a positive initiative. At the same time there should be continuing support for the links and partnerships that have already been shown to work effectively. These include the sort of school links with higher education described by Lawley *et al* in Chapter 13 as well as the Sussex Coastal Highway or 'progression accord' which forms the backdrop to the progression initiatives outlined by Harding in Chapter 17. As Blythman and Orr argue in Chapter 10, for continuing success progression initiatives should be embedded within the working culture of institutions. That means continuous funding, not shifting resources from one initiative to another according to the 'spin' of the day.

The rejection of higher education

It seems that many young people no longer automatically accept that a university degree is the passport to a better job that it once was, but regard it as a venture full of risks and uncertainties. Research shows us that they are right. The kind of job that graduates can expect and the salary that they can anticipate is, of course, positively influenced by the possession of a degree. But a graduate's place in the labour market is also influenced by class, 'race' and gender with white, middle class males continuing to command the highest salaries.

In terms of status and identity the possession of a degree is not necessarily seen as an advantage. For example, some young men find it hard to reconcile the idea of studying with their version of masculine identity. For most students without a family tradition of higher education, going to university entails an emotional and cultural readjustment as we have seen in Chapters 1, 2, 6 and 7. As Burke (2002) points out, this is the case for mature students even when their motivation for returning to study is clearly about change and an opportunity to 'find themselves'. The process of individual exploration is never easy but it seems that the real problem for those considered 'non-traditional' students is that in order to succeed in education, they are required to reject their own culture and values and accept middle class values.

Quite apart from these complex issues of identity related to structural inequalities, there also seems to be something of a cultural shift in what assigns status to individuals, with lifestyle and leisure becoming more important. As Ball, Maguire and Macrae suggest, 'Young people may well invest less of themselves in work and educational identity and more in their social/leisure selves' (2000: 67). This affects both the decision to participate in higher education and the importance attached to study if young people decide to continue. As we have seen, it is essential for most students to work in order to support themselves while they study. However, they also need to work in order to maintain their lifestyle and social life and this results in the higher education experience having less prominence in their lives than has previously been the case for undergraduates. Students living at home often continue with the same work patterns, family responsibilities, leisure activities and social networks that they employed while at school or college.

This is a very different experience to the three years 'up' at university that has traditionally been associated with undergraduate study. However, the new pattern can lead to an extremely useful combination of skills, knowledge and experience that might be useful, as Ball, Maguire and Macrae point out, '...in the "risk" society where "good" qualifications, working hard and "not causing trouble" might not be a guarantor of a straightforward and unproblematic transition to adulthood and financial independence...' (2002: 69). It may be the case that, in some ways, young people whose identities and position in society are fluid and as yet undefined are better able to see the realities and possibilities of our emerging 21st-century global culture.

A higher education agenda for the 21st century

As we discussed in the Introduction it was traditionally assumed that only a fraction of the population had the ability to benefit from higher education and when the Robbins report proposed an expansion of university places in the 1960s there were accusations that 'more would mean worse'. The same argument about 'standards' is still being espoused 50 years on by those who oppose change in higher education and defend elitism. A recent outburst from Chris Woodhead, former Chief Inspector of schools, illustrates this: 'What is wrong with traditional virtues, what is wrong with high standards, demanding intellectually rigorous academic education which by definition only a few can benefit from?' (Woodhead, 2002).

The assumption that high 'standards' are something that only some can attain is mistaken. The notion that learning is something only for the few was the reason given at different times in history for excluding various groups from education – including women and black people – with the argument that they were too stupid to benefit. Such arguments have since been disproved by a readily observable reality, though not without struggle.

Higher education needs to change if we are to effectively relate participation to the needs and aspirations of young people from backgrounds with no family tradition of higher education. A theme running throughout the contributions to this book is that young people increasingly relate very differently to the risks and benefits of higher education. They no longer see a university education as a guarantee of success. Those who choose to progress to higher education increasingly do so on different, 'non-linear' and complementary routes that enable them to simultaneously satisfy other material and social needs as well as gain a degree. Traditional middle class images of the road to university are being replaced and amended by a host of new approaches. With them come new attitudes to knowledge and new concerns about the purpose and content of education. It is clearly time to discard the 'old' models of progression on which government policy is based, and instead move to develop new models that resonate with and cater for the realities, needs and aspirations of young people recorded by contributors to this book.

Standards, judgements and league tables are not neutral ideas but reflect the values of the people who make them and use them. The contributions to this book show starkly how higher education systems in the UK today are loaded against students from the lowest socio-economic groups and how the policies designed to redress the bias are themselves biased, reflecting predominantly middle class values. Real educational opportunity can only be achieved by taking a completely different stance, one that values all contributions equally, respecting the insights that different backgrounds and experiences offer, rather than trying to make us all middle class. To achieve social justice people must have equal access to education and training throughout their lives. This does not mean we should discuss learning and the products of learning as if they were just commodities. Teaching, learning and curricula are part of our social fabric and must develop and change to support the move into a new social era for higher education.

This is not about handing down educational opportunities to the excluded classes; rather it is about learning to value education and educational achievement in a different way and develop fresh insights and new knowledge to the benefit of society as a whole. The challenge is not something that just faces individuals, institutions or even nation states. The global nature of our society, the growth of technologies which permit transglobal exchanges of knowledge and information and the growing capacity to store knowledge and information mean that access to knowledge and the capacity to utilize it are global issues which determine both our identity and our very means of existence. Widening participation is crucially important. Without it we cannot secure social justice and equal access to the world's wealth. Though information may have gone global, as Bauman (2001) has pointed out, 'one thing which has thus far escaped globalization is our collective ability to act globally'. He argues that securing a universal right to a secure dignified life needs to begin with a new moralism and a new attitude towards advantage.

The debate about the future and the purpose of learning in higher education needs to go forward. This means moving away from outdated ideas about limited access to education and leaving behind the curricula of the 19th and 20th centuries. We should look to the future and develop a new curriculum and innovative approaches to teaching and learning that will enable students to develop the skills, knowledge and understanding to equip them for the challenges of the 21st century.

References

Ball, S, Maguire, M and Macrae, S (2000) *Choice, Pathways and Transitions Post-16*, Routledge/Falmer, London

Bauman, Z (2001) 'Quality and inequality', *Guardian*, 29 December

Burke, P J (2002) *Accessing Education: Effectively widening participation*, Trentham Books, Stoke-on-Trent

Gamarnikow, E and Green, A (1999) Developing social capital: dilemmas, possibilities and limitations in education, in *Tackling Disaffection and Social Exclusion*, ed A Hayton, Kogan Page, London

Gewirtz, S (2001) Cloning the Blairs: New Labour's programme for the re-socialization of working class parents, *Journal of Education Policy*, **16** (4), pp 365–78

Giddens, A (1998) *The Third Way*, Polity, Cambridge

Giddens, A (2002) *Where Now for New Labour?* Polity, Cambridge and Blackwell Publishers, Oxford

Hodge, M (2001) article in the *Guardian*, 6 November

Hodgson, A (1999) Analysing education and training policies for tackling social exclusion, in *Tackling Disaffection and Social Exclusion*, ed A Hayton, Kogan Page, London

NATFHE (2000) *Dismantling the Ivory Tower:* appendix to submission to Higher Education: Student Retention, Education and Employment Select Committee Enquiry

National Committee of Enquiry into Higher Education (NCEHE) (1997) *Higher Education in the Learning Society*, HMSO, London

Paczuksa, A (2000) Further education and higher education: the changing boundary, in *FE and Lifelong Learning: Realigning the sector for the twenty-first century*, ed A Green and N Lucas, Bedford Way Papers Institute of Education, London

Reay, D (2001) Finding or losing yourself? Working-class relationships to education, *Journal of Education Policy*, **16** (4), pp 333–46

Stuart, M (2002) Standards, Standards, Standards: the unintended consequences of widening participation? *Journal of Access and Credit Studies*, **3** (2), pp 143–53

Universities UK (2002) *Social Class and Participation*, London

Watson, D and Bowden, R (1999) Why did they do it? Conservatives and mass higher education, *Journal of Education Policy*, **14** (3), pp 243–56

Woodhead, C (2002) article in the *Guardian*, 23 March

Woodrow, M (2001) *From Elitism to Exclusion: Good practice in widening access to higher education*, CVCP, London

Young, M F D (1999) Some reflections on the concepts of social exclusion: beyond the Third Way, in *Tackling Disaffection and Social Exclusion*, ed A Hayton, Kogan Page

Index

A level   14, 27, 29, 40, 59, 125,
    126, 155, 183, 228
  gap between GCSE and A level   59
Abitur   42
academic culture   150
academic labour   174
academic standards   184
academic/vocational divide   42
Access courses   14, 137, 155, 204,
    225–33, 256
Accreditation of Prior Experiential
    Learning (APEL)   117, 230
action research   243
admissions criteria profiles (ACPs)   139
admissions process   137–48, 155
advice and guidance   13, 140–43,
    173, 212–24, 218, 237, 262
Age Participation Index (API)   256
alliances   170, 171

baccalaureate   61, 63–65
Barnett, R   7, 151
barriers to higher education   8–9, 10,
    12–15, 115, 198, 203
Beck, U   24, 108, 123, 131–33
Bernstein, R   232, 255
Birkbeck College   227
Blair, Tony   90, 103
Blunkett, David   70, 71, 72, 85, 103
Bourdieu, P   10, 23, 25, 143–44
BP Oil   193
Britasians   26

BTEC   199, 204
buddying   242; *see also* mentoring

career choice   9, 142, 180, 183,
    215, 216
careers service   13
Centres of Vocational Excellence   103
choice   9–11, 23–38, 106, 212
clearing system   91, 92, 93, 94, 95,
    96, 138–39
Commission for Racial Equality (CRE)
    172
Compact Scheme   202, 203, 205
competence   51
competition   94–96, 160, 261
completion   154, 155
Council for National Academic Awards
    (CNAA)   159
credentialism   127–28
credit framework   230
Cubie report   77–79, 83
cultural capital   25, 38, 109,
    143–44, 182
curriculum development   102,
    146–47, 206, 236, 229
curriculum matching   208
  in higher education   157, 161
Curriculum 2000   57, 62, 63, 222,
    263

Dearing report   15, 71, 79–81, 179,
    201

debt *see under* students
deficit model   106, 259
democracy, demands for   3
disability   98
discrimination   197
drop-out rates   56, 264

Educational Maintenance Allowance
    (EMA)   82, 83
elitism   23, 24–25, 37, 197
employability   110
empowerment   2, 5–6, 16
engineering   96–102
Enlightenment, the   3
entry qualifications   91, 116–17,
    139, 180, 181, 205
equal opportunities   2, 4–5, 172–73,
    174, 178, 184
ethnicity   26, 41, 92, 98, 107, 112,
    114, 129, 189–99, 225
Excellence Challenge   221, 262
exclusionary practices   146
expansion of higher education   14,
    55–57, 113, 150, 157, 169,
    173, 213
extended degree   69

Fachhochschulen   42
financial support for students   14,
    115, 141, 215, 231, 265
Foucault, M   165, 174–75
foundation degrees   55, 134, 268
14+ education   57, 60
14–19-year-olds   58, 60
Fryer, R   201
funding   14, 69, 264

gap year   214
GCSE   59, 183, 184
    achievement of 5 A–C passes   59, 61
    gap between GCSE and A level   59
Giddens, A   123, 131–34, 258
globalization   6, 129, 268
GNVQ   59, 204
government policy   90, 256,
    267–69
graduation   5
growth of professions   3
Gymnasium   42

habitus   23, 143, 147
hardship   69, 186
Hardy, T   4
high-flyers   191, 207
Hodge, Margaret   90, 224
Hodgson, A   55, 56, 58, 256

industrialization   3, 6
Inner London Education Authority
    (ILEA)   173, 200
Institute for Learning and Teaching
    (ILT)   159
Institute for Public Policy Research
    (IPPR)   84
institutional change   165–76
institutional culture   166–67
institutional structure   169

Jude the Obscure   4

Keep, E   59, 123
Kennedy committee   15, 170, 201
key skills   61, 97
knowledge economy   70

labour market   6, 42, 56, 127–30
Learning and Skills Council (LSC)   60,
    241
learning and skills sector   60, 103
lifelong learning   133, 231
loans   115, 116
London Enterprise Agency (LENTA)
    192
Lovett, William   4

management culture   167
manufacturing, decline in   129
marketization   174
MASN   103, 160, 261
mathematics   154
    students of   26–37
mature students   12, 42, 115, 124,
    155, 235–43, 257
media studies   156
medical schools   166, 178–87
mentoring   13, 52, 182, 189–99,
    221; *see also* buddying
meritocracy   52, 114
micropolitics   173

middle class students   9, 72, 111, 113, 166
Mirza, H S   34, 114
Modern Apprenticeships   58, 59, 60
Modood, T   34
modular programmes   153–54
monastic origins of universities   2
Morris, Estelle   69, 72, 103
mutual improvement societies   5

National Audit Office (NAO)   40, 152
National Lottery   195
New Labour   1, 25, 69–73, 257
new technologies   6, 7
non-participation in higher education   106–18
'non-traditional' choosers   14, 17, 25, 38
'non-traditional' students   14, 89, 148, 152, 153, 215, 217, 246, 264
nursing   139, 151–52
NVQs   158

Open College Network   155

Palgrave paper   2
parental support   45
participation and achievement   58
participation in higher education   7
   by ethnic minorities and women, increased   59
partnerships   161, 201–11, 266
part-time work   41, 43, 65, 153
Passeron, J-C   23, 25
pathways into education   180
Piatt, W   59, 84
positive discrimination   180
poverty   258
pragmatic choosers   27
Princess Ida   5
professional knowledge   5–6

qualifications system   13, 155, 263
Qualifying for Success   61
Quality Assurance Agency (QAA)   26, 104, 145, 155–56, 228
recruitment   152

Rees report   79
reflective practitioners   159
reflexive modernization   130–34
reflexive self-awareness   138
regional partnerships   245
Research Assessment Exercise (RAE) 94
Responsive College Unit (RCU)   250
retention   38, 101, 190, 223
Rights of Man   3, 4
risk   11, 24, 49, 76, 108, 111–18, 215, 268
Robbins report   8, 92, 256
Robinson, P   59, 84
role models   41, 48, 194
Rose, J   4, 5, 6
Russell Group   103, 104, 159, 215

St Mungo's Trust   227
school improvement literature   171
Scott, Peter   3, 103, 149, 150, 151, 153
selectivity   12, 146, 261
service sector   6
sexism   173
Shakespeare, William   5
16–19-year-olds   57, 206
slowdown in the system   17, 58
social capital   10, 11, 25, 259
social class   1, 31, 44, 92, 106, 107, 152, 184
   and participation   44, 60, 106, 225
social engineering   82
social inclusion   122, 134
Southampton School of Medicine   178–87
Spours, K   55, 56, 58
student demand   89
Student Voice   235–43
students
   debt   74–76
   financial support   14, 69–85, 265
   loans for   71, 73–74, 213
   mature see mature students
summer schools   221
Sunday schools, socialist   5
supercomplexity   7
supply of students   55, 56
Sussex Coastal Highway project   245–54

tacit knowledge   48
targets   89, 257
Thatcher, Margaret   256
Third Way   257
Thompson, E P   5
transition   22
  into employment   51
  into higher education   13, 223,
    235–43, 265
tuition fees   40, 116, 130, 134, 251
tutorial support   220

universities, monastic origins of   2–3
Universities and Colleges Admissions
    Service (UCAS)   94, 137–40,
    142, 146, 166, 182, 205, 219,
    237, 238, 239, 241

voluntarism   3

Watson, Sir David   150
widening participation
  policy   74, 84, 106, 149, 186,
    261, 263
  students   93, 102
women
  entry to higher education   5, 7
  participation in higher education
    90, 125–26
women's rights   4
Woodhead, Chris   156, 267
Woodrow, M   24, 37, 106, 210, 256
work, part-time *see* part-time work
Workers' Education Association   5
working class students   4, 8, 40, 48,
    109, 112, 115, 118

Young, M   24
Young, M F D   13, 145, 161